A treatise of the virtue of humility. ... By Alphonso Rodriguez. The fourth edition, revised and amended from the Latin edition.

Alfonso Rodríguez

ECCO
PRINT EDITIONS

Eighteenth Century
Collections Online
Print Editions

Gale ECCO Print Editions

Relive history with *Eighteenth Century Collections Online*, now available in print for the independent historian and collector. This series includes the most significant English-language and foreign-language works printed in Great Britain during the eighteenth century, and is organized in seven different subject areas including literature and language; medicine, science, and technology; and religion and philosophy. The collection also includes thousands of important works from the Americas.

The eighteenth century has been called "The Age of Enlightenment." It was a period of rapid advance in print culture and publishing, in world exploration, and in the rapid growth of science and technology – all of which had a profound impact on the political and cultural landscape. At the end of the century the American Revolution, French Revolution and Industrial Revolution, perhaps three of the most significant events in modern history, set in motion developments that eventually dominated world political, economic, and social life.

In a groundbreaking effort, Gale initiated a revolution of its own: digitization of epic proportions to preserve these invaluable works in the largest online archive of its kind. Contributions from major world libraries constitute over 175,000 original printed works. Scanned images of the actual pages, rather than transcriptions, recreate the works *as they first appeared.*

Now for the first time, these high-quality digital scans of original works are available via print-on-demand, making them readily accessible to libraries, students, independent scholars, and readers of all ages.

For our initial release we have created seven robust collections to form one the world's most comprehensive catalogs of 18th century works.

Initial Gale ECCO Print Editions collections include:

History and Geography
Rich in titles on English life and social history, this collection spans the world as it was known to eighteenth-century historians and explorers. Titles include a wealth of travel accounts and diaries, histories of nations from throughout the world, and maps and charts of a world that was still being discovered. Students of the War of American Independence will find fascinating accounts from the British side of conflict.

Social Science

Delve into what it was like to live during the eighteenth century by reading the first-hand accounts of everyday people, including city dwellers and farmers, businessmen and bankers, artisans and merchants, artists and their patrons, politicians and their constituents. Original texts make the American, French, and Industrial revolutions vividly contemporary.

Medicine, Science and Technology

Medical theory and practice of the 1700s developed rapidly, as is evidenced by the extensive collection, which includes descriptions of diseases, their conditions, and treatments. Books on science and technology, agriculture, military technology, natural philosophy, even cookbooks, are all contained here.

Literature and Language

Western literary study flows out of eighteenth-century works by Alexander Pope, Daniel Defoe, Henry Fielding, Frances Burney, Denis Diderot, Johann Gottfried Herder, Johann Wolfgang von Goethe, and others. Experience the birth of the modern novel, or compare the development of language using dictionaries and grammar discourses.

Religion and Philosophy

The Age of Enlightenment profoundly enriched religious and philosophical understanding and continues to influence present-day thinking. Works collected here include masterpieces by David Hume, Immanuel Kant, and Jean-Jacques Rousseau, as well as religious sermons and moral debates on the issues of the day, such as the slave trade. The Age of Reason saw conflict between Protestantism and Catholicism transformed into one between faith and logic -- a debate that continues in the twenty-first century.

Law and Reference

This collection reveals the history of English common law and Empire law in a vastly changing world of British expansion. Dominating the legal field is the *Commentaries of the Law of England* by Sir William Blackstone, which first appeared in 1765. Reference works such as almanacs and catalogues continue to educate us by revealing the day-to-day workings of society.

Fine Arts

The eighteenth-century fascination with Greek and Roman antiquity followed the systematic excavation of the ruins at Pompeii and Herculaneum in southern Italy; and after 1750 a neoclassical style dominated all artistic fields. The titles here trace developments in mostly English-language works on painting, sculpture, architecture, music, theater, and other disciplines. Instructional works on musical instruments, catalogs of art objects, comic operas, and more are also included.

old books. new life.

The BiblioLife Network

This project was made possible in part by the BiblioLife Network (BLN), a project aimed at addressing some of the huge challenges facing book preservationists around the world. The BLN includes libraries, library networks, archives, subject matter experts, online communities and library service providers. We believe every book ever published should be available as a high-quality print reproduction; printed on-demand anywhere in the world. This insures the ongoing accessibility of the content and helps generate sustainable revenue for the libraries and organizations that work to preserve these important materials.

The following book is in the "public domain" and represents an authentic reproduction of the text as printed by the original publisher. While we have attempted to accurately maintain the integrity of the original work, there are sometimes problems with the original work or the micro-film from which the books were digitized. This can result in minor errors in reproduction. Possible imperfections include missing and blurred pages, poor pictures, markings and other reproduction issues beyond our control. Because this work is culturally important, we have made it available as part of our commitment to protecting, preserving, and promoting the world's literature.

GUIDE TO FOLD-OUTS MAPS and OVERSIZED IMAGES

The book you are reading was digitized from microfilm captured over the past thirty to forty years. Years after the creation of the original microfilm, the book was converted to digital files and made available in an online database.

In an online database, page images do not need to conform to the size restrictions found in a printed book. When converting these images back into a printed bound book, the page sizes are standardized in ways that maintain the detail of the original. For large images, such as fold-out maps, the original page image is split into two or more pages

Guidelines used to determine how to split the page image follows:

• Some images are split vertically; large images require vertical and horizontal splits.
• For horizontal splits, the content is split left to right.
• For vertical splits, the content is split from top to bottom.
• For both vertical and horizontal splits, the image is processed from top left to bottom right.

Let this minde be in You, wch was in CHRIST IESUS
who being in y.^e Form of GOD, thought it not Robbery
to be Equal with GOD but made himself of no Repu
tation & took upon him y.^e Form of a SERVANT
Phil.2 v 5.6.7.

J. Trye inv & sculp

A TREATISE OF THE VIRTUE OF HUMILITY.

WHEREIN

That *First* and truly *Cardinal Virtue* of *Christian Morality* is Explained, Recommended, and Enforced, not only from the Scriptures, but also from the Writings and Examples of the Saints, and Primitive Fathers of the Church.

By ALPHONSO RODRIGUEZ.

The Fourth Edition,

Revised and Amended from the Latin *Edition.*

WITH

A PREFACE concerning the Author. Wherein some Cautions are given, against the Danger of reading *Popish*, and other unorthodox or suspected Books.

A Chapter also is added shewing, how *Children* may be trained up to the Virtue of HUMILITY.

Be cloathed with Humility———— 1 PET. v. 5.

LONDON: Printed for C. RIVINGTON, at the *Bible* and *Crown* in St *Paul's Churchyard.* 1733.

B♔L

PREFACE
To the READER.

Concerning the AUTHOR, and the Reaſon of this Edition; wherein ſome Cautions are alſo given, againſt the Danger of reading *Popiſh* and other unorthodox or ſuſpected Books.

THE Reviſal of this ſmall Treatiſe upon *Humility*, being a Task I impoſed on myſelf, and the Product of ſome leiſure Hours, it ſeems neceſſary I ſhould acquaint the Reader with my Reaſons for promoting a *New Edition*, and my Deſign in ſo doing.

ON my firſt Peruſal of the Book, in it's *former Edition*, I could not but obſerve many excellent Rules contained therein, for the Attainment and Practice of *Humility*, with a Spirit of great Piety and Unction throughout the Whole. But withal,

A 2　　　　　　ſuch

such Incorrectness in the Style and Expression, and so many Errors of the Press occurr'd almost in every Page, that in pure Respect to the pious (but then to me unknown) Author, and for my own private Use, I made such Amendments as might clear his Sense from any palpable Blemishes. —— At the same time wishing to see a more correct Edition, that so the Benefit, which I have heard many acknowledge to have received from it, even under all those Disadvantages, (and I trust that I also have received,) might be made thereby the more Extensive.

But, on a further and more attentive Review, I discerned some Mistakes of worse Consequence, than were to be charged on the Style or the Impression :—certain Strains of *Popish* Fanaticism appear'd, and then discover'd what *Communion* the Author belong'd to. This determined me therefore to examine the more accurately into the Doctrine, as well as Phrase ; and what I found erroneous or unsound, I took the liberty to correct, or expunge.

Thus far I had proceeded, having nothing to work upon, but the Edition last published in 1714.—— Since then, meeting with a *Latin* Edition of all the Author's Works, and also a Translation into *English* of this particular Treatise on *Humility*, which was printed at *Rouen* in 1631. I was not a little pleased with the collating them together, altho' it encreased my Trouble, and I had all my Work to go over again.

I found

I found that the Author was one *Alphonfo Rodriguez*, a *Spanish* Jefuit; that this Treatife is but a Part of a larger Work, which is called,——*The Exercife of Perfection*; was originally written in *Spanish*, and, as the Publifher of the *Latin* Edition (at *Gologn* in 1677.) informs us, " had " been tranflated into moft Languages, and ob- " tained fo univerfal an Efteem with all religi- " ous Perfons, that fcarce a Family was without " it. That next to *Kempis*, no Author had " written better, or with more Juftnefs, con- " cerning *Spiritual Religion*, or the *Interior* " *Life.*"

THE like Character is given him by the Author of the *Pacific and Myftic Theology.*—— *Scripfit fatis methodicè*, &c. " He wrote with " good Method, by way of Rules and Precepts; " to which he added fundry Examples out of " the Lives of the Fathers, Hermits, and other " Saints: Delivering all in a Style fo eafy and " plain, as muft render his Book no lefs plea- " fant, than ufeful and intelligible to the mean- " eft Readers."

THE firft Tranflation into *English* of this little Treatife on *Humility* in 1631, feems to have been from the *Spanish*, but appears much infe- rior to the *Latin* Verfion, if we, who are unac- quainted with the Original Language, form our Eftimate from the Character, that is given of the Author.

THE Edition which the late Reverend and Learned Dr *H. Hammond* is said to have recommended to the Press, is plainly a Copy from this old *English* Translation, by some *Protestant* Reviser, who left out what he judged favour'd of *Popery*, and made some few Alterations; but not in the Style, nor with sufficient Care to preserve the Connexion. Yea in many Places some excellent and sound Passages were thrown out; which are now restor'd.—— This Edition was publish'd in 1654. and is called the *first*, without Notice taken of that in 1631.—— What is called the *second*, came out in 1673.——And by this reckoning, the present Edition (succeeding the former in 1714.) is called the *Fourth*.

IT might seem more curious than useful, to be thus particular in the detail of the Author's Character, and of the several Editions, which this little Book has gone through amongst us, were it not to introduce the Caution I have bound myself to give the Reader, against the Dangers of conversing *too freely* with Authors of other Communions, and especially the *Romish*.

THE unhappy Effects I have often observed of that unguarded Liberty taken by the Laity of our Church, promiscuously to read *all kinds of Books*, without Choice or Distinction, has made me as often wish (seeing the wise Custom of having spiritual Guides for this Purpose, is not retain'd, or at least observ'd, as it ought, in our Church,) that some abler Hand would write

a pro-a proper Treatife to fupply that Defect, and to direct all, efpecially young Beginners, *in the Choice of their Authors*; in order to warn them, not only from fuch Books as may corrupt their Morals, but thofe alfo, which may miflead their Judgment, and taint their Principles.

I FEAR it may too truly be faid, that fome that are called *Good Books*, have done more harm in the World, than notorioufly *Bad ones.* ——Where fuch have any latent Poifon in them, they deceive under the fpecious Shew of Piety, and *infenfibly* deftroy. Of this fort none have done more hurt to *Proteftants*, than the *Spiritual Books* of the *Romifh* Church. It's Tenets, (I mean thofe from which we have Reform'd) are fo apparently erroneous and corrupt, it's Doctrines fo blended with Untruths, it's Worfhip fo over-run with Superftitions, no lefs abfurd, than inconfiftent with the Spirit of Chriftianity, that I am perfwaded no Church of *England* Man, of tolerable Judgment, would ever turn Profelyte to that Church, were it not for an uncommon Strain of feeming Piety and Devotion in their *fpiritual Books*, which dazzles the Eyes, and biaffes the Mind of the unwary Reader. ——It feems impoffible to fuch a one, that Men, who in his Opinion write fo pioufly and well, fhould be of a *bad Religion*; or that a Church fhould have any damnable Errors, which produces, as he thinks, fuch *excellent and holy Men.* —— And to fecond this firft Impreffion made on his Judgment, another plaufible Argument is put in his Head, that furely it muft be very *uncharitable*, and the Sign of a *partial* and *narrow*

A 4 Spirit,

Spirit, to condemn Men, who are generally esteemed the best Instructors in *Perfection*, and have written such excellent Tracts on the most *spiritual Points* in Divinity, and consequently, he concludes it highly unjust, to condemn *a Church*, in whose Bosom such *Seraphic* Teachers have been trained.

THUS *Kempis*, thus *Bona*, thus *Parsons* and *Gother*, thus our *Rodriguez*, and others, have with great Success been employ'd to press Men into the Service of *Popery*, and drawn over Multitudes of Converts to that Church.

THE *Lives* also *of their Saints* are another ensnaring Bait to weak *Protestants*.—— I have more than once observed the intoxicating Effect of such Books.—— To pass from admiring the *Life*, to embracing the *Religion*, of one we think a *Saint*, is a kind of natural Transition. Let all therefore who incautiously drink too freely of *Babylon's* * *Golden Cup*, beware lest their Heads turn giddy.—— *Let him that thinketh he standeth, take heed lest he fall.*

THEY are the *Religious* and more *piously disposed* of our Brethren, who are in greatest Danger of falling a Prey to these Seducers.—— Such (especially if Novices) are inclined to judge of Religion, more by it's Heat, than by it's Light, by Imagination rather than Judgment; and, till they have deeply tasted of the Scriptures, those true *Wells of Salvation*, and had

* Revel. XVII. 4.

long

long Experience in the ſpiritual Life, they are apt to frame to themſelves wrong and diſproportionate Ideas of *Perfection*: the Figure they paint in their Fancy, is above and beyond the Life, and the Schemes they draw, are too ſtrict and Impracticable. —— This not only tempts to Vain-glory, but lays them the more open to Deluſion.——If any *Perfectioniſt* or *Myſtic* Writer fall in their Way, they haſtily ſwallow his Notions, without obſerving the Danger, or regarding any friendly Warning, 'till ſad Experience convince them of their Miſtake. —— Againſt ſuch Conſequences, there can be no better Preſervative than *Humility :*——Whoever makes not *this* the firſt Round in the *Scale of Perfection*, will infallibly fall into one of thoſe dangerous Extremes, *Preſumption* or *Deſpair.* —— And to ſuch Perſons, this little Book is more eſpecially recommended, and moſt humbly Dedicated.

HUMILITY indeed is ſo ſure a Defence againſt all *dangerous* Errors in Religion, that no Book ſeems leſs unſafe to read, than one upon this Subject. ——But alas! there is a *falſe*, as well as *true Humility*; and this Virtue has ſuffered great Adulteration among the *Roman* Dealers. —— Where any Symptom of this kind appeared in the following Treatiſe, I have endeavoured to rectify the Error, or left the Paſſage quite out.

I MUST do the Author the Juſtice to own, that the *vicious* Extream of *Humility*, is not ſo much to be found in his *Rules and Precepts*, as

A 5   in

in the *Sayings* and *Examples* of some modern *Popish* Saints; and these, possibly, are rather *Legendary Tales*, than true History; They are therefore deservedly omitted, not only as *bad Examples*, but probably *Untrue* *. And this suggests another Caution against *Romish* Books:——— They are often stuff'd with *such* Stories.——— The Lives of their *Saints*, are generally as *Romantick* and beyond the Life, as their *Miracles* are feign'd, and contrary to Truth.

ANOTHER thing I must commend in the Author:——— he every where keeps clear from the *Popish* Doctrine of *Merits*. He over and over excludes it from the Character of the *Humble* Man, and makes it wholly inconsistent with the Virtue, he is recommending to his Readers. So that I must own, he is as free from Errors peculiarly *Romish*, as any *Popish* Writer that I know.

IF I may presume to offer some Advices for the Direction of Beginners (who are adult Members of our Church) in their *method of Reading* Religious Books, in order to settle them in right Principles, and, by way of Antidote, against the infectious Influence of *Popish*, or other *Unorthodox* Books,———

---

* *Two or three* whole *Chapters in the* Popish *Editions contain such* Examples *of* Humility, *as are, if true, not fit for* Imitation, *and are therefore left out in this.*

1. THE

1. THE first may be this; for all who are sincere Converts to *Religion*, and are touched with a Sense of Sin, a fear of God, and defire to pleafe him; (for 'tis in vain to talk to others, who have none of thefe Sentiments, and are deftitute of the Spiritual Life:) For thefe, I fay, the firft neceffary Step is to become *as little Children* again, and go back to the Fundamentals, or *firft Principles of the Doctrine of Chrift*——In his School the firft Clafs is *Humility.*—This agrees with his own Rule †. And, under Him, nothing can better inftruct them *in thefe Principles*, than our own Catechifm —— This fhould be well ftudy'd; firft, in the Words of the Church; —— then with fome good Expofition ——Examine every Proof by the Bible; take nothing upon Truft : —— mark what you do not underftand, and confult your Minifter.——Continue this Study, till the Judgment be thoroughly grounded in the Nature and Tenour of the *Baptifmal Vow.* And when the Mind is fix'd in this, as a *Firft* and undoubted *Principle*, that the End and Defign of our *Covenant* is,—— 1. On God's part, to re-unite us to himfelf, by the Mediation of his Son Jefus Chrift, and make us everlaftingly Happy: that, 2. On our parts, we ftand engaged to *Repent* of all our Sins; to *Believe* all the Articles of the Chriftian Faith ; and to pay a conftant and uniform *Obedience* to all the Laws of God ,

† Matth. xviii. 3,

2. THE

2. THE next thing should be, with great Serioufnefs and Attention to begin the Bible and read it thro'.——Read it firft without Notes;——what is too difficult to underftand, may be left to a future Reading;——yet skip no Part over. Remember the *Eunuch*, who was reading *Ifaiah*.——Tho' he underftood not *then* what he read, God provided him a Teacher to explain the Meaning.——The humble Student of God's Word, fhall never want a *Philip* to expound it. —— We fhall alfo be *taught of God*, if we *pray for his Teaching*.——To which let me add, that our *firft Rule*, if duly obferv'd, will prove a fure Key for *opening* and *interpreting* the whole Scriptures. For,

3. THIS is to be laid down as a ftanding Maxim, that the whole Bible is, in effect, but a Comment upon, and Expofition of, the Covenant between God and Man: That it's whole Defign is to teach us, (more at large,) what God is, *in Himfelf*, and what *to Us*;——*Why* we muft be re-united to him through Chrift, before we can be faved; and *How* that is to be done:——to teach us alfo, what we *were*, what we *are:*—— *Why*, and *How* we are to *Repent*, and particularly *what* we are to repent of. 2. What thofe *Articles* of *Faith* are, which we promifed to *Believe*, and *how* we are to believe them. 3. What the *Laws* and *Commands* of God are, which we promifed to *Obey*, and *in what Manner*.

4. AND here it may be of Ufe to underftand, that the Covenant, which both *Papifts* and *We*
enter

enter into in Baptifm, is the very fame : Our Baptifmal *Form* and theirs, our Stipulations and theirs, our Privileges and theirs, being the fame. The Scriptures, which contain the Effential Articles of that Faith, into which we and they are Baptiz'd, being alfo the fame. The beft Criterion therefore for knowing *which* Church, *Theirs* or *Ours*, is the moft Orthodox, is not to judge by the *Writers* of either Side :——— The only fure Mark is this ;——— " That Church, " which expounds her *Baptifmal Vow* moft a- " greeably to the Scriptures, on which *alone* it " is founded, is certainly the Beft and moft " Orthodox Church : and thofe Members, who " live moft conformably to that Vow, as *fo* " explained, muft certainly be the Beft, and " moft Orthodox Chriftians."

5. IN reading the Scripture (after a firft or fecond curfory perufal) the *Letter* ought to be *well* ftudied, but the *Spirit* of it *much more*. That is, in every Precept or Prohibition, every Threatening or Promife, every Hiftory or Ex- ample, the Reader fhould chiefly ponder the *Spiritual* ufe, which he, and every Chriftian is to draw from thence : fhould ruminate well thereon by Meditation, chewing as it were the Cud, and preparing it for his own Food ; then inwardly digefting the fame, for the Health and Nourifhment of his Soul. ——— To dwell fo long on the Lives and Actions of the Saints of both Teftaments, till he extract the Quinteffence and Marrow, and by a holy Chymiftry, tranfmute their very Temper and Spirit into his own Na- ture and Subftance.——— Till he hath learned the

Art

Art of tranfcribing *their* Faith, *their* Devotion, *their* Love of God, *their* Patience, *their* Meek-nefs, and all thofe amiable Qualities, which render'd *them* fo dear to Heaven, and their Me-mories fo precious to all Ages. —— This holy Skill of affimilating ourfelves to thofe *undoubt-ed* Worthies, but above all to the moft perfect Pattern of our deareft R E D E E M E R's Life and Converfation, is the moft infallible Inter-pretation of the Scripture: He that has acquired this Art, has found out the true Secret of right-ly underftanding the whole Bible. —— His Pra-ctice is the beft Critic; a Living Commentary. ——By the fame Rule he frames his Judgment of all *Human* Compofitions.——The nearer any Doctrine comes to that *furer Word of Prophecy,* the Scripture; that is, the more Confonant it is to the grand Charter of his Salvation, the *Baptifmal Covenant*, which is founded thereon, the nearer he knows it to be to the Truth. —— By this Standard or Touchftone, he dif-cerns and approves what is Orthodox in them; by this he rejects what is Wrong.——What our Lord fays of his Sheep, that *they follow Him, becaufe they K N O W His Voice; but a Stranger they will not follow, but will flee from him, for they K N O W N O T the Voice of Strangers,* (John x.) is juftly applicable to fuch faithful Students of his Word:——they readily diftinguifh Evangelical Truths, from the moft plaufible Pretences of Falf-hood and Error: ——The Teachers of *unfcriptu-ral* Doctrines are *Strangers* to them, they *know not their Voice;*——their Tenets are ftrange and unknown to them, and therefore they *flee from,* and avoid them. But,

FOR

FOR the very fame Reafon, they cannot but love and adhere, with all poffible Attachment, to the Church of *England*; becaufe they find her Doctrine fo exactly parallel to the holy Scriptures, yea rather to be the very fame. For what her peculiar Doctrine is, the pious Student collects not (as we have faid) from a Multitude of *private* Writers, but from thofe public and authentic Syftems, which bear *her own Stamp*, and are publifhed by her immediate Authority; to wit, her *Catechifm*, her *Articles*, and her *Homilies*; but more efpecially from the *Leffons*, which fhe has appointed for every Day in the Year; and ftill more particularly from thofe Leffons and portions of Scripture, fhe has felected for our Inftruction on the *Sundays*, and *Festivals* throughout the Year.——Thefe laft he gives the more diligent heed to, and, upon due Examination, and attentively confidering her End and Scope in the Choice of them, finds to contain her whole Doctrine, and to be the compleateft Syftem, and moft perfect Body of Divinity. As for other Syftems he meets with, however celebrated the Writers may be, or of what Communion, he regards them no farther, than they correfpond with thefe. *A Man of Underftanding trufteth in the LAW, and the Law is faithful unto him as an Oracle.* Ecclus. xxxiii. 3.

THESE Advices are chiefly calculated for the Ufe and Capacity of ordinary and grown up Chriftians; yet will not be unufeful to the greateft Scholars, if Students alfo in *Humility*.— A larger
Compafs

Compaſs of Reading, and other Studies, may make a fine *Preacher*, a profound *Philoſopher*, or acute *Diſputant*; the Study I have recommended, is the ſurer way of making a *good Man*. Pride indeed will deſpiſe and hate ſo plain, ſo low and humble a Way; becauſe *it hates Humility* †. But, where *Humility* is, there we are ſure is Wiſdom, there every Virtue will attend; —— not only to improve our Morals, but to ſecure the Judgment from every *dangerous* Error: which is the End I propoſed in the foregoing *Advices*.

He that has taken this Method, may ſafely be truſted to read any other Sort of Writers.—— If furniſh'd with the above Touchſtone, he will diſtinguiſh *the Precious from the Vile*, he will ſeparate the good Ore for his own Uſe, and reap a Benefit from what is Good, in ſuch Books, without being hurt by what is Corrupt, or deceived by Varniſh and Shew; according to the Import of that Promiſe of our Lord, to all True Believers, *they ſhall take up Serpents, and if they drink any deadly Thing, it ſhall not hurt them* *.—— Yea ſuch a one will rather grow more and more convinced of the *Scripture*'s Uſe and Excellence, more firmly adhere to his own Church, whoſe Doctrines he finds to be all pure Sterling; her Devotions, as free from Enthuſiaſm, as they are from Superſtition; that as her Precept, ſo her Practice, is, *to pray with the Spirit, and to pray with the Underſtanding alſo*. That her admirable *Form* exemplifies *the Rule*. and the ſo-

---

† *See* Ecclus xiii. 20.   * Mark xvi. 18.

ſemn

lemn Sedateneſs of her *Common Prayer*, corre-
ſponding with the Solidity and Nervouſneſs of
her *Inſtructions*, it may well be ſaid, both of
her Liturgy and her Doctrines, what DENHAM
ſaid of her *Thames*;

Tho' deep, yet clear, tho' gentle, yet not dull,
Strong, without Rage, without o'reflowing, full.

HOWEVER rapturouſly ſome Writers of
Proteſtant or *Popiſh* Denomination, may talk of
Divine Love,——of the *Soul's Abſorpſion, Ingulf-*
ment, &c. *into God , Entering into his Simplicity*
and Unity, and that bold Word *Deification,*
with many more like unwarrantable Expreſſions; he ſees plainly they are the Language of
a *heated Fancy,* rather than *of Scripture*; fitter
to blow up the Mind into a wild Enthuſiaſtic
Devotion, and Spiritual Pride, than to edify or
improve.

WHEN the ſame ſort of Guides take upon
them to point out the Way to *Perfection,* the
Soul that has firſt formed her Judgment on the
firm Baſis of *Scripture,* according to the Method
here preſcribed, will diſcover this very material
Defect in theſe Inſtructors, that their Rules are
generally too looſe and indefinite, as to the
firſt ſetting out; too high and impracticable as to
the End propoſed.——They are not clear or expli-
cite enough in ſtating the Point, *whence* Perfection is *to commence,* nor in deſcribing the proper
Degrees, *by which* it is to be *aſcended to* ——
No wonder then they exceed the due Bounds,
deviate

deviate into wrong Channels, and commonly run into Extreams.——Among many others, my Author furnishes us with an Instance of this Charge.——In a very large Volume, on the Subject of *Perfection*, he says many fine things under scattered Heads, but not one Chapter do I find to direct us to the Stage, *from whence* we are to start, and *Begin* the glorious Race. But our *better Guide* the CHURCH, has, with all possible Plainness, appointed *this* wise and rational *Order*, that *Repentance* should begin the Race ; *Faith* shew and lead the Way , *Obedience* finish the Course, and win the Crown. And our *best Rule*, the SCRIPTURE hath, with like Plainness, determined, that no one shall *receive* the Crown, except he strive *lawfully* *, that is, conformably to the Laws and Orders of the Race. —— Why should we then desert our own *Guide*, to follow those, who know so little of the Way ?——Why forsake our own *Rule*, for such uncertain Lights ? Why *hew to ourselves Cisterns, broken Cisterns, that will hold no Water* ?

I MUST not dissemble it, that the Teachers, on *either* Side, are too regardless of *this* true Order of our Christian Race, which our Excellent Church hath delineated to us.——*Humility*, by stooping low, will discern and pursue it But, alas ! worldly Wisdom and human Learning, are too apt to despise, or overlook so plain a Rule.

* 2 Tim. ii. 5.

NEITHER

NEITHER muſt I deny, that tho' *We* have the clearer Light, yet the *Roman* ſeems to have the greater Warmth:——We have Knowledge, but, alas! without Zeal: they have Zeal, but without Knowledge.—— God grant the needful Supply of our reſpective Wants, giving *us* a further Meaſure of the Fervour of his Spirit, *them* a greater Degree of his divine Truth.——Here only lies the right Center of Union; and when they and we are led, by the hand of *Humility*, to *meet* in this true Point, and are mutually agreed to worſhip Him both *in Spirit AND in Truth*, then ſhall we ſoon become One Church, and One Body.

I WOULD not be underſtood by any Thing I have ſaid, to condemn, in general, all Books written by Authors of a different Communion from our own; nor to cenſure any, farther than they contain Doctrines Unorthodox, or Unſound; I mean, ſuch as agree not with the Divine Truths delivered to us in Holy Scripture Theſe *Divine Truths*, like the Divine Promiſes, *belong to Us, and to our Children* They are as the Current Coin of the Kingdom of Heaven, neither to be Depraved, nor yet to be Engroſſed by any one particular Sect or Species of Chriſtians. The *Firſt*, (to wit, the Debaſing this Heavenly Coin with any Impure Allay) were a Kind of High Treaſon againſt God. The other, (namely, confining *to ourſelves* the common Property and Birthright of every Chriſtian) is an Act of a Narrow and Contracted Spirit, no leſs injurious to Others, than inconſiſtent with a true Chriſtian Charity. Nevertheleſs

thelefs, on the other Hand, to fuffer our Eyes
to be blinded, and our Judgments bribed, by
any, the moft Holy, but Mifapplied Truths,
in favour of Falfhood and Error, is not only
a Weaknefs inconfiftent with Chriftian Prudence,
but a moft inexcufable Fault in any Member of
the Church of *England*, which has fo well provided againft fuch Dangerous Deceptions.———
'Tis no new Stratagem of Satan [*fub fpecie recti
falfis illudere*] to Deceive under the Appearance
of an Angel of Light, and to cover his Baits
with Words of Scripture: But our Lord has
fet us the Pattern, how to guard againft fuch
Temptations, in his wife Conduct, when affaulted in the fame Manner.——But, if I may
prefume to offer my Opinion, with refpect to
the prefent Queftion, the Truth of the Cafe
feems to be this:——As in the dark and Fabulous Ages of *Heathenifm*, God was pleafed by
Philofophy to communicate many Noble, not
only Natural, but Moral and Divine, Truths to
the *Gentiles*, in order to preferve fome Rays
of that Heavenly Light amongft them, which
their *Idolatrous Superftitions* had well nigh ex-
tinguifh'd; fo in gracious Compaffion to thofe
Souls, who had long been involved in the Dark
and no lefs Fabulous Times of *Popery*, the fame
good Providence has at fundry Times, and in
divers Manners, raifed up fome Eminent Lights
in the *Roman* Church, who by their Devout
Writings, might preferve amongft them, the
Main and Effential Principles of *Virtue* and *Piety*,
which the grofs Errors *in their Worfhip*, would
otherwife have totally deftroy'd. —— This was
the Fire in the Embers,——this the Holy Seed,

by

by which his Church was to be Preserved and Perpetuated.——As the *Pagan* and *Popish* Idolatry differ very little in the *Form*, so the bad *Effects* of both have been *the very same*, according to the wise Man's Remark (Wisd. xiv. 12.) the *devising of Idols was the Beginning of Spiritual Fornication, and the Invention of them the Corruption of Life.*——To prevent therefore, as far as possible, this *Corruption of Life*, which has been the necessary Consequence of *Modern*, as well as *Antient* Idolatry, was the End and Design of Divine Wisdom, in raising up some admired Writers in the *Heathen* and *Papal* World, to " give Light to them that sat in " Darkness, and in the Shadow of Death, and " to guide their Feet into the Way of Peace." But to *US*, who freely enjoy the full Benefit of the Gospel-Day, *such Lights* are of as little Use, as Candles at Noon——For *Us* to prefer a *Romish* Author's *Religion*, because of some genuine Truths in his Book, —— would be no less unwise, than to espouse the Religion of *Plato* or *Cicero*, of *Epictetus* or *Seneca*, because their Works shine with some extraordinary Sentiments of Moral Virtue——The Design of God, in setting up such Lights, was no doubt to expose the Errors of *Paganism* and *Popery* We should quite thwart that Design, if we suffer ourselves, by the same Lights, to be betray'd into those very *Errors*, and consequent *Corruptions*, which they were intended to prevent.

THE short is, the *Popish* Church, *as Popish*, teacheth *nothing but Error*, both in Doctrine and Worship,

Worſhip; yet hath produced many Authors eminent for their Pious and Good Books: The Church of _England_, in _Herſelf_, is perfectly Pure and Orthodox, _without Spot or Wrinkle_, ——whatever Truths the _Romiſh_ hath, _She_ hath alſo; but without the leaſt impure Mixture. But I ſay not the ſame of her Teachers, that _All_ of them are free from every Tincture of Error. —— What then is to be done?——— If the foregoing Rules be faithfully obſerved, we ſhall neither be drawn away to deſert our own Church, when we obſerve any _Unſound_, or even _Antichriſtian_ Doctrines, in any which call themſelves _Proteſtant_ Writers; nor by the fair Shew, and glowing Expreſſions of Piety, that we meet with in _Romiſh_ Books, be tempted to eſpouſe the Errors of _Rome_.——The ſame Rule holds equally Good, as to all other _Heterodox_ Opinions in Religion. In a Word, wherever I meet, in _Romiſh_, or other ſuſpected Writers, with any _Divine Truths_, I take them, not as _Theirs_, but as Ours, in _Chriſt_; according to that ſolemn Act of Donation by His Apoſtle; —— " _Let no_
" _Man glory in Men, for ALL THINGS ARE_
" _YOURS. Whether Paul, or Apollos, or Cephas,_
" _or Life, or Death, or Things preſent, or Things_
" _to come, ALL ARE YOURS_ †."

AND this Conſideration may ſerve for a ge-neral and ſufficient Juſtification for the Members of our Church, Tranſlating or Excerpting from _Romiſh_ Authors, whatever _Chriſtian_ Truths they meet therein. If in their Dunghil we diſ-

---

† 1 Cor. iii. 21, 22.

cover any fuch precious Jewels, we may lawfully take them as *Our Own.* ———— In this we
are not Plagiaries, but Proprietors, for fo our
Charter runs,——— *All is Yours.* The *Romanift*
is welcome to make Reprizals, and to take
every Divine Truth he can gather out of *Our*
Writers. ——— Thefe facred Mines are open to
all, and common to all: I plead not againft
the Ufe, but the Abufe and Mifapplication of fuch
Things, as in Themfelves are truly Excellent.
And while Scripture itfelf is wrefted to maintain Error, fuch Caution as I have given, cannot feem unneceffary, nor unfeafonable What
was it that God blamed in the Three Friends
of *Job* ? — not any Expreffions they had ufed,
to difplay the Divine Power and Juftice, but
the wrong Application they made of thofe
noble Sentiments, in Derogation of his Providence and Mercy, as well as contrary to the
Charity and Compaffion, which was due to
that illuftrious Sufferer. ——— To conclude, the
more excellent any Thing is in itfelf, the more
pernicious the Abufe, and the greater Caution
requifite, *that we be not Deceived.*

I HAVE in the *Title Page* called *Humility* a
Cardinal Virtue, and perhaps fome will be fright-
ened at a Word that feems to carry a *Popifh*
Sound. On the other hand, the mere *Acade-
mic,* who has drawn his *Ethics* more from the
Plan of *Ariftotle* and *Cicero,* than from the School
of Chrift, will difpute or defpife fuch new Philofophy, which ufurps a Title, that he has long
been taught to give to *Prudence, Juftice, Tempe-
dance,* and *Fortitude.* ——— I intreat both to put

on

on fo much *Humility*, as to hear with Patience what I have to fay, in defence of myfelf
and it.

CARDINAL, that is, *Principal* or *Chief*,
takes it's Origin from a Word that fignifies a
Hinge, on which the Door turns when it opens
or fhuts. Hence the *chief* Points of the Heavens,
are called *Cardinal Points*. —— Certain Prelates,
who are *chief* of the Ecclefiaftic State in *Rome*,
are ftiled *Cardinal*. Hence, in a Word, (befides
many other Things) the primary or principal
Virtues have been fo called by the *Gentile* Moralifts.

IT is not to be denied, but that the Author of
the Book of *Wifdom*, * has given a kind of Sanc-
tion to that Diftribution of *Ethics* into thofe *Four
Cardinal Virtues*, where he faith, *if a Man love
Righteoufnefs, her* [i. e. Wifdom's] *Labours are
Virtues, for fhe teacheth* Temperance *and* Prudence, Juftice *and* Fortitude ; *which are fuch things
as Men can have nothing more profitable in their
Life.*—It appears indeed by this Paffage, that
this Writer was fome *Helleniftical Jew*, who
was converfant in the Heathen Moralifts. Yet
'tis to be obferved, that altho' he name thofe
Four Virtues, he calls them not *Cardinal*, or the
Principals, whence other Virtues are derived ;
but afferts rather, that thefe *Four* (and confequently all *other* Virtues) do flow from *WIS-
DOM*; [he means, from the Knowledge and
Fear of God, or true Religion,— and this I

* Chap. viii. 7.

heartily

heartily subscribe to. —] These *Four* then are no more than so many Streams issuing from *that* Fountain: and by the *true Solomon* we are assured, that *this Wisdom* dwells: Ever with *Humility*; for so he affirms, *Prov.* xi. 2. *With the Lowly is Wisdom.* So that in Fact, if any Virtues are to be called *Cardinal*, they are these two, *FAITH* and *HUMILITY:* The first, being, as it were, the *upper*, the other the *lower* Hinge, on which the Gate of true Felicity turns. Consequently on *these Two*, every other Virtue must depend. By these only, our Entrance lies to that *Summum Bonum*, or soveraign Good, which all the World is in quest of;——but was impossible for *Heathen* Philosophy to discover, because it understood neither the one, nor the other;——neither *Faith* nor *Humility*. And I must own, it has often astonished me to see Christians, yea Christian *Divines*, treading so servilely in the Steps of *Heathen Masters*,—— Blind Guides;——rather than follow the Path of that Divine Master, whose Service they profess, and whom they acknowledge to be the *Way*, and the *Truth*. But how can it well be otherwise, when our Schools of Learning are *Heathen* still?——*Heathen* Gods,——*Heathen* Morals are instill'd into our Youth, before they are duly season'd with the Faith and Doctrines of the Gospel. And is not this the Reason, why our Religion and Morals are so leaven'd with *Heathenism?*—— This I verily think may with Confidence be affirmed, that such prepossessing the Minds of young Students with *Profane* Authors, and the too common Practice of most grown Persons Reading *any* Books that fall in their way, rather than the Bible, before they are well fettled in the *Scriptural Grounds* of Religion, is the main Caufe of that Diverfity in Opinions, that Scepticifm or Indifference in Religion ; that Neglect, yea Contempt of the *Scriptures*, which fo generally prevails amongft us. — And what Remedy for this, but, [*retror fum vela dare*] turning back to the Fountain Head, and beginning again with our *Firft Prin ciples* (as hath been advifed.) — As to putting the *Bible* into young Childrens Hands as a *School Book*, for the fake of teaching them *to Read* ; this, I fear, has contributed much to fink its Value and Authority amongft us. — How much better were it, if only fome Extracts were made, and publifhed, out of the *Hiftorical* and *Sapiential* Books, for the ufe of Schools ; and that the Reading of the whole might be refer-ved, to a more competent Age, and riper Judgment !

B u t to return :——*Virtue* is either *Moral* or *Divine*, the latter is what we properly call *Re ligion*, and depends, as we faid before, upon *Faith* —— The other is the proper Subject of *Ethics*, and it's End is to regulate *our Manner* or thofe Duties, which we owe to our Neigh bour and ourfelves. Thefe Duties, I cannot but think it more confonant to Truth, and indeed more agreeable to the Scriptures, to range under the *feven* following Heads, (as fome of the an tient Fathers have alfo numbered them, in op pofition to the *feven Deadly Sins*,) namely, *Hu-mility, Benevolence, Liberality, Chaftity, Tempe rance, Meeknefs*, and *Diligence.*

T

THESE *seven*, if confidered as General Heads, and fpreading themfelves into feveral Branches, which naturally fpring from them, do more truly deferve the Name of *Cardinal*, than that old Heathen Quaternion of *Prudence, Juftice,* &c.

IT feems alfo more *Scriptural*, both as to the Species, and likewife the Number of them; the *Septenary*, (as appears in many Inftances) is a kind of *facred* Number, and by fome called the Number of *Perfection*.——We read of the *feven Gifts of the Holy Ghoft*, the *feven Spirits of God* —— the *feventh Day*, the *feventh Year*, and Wifdom's Houfe, is faid to be builded with *feven Pillars*.——And that by thefe *Pillars* may be underftood the *feven Virtues*, we have been fpeaking of, I need only appeal to the Authority of St *Chryfoftom*, and to his Expofition of this very Allegory. — *Quamvis plures fint Spiritus Virtutum, tamen Septem dicuntur*, &c. " Altho', *faith he*, the Spi-
" rits [or Kinds] of Virtues be divers, yet they
" are ufually called *Seven*, becaufe from thefe
" *Seven*, all the particular kinds of Virtues do
" proceed, and this is fignified to us by *Solomon*,
" where he faith, *Wifdom hath builded her Houfe*,
" *fhe hath hewn out her SEVEN Pillars.*
Prov. ix.

IF it be granted then that thefe *feven* are *Pillars*, or *Principal* Virtues; 'tis ftill more evident, that *Humility* is the *Firft*, and Chief of all (For the further Proof of which, I need only refer the

candid

candid Reader to the *second* and *third* Chapters of the enfuing Treatife ,) —I hope therefore it will be granted alfo that *Humility* has a juft and undoubted Title to be called, —— The *FIRST*, and *truly CARDINAL Virtue, in Chriftian Morality.*

HAVING already exceeded the due Bounds of a Preface, I ought not to trefpafs further on the Reader's Patience. But as I expect none but the Candidates of *Humility* will be of that Number, I the rather prefume on the hopes of Pardon, while I proceed to mention two Things which in juftice to the Publifher, and the Subject, I could not well omit.

IT has been remarked, and, as far as I can judge, with fome Reafon too, that no Virtue has been *lefs treated of,* than This. The *Popifh* Tranflator of the following Piece, upbraids the *Proteftants,* that they had no Book then extant on the Subject: And Mr *Norris,* before his Treatife *concerning this Virtue,* at the fame time that he obferves the very great and feafonable Importance of the Subject, confeffes alfo the *exceeding little that had been profeffedly written upon it.*—— Whatever other Reafons there may be for fuch fcarcity of Writers upon *Humility,* I fear this may juftly be affign'd for one, that it is owing to the fcarcity of Readers: Few Authors caring to write, or Printers to publifh, what few affect to read, and fewer are like to buy.——A reafonable Inducement this, for the publifhing, even fo little a Book as this, *by Subfcription,*

ſcription; that ſo no Damage may be ſuſtained by the Undertaker, who propoſes little more Profit by the Impreſſion, or expects it, than the Benefit which may accrue to the ſerious Reader. Wretched Times! *Atheiſm* and *Immorality* ſtand in no need of ſuch a Precaution. —— The *beſt* Books are grown mere Drugs: while the *worſt* make their way thro' *repeated* Editions: and the more Impious they are, the briſker the Sale!

BUT of all Subjects, none ſo unlikely to recommend a Book, as this of *Humility*. However *common* and approved, *Humility* may be in Profeſſion and Pretence, 'tis certain nothing is more *rare* to be met with in Practice; nothing *leſs underſtood* in Theory, than it. Bear with me therefore, gentle Reader, while I draw ſome general Character and Deſcription of this moſt excellent, but moſt neglected Virtue, which will alſo ſerve as no improper Introduction to the enſuing Diſcourſe.

HUMILITY is, properly, the due Knowledge and right Eſtimate of ourſelves, grounded on the right Knowledge of God.

IT is the higheſt Act of *Juſtice* †, it's trueſt Weights and Meaſures, by which is rendered what is ſtrictly owing to God, our Neighbour, and Ourſelves.

---

† —— *Jus ſuum unicuique tribuens pro Dignitate ſua* ——Cic.

No Man can poſſibly know *Himſelf* aright, except he have a right Apprehenſion of GOD, Man being the Image or Copy, and *God* the moſt perfect Original, of all Excellence.———A View therefore of the infinite Perfections of God, demonſtrates to Man his vaſt Inferiority and Defects.———The Senſe of his preſent Corruption and Degeneracy from his primitive Rectitude, confounds his *Pride*; and both together evince the Neceſſity and Reaſonableneſs of *Humility*.

A Conſciouſneſs of the infinite Diſtance and Diſproportion there is between the eſſential Perfections of the *Divine*, and thoſe of *Created* Nature, is the proper *Humility* of *Angels* and glorified Spirits: The Conſciouſneſs of our deviation from the divine Likeneſs, is the proper *Humility* of *Man*, being the only right Foundation of that *Poverty of Spirit*, which is to bring us back to God, and reſtore his Image.

HUMILITY therefore is the firſt Moral Virtue we are capable of, and called upon to practiſe, conſequently the *Root* and *Parent* of all others.———For,

WHAT are all the *Social* Virtues of *Benevolence*, &c. what the Duties we owe to *ourſelves*, of *Temperance* and *Sobriety*, *Chaſtity* and *pureneſs of Life*, but the neceſſary Iſſues of *Humility*?——— Yea what is Religion and Piety itſelf, but a Ray of the divine Majeſty, reflected from a deep Senſe of of our Want and Dependance;—of *Our* spiritual Poverty, and His plenitude of Perfections?

WHAT are all acts of Submission to the divine Will; What is Gratitude for his Benefits and Mercies, or Joy in his great Goodness; What are all acts of Repentance, Confession, and Prayer, but so many several acts of *Humility?*

HUMILITY then " is no mean abject Quality, but the greatest Height and Sublimity of " the Mind; 'tis the Endowment of highborn " and well educated Souls, who are acquainted " with the true Price of excellent Things. They " know too well the little worth of Riches, " Beauty, *&c.* to value themselves for them, or " to despise those who want them: Their study " is to surmount themselves, and all the little " Attainments they have hitherto reach'd; and " still to aspire to higher and more noble " Things.

" BUT the truest, most genuine, and purest " *Humility*, doth not so much arise from the " Consideration of our *Faults* and *Defects*, (tho' " every Advance in Piety discovers them the " more,) " as from a calm and serious Con- " templation of the *Divine Attributes* for " by fixing our Eyes on the infinite Greatness " and Holiness of God, we are best convinced " of our own Meanness: This will sink us to " the very Bottom of our Beings, and make us " truly appear as nothing in our own Sight,
" when

" when beheld from fo great a Height. This
" is in reality, the greateſt Elevation of Soul :
" and nothing in the World is fo Noble and
" Excellent, as the Sublimity of *Humble*
" Minds.",

IF any objeƈt to the Plainneſs of the Phrafe
in the following Traƈt, let *Humility* herſelf
plead my Excuſe : A plain Dreſs becomes her
beſt. What I aim'd at, was a neat, yet
humble Stile ; and therefore in the Amendments
I ſtudied rather to Smooth, than to Embelliſh
it, that fo every part of *Humility's* Garb might
appear of a Piece with the reſt, and be like
her Lord's Coat, *without Seam* or *Rent throughout.*——But to the *Humble* Reader, this Ad-
vertiſement, perhaps, is needleſs. —— Let
us rather pray the great Maſter of this Virtue,
to inſtruƈt both *Reader* and *Editor* in this Firſt
and moſt Important Leſſon of his School,
and that he will transfuſe the whole Spirit and
Subſtance of this little Book into our Hearts,
and Lives, that fo we may come to know thee,
O Father, and Jeſus Chriſt, whom thou haſt
ſent : that fo we may come to know Ourſelves.
——This is Life Eternal ; —— This our trueſt
Wiſdom, —— our only Happineſs. This, in a
word, is *true* HUMILITY.

***

* The pious Profeſſor *Franks* in an excellent Book
of his, newly publiſhed in *Engliſh*, called, *Chriſt the
Sum and Subſtance of all the Scriptures*, adviſes the
Reader

Reader of them to begin *with the New Testament* :
——This Rule of his seems contrary to what I have offered in the second Article of the foregoing *Advices*, and has been made an Objection thereto. — In answer to which, I crave leave to observe, That if the different *Occasion* of the Advice on either side be considered, it will appear that I do not in the least clash with that great and Holy Man. —— The Subject, he treats of, is the great Fundamental of our Faith, *the Divinity and true Nature of Christ*, And with respect to *this* Doctrine, his Advice, no doubt, is right, and his Rules excellent Whereas my Argument being more general, and relating to the reading of the Bible with respect to the whole Extent of our Vow in Baptism, I humbly conceive the Method which I have, with great Deference to better Judgments, been recommending, to be the most proper for that purpose.——But if we consult the Passage wherein his Advice is contained (p 12.) we shall not find the least Appearance of Disagreement. For he supposes of his Reader, before he enters on the Study of the Scripture, for the Purpose he is recommending, " that the *whole Bible*, or *all* the Writings of the Old " and New Testaments, have been *Once at least* " *read over*, and the Course of things described in " both Testaments, summarily understood by such " Perusal ; but *afterwards* (as he goes on) when the " more solid, and more proper Knowledge of Divine Truth comes to be discuss'd by a nicer and fuller " Enquiry, from the Foundation now laid, the most " convenient Method for understanding the Doctrine [*of Christ's Nature and Divinity*] is chiefly, and in " the First Place, *to begin* with the Writings of the " *New Testament*, to meditate upon them with the " greatest Industry, and to render them familiar to " us."——This, doubtless, is the most proper and effectual Method for attaining the great End by *him* proposed

propofed ; and the Rule is a good One, if I may prefume to appeal to my own Experience. Indeed it has long appeared to me the moft profitable Way of reading the Scriptures, that after the firft and fecond *thorough* Perufal, (which alfo the excellent Mr *Franks* approves of, as neceffary to gain a general Knowledge of both Teftaments, as to Facts and the Courfe of Things therein defcribed,) if the Perfon be. ferioufly minded to be firmly grounded in the *whole* Doctrine of Religion, fo as to fettle his own Principles, and to fortify himfelf againft every dangerous Error, fuch Reader fhould then adapt his Study of the Bible to the Plan of his Baptifmal Vow. Firft, with a profeffed View to God ; to note and obferve more particularly, what He is *in himfelf*, and what *to us, &c.* according to my third Head of Advice. —— This will give a general Idea of the Ground of that firft Branch of our Covenant, which contains the great Privileges that it configns to us. And this fhould be the main Bufinefs of One thorough Perufal ——The next fhould be with a fpecial View to MAN, to fhew us what we *were*, what we *are*, (as is above advifed) that is, to know Ourfelves, the Cafe of our Fall, and the Nature and Effects of Sin. — This the Old Teftament is moftly calculated to inftruct us in, and therefore with refpect to *Repentance*, it feems the moft proper for us to *begin* with, and attentively perufe. The next fpecial Perufal fhould be with regard to the *Chriftian Faith*, and here the Law as the (divinely appointed) Schoolmafter to Chrift, fends us to the Gofpel. Here then Mr *Franks*'s Advice moft aptly takes Place, that the New Teftament fhould be the *firft* and chief Subject of our Study, yet not fo much a diftinct Study, as explanatory of the Old, in order to fettle and confirm our *Faith* in *Chrift*. But whofo defires to be a Scribe throughly inftructed, and

to

to be perfe&t in every good Word and Work, will take the pains to give the *whole* Bible another thorough reading, with an Eye chiefly to the third Part of his Baptifmal Promife, the Duty of *Obedi- ence*, and the pra&ical Parts of Religion; more- efpecially attending to the Hiftorical and Sapiential Books; to the Examples and Chara&ers of good and bad Men in *both* Teftaments, the Promifes and Threatnings of God, Rewards and Punifh- ments. And as before he remark'd the *Vices* he was to renounce, now he notes down the *Vir- tues* he is to pra&ife; and by the Purity of the Chriftian Morality, corre&s or improves the De- fe&s and Imperfe&ions of Natural or Jewifh Righ- teoufnefs, knowing that Chrift came to *fulfil the Law*, not only in his Paffion and Sufferings, but by his *Obedience*.

But whofoever cannot find Time for purfuing fuch a Plan as this, let him but diligently attend to the *Leffons*, which our moft Excellent Church has appointed for her *Faft* and *Feftival* Seafons, and par- ticularly the *Firft Leffons* for every *Sunday* through- out the Year, and he will with no lefs Pleafure than Profit obferve, that her profeffed Defign is to inftru&t us in the Nature and Obligations of our *Baptifmal Vow*; and that fuch *Sele&* Portions are moft aptly Styled *Proper* Leffons, as having a fpecial Eye to one or other of the Branches of our *Holy Covenant*. Which being the Grand *Charter of Chriftianity*, fhe makes it her principal Bufinefs, all the Year round, to Inculcate and Explain on thofe High- Days. —— And I would to God, that her Teachers would take the Hint, and follow *Her* Example!

O F

OF THE
VIRTUE
OF
HUMILITY.

CHAP. I.

Of the Excellency of the Virtue *of* Humility,
and how great need we have thereof.

EARN *of me,* faith JE-
SUS CHRIST *our* SAVIOUR,
*for I am meek and lowly in
heart , and you shall find rest
to your souls ,* Matth. xi. 29.
" The whole Life of our
" Lord upon Earth (*faith*
" *St* Auguftine *) was led for our Inftructi-
" on ; He was the Mafter and Teacher of
" all the *Virtues,* but especially of this of
" *Humility,* which He defired we fhould
" chiefly learn." And this Confideration

* De vera Relig

B   alone,

alone, may well fuffice to let us underftand both the great Excellency of this *Virtue*, and the great need alfo we have thereof, fince the Son of God himfelf came down from Heaven to Earth, to teach us the Practice, and to be Himfelf our Inftructor therein; not by word of Mouth only, but more particularly by his Actions. For indeed his whole Life was an Example, and lively Pattern of *Humility.*

St *Bafil* * runs thro' the whole Life of CHRIST, and from His very Birth obferves and fhews, how all His Actions tended in a moft particular manner to teach us this *Virtue.* " He would needs (*faith he*) be born
" of a Mother, who was poor, in a mean
" open Stable, be laid in a Manger, and
" wrapped in homely fwaddling Cloaths,
" He would be circumcifed like a Sinner,
" and fly into *Egypt* like a weak and help-
" lefs Creature; chofe to be baptized a-
" mongft Publicans and Sinners, like one
" of them When afterwards they had a
" mind to do Him Honour, and make
" Him their King, He hid himfelf; but
" when they put Difhonour, and Affronts
" upon Him, He then prefented himfelf
" to them When he had any extraordi-
" nary Honours paid Him, yea by Perfons
" who were poffeffed with the Devil, He
" commanded Them to *hold their Peace*,

* Serm de Humilit

" but

" but when they thought fit to reproach
" and fcorn him, He then *held His Peace,*
" and reviled not again. And near the
" end of His Life, that He might, as
" it were, leave this Virtue to us by His
" laft Will and Teftament, He confirmed
" it by that extraordinary Example of
" Wafhing his Difciples Feet; as alfo by
" undergoing the Ignominious Death of
" the Crofs" St *Bernard* alfo, fpeaking
of his Nativity, faith, " The Son of God
" abafed and leffened himfelf, *by taking our*
" *Nature upon Him*, and would have His
" whole Life be a Pattern *of Humility*, that
" fo He might firft Teach us *by His Acti-*
" *ons*, what He was to Teach us *by His*
" *Words*" A ftrange way of Inftruction
this!— But why muft fo high a Majefty be
abafed fo low? " To the end that from
" thenceforth there might not fo much as
" one Man be found, who fhould prefume
" to be proud, and exalt himfelf upon the
" Earth. It muft be a moft fhameful
" Infolence, when Majefty empties itfelf,
" for a little Worm to fwell and grow
" proud." It was ever indeed a ftrange
Folly, a ridiculous kind of Abfurdity,
for Man to be proud; but how much more
abfurd muft fuch Infolence *now* be, fince
the moft High God hath humbled and
abafed Himfelf! The Son of God, who
is equal to the Father, takes upon Him
the form of a Servant, and vouchfafes to

be humbled and defpifed, and fhall I, who am but Duft and Afhes, feek to be honoured and admired?

With good reafon therefore did the Saviour of the World declare Himfelf the Mafter of *Humility*, and would have us to learn it of Him. Neither *Plato*, nor *Socrates*, nor *Ariftotle*, did ever Teach Men this *Virtue* When thofe Heathen Philofophers were treating of the Moral *Virtues* of *Fortitude*, of *Temperance*, of *Prudence*, and *Juftice*, they were fo far from having *Humility*, that they fought, even by thofe very Writings of theirs, and by all the *Virtues* they taught, to be Efteemed, and to tranfmit their Fame to Pofterity It is true, there was a *Diogenes*, and fome others like him, who profeffed to contemn the World, and to defpife themfelves, by ufing mean Cloaths, and practifing certain other Aufterities, and great Abftinence; but even in this they were extreamly proud, and fought even, by thofe Means, to be obferved and efteemed, whilft they themfelves defpifed others; as was wifely noted by *Plato* in *Diogenes*. For one Day, when *Plato* had invited certain Philofophers, and amongft them *Diogenes*, to his Houfe, he had his Rooms well furnifhed, his Carpets laid, and fuch other Preparations made, as might be fit for fuch Guefts. But *Diogenes*, as foon as he entred in, began to foul thofe fair Carpets with his dirty Feet, which

Plato

Plato obferving, afked him what he meant. *Calco Platonis faftum,* faith *Diogenes,* I am trampling upon *Plato's Pride.* But *Plato* made him this good Anfwer, *calcas, fed alio fiftu,* you trample indeed, but with another *kind of Pride,* infinuating thereby, *that the Pride, wherewith he trod upon* Plato's *Carpets,* was greater than *Plato's Pride in ufing them.*

The Philofophers underftood nothing of that Contempt of themfelves, wherein Chriftian *Humility* confifts, nay they did not fo much *as know Humility,* even by Name. fo true it is that this *Virtue* was properly, and only Taught by Chrift our Lord St *Auguftine* obferves, how that the Divine Sermon made by Him on the Mount, began with this *Virtue*; *Bleffed are the Poor in Spirit, for theirs is the Kingdom of Heaven.* For both St *Auguftine,* and others affirm, that by *poor in Spirit,* fuch as be *humble* are to be underftood. So that the Redeemer of the World begins his Preaching with this, He continues it with this, and he ends it with this. This was He teaching us all his Life long; this doth He defire that we fhould learn of him, " *He faith not,* (as " St Auguftine *obferves)* Learn of me to " Create Heaven and Earth, Learn of me " to do wonderful Things, and to work " Miracles, to cure the Sick, to caft out " Devils, and to raife the Dead, but " *Learn of me to be Meek and Lowly in*
B 3 " *Heart.*

" *Heart.*"—For better is the humble Man who serves God, than he that works a Miracle —That other way is plain and safe, this, full of Stumbling-Blocks and Dangers

The Necessity we all have of this *Virtue* of *Humility* is so great, that without it, *a Man cannot take one Step in the Spiritual Life.* St *Augustine* saith, * " It is necessa-
" ry that all our Actions be constantly ac-
" companied, and well fenced by *Humility,*
" both in the beginning, in the middle,
" and in the end thereof · if in this we re-
" mit our Care, and suffer Self-compla-
" cence, and vain Thoughts to enter in,
" the Wind of Pride will carry all away."
It will avail us little, that the Work itself is very good; nay in *good* Works, we have the more Cause to fear the Vice of vain Glory, and Pride. " For the other Vices
" have relation only to Sins, and forbidden
" Objects; *Envy, Luxury,* and *Wrath,*
" carry always a kind of evil Mark upon
" them, that we may take the better heed
" to avoid them." Whereas *Pride is Virtue's unwelcome Attendant* †, and ever treading as it were upon the Heels of good Works, that so it may destroy them. Many a Man has set out with a prosperous Gale towards Heaven, and at the beginning

* Epist 56
† Virtutum ingrata Comes *Claud*

of

of the Action had raifed his Heart thither, and directed all to the Glory of God, when fuddenly a Wind of Vanity arofe, and caft him *on a Rock* By raifing in him a Defire to pleafe Men, to be honoured and efteemed by them, and taking fome vain Contentment therein, the whole undertaking is fullied and depraved To the fame Purpofe both St *Gregory*, and St *Bernard* fay very well· " He that affembles the other Virtues without *Humility*, is like a Man, who " carries a little Duft or Afhes againft the " Wind, in which cafe the Wind will be " fure to fcatter, and carry it all away.

C H A P. II.

That Humility *is the Foundation of all the other* Virtues.

ST *Cyprian* faith, " *Humility* is the Foun
" dation of all Holinefs." St *Hierom*
calls it " The *Firſt* and *Principal* Grace of a
" Chriftian." St *Bernard* faith, " *Humility*
" is the Foundation and Preferver of the o-
" ther *Virtues*." St *Gregory* in one Place calls
it the Miſtrefs and Mother of every *Virtue* ;
he faith alfo, in another Place, that it is
the Root, and very Spring-head of *Virtue*.
This Comparifon of the *Root*, is very
proper, and doth moft aptly exprefs the
Properties and Nature of *Humility*. For
firſt, faith he, as the Root fuftains and
fupports the Flower, but when the Root
is pluck'd up, the Flower doth inftantly *dry and wither*, fo every *Virtue* whatfoever is inftantly loft, if it fpring not from,
and continue not in, *the Root of* Humility.
Again, as the Root lies under Ground, and
is trampled and trodden upon, having no
Beauty or Odour in itfelf, and yet the Tree
receives it's Life from thence ; juſt fo the
humble Man is dif efteemed, and defpifed ;

feems

feems to carry no Luftre nor Brightnefs in himfelf, but is caft afide in a Corner, lies buried and forgotten; and yet this is the very thing that conferves him, and makes him thrive. Laftly, to the end the Tree may grow, and continue, and bear much Fruit, it is neceffary that the Root lie *deep* in the Ground, and how much the deeper it lies, and more covered with Earth, fo much the more Fruit will the Tree bear, and fo much the longer will it continue, according to that of the Prophet *Ifaiah,* * *It fhall again take Root downward, and bear Fruit upward;* fo the fructifying of a Soul in *Virtue,* and the conferving it therein, confifts in laying a low Root of *Humility:* The more *humble* you are, the more will you profit and grow in Virtue and Perfection. To conclude, as *Pride is the Beginning and Root of all Sin,* according to the wife Man ||, fo *Humility* is the Foundation and Root of every Virtue.

Objection. But fome perhaps will object and fay, how can you affirm, that *Humility is the Foundation of all Virtue,* and of the whole Spiritual Building; when we are commonly taught by our Divines, that *Faith* is the Foundation; according to that of St *Paul, Other Foundation can no Man lay, than that is laid, which is Jefus Chrift †;* that is, *Faith* in Jefus Chrift. To this

Aquinas anſwers well. " Two things are
" requiſite for the well founding of a
" Houſe, firſt it is neceſſary to open the
" Ground well, and caſt out all that is
" looſe, 'till at length you arrive at a firm
" Bottom, whereon you may build ſafely :
" When this is done, you begin to lay
" the *firſt Stone*, which with the reſt then
" laid, is the principal Foundation of the
" Building After this manner (*continues*
" *he*) do *Humility* and *Faith* comport to-
" gether, and aſſiſt each other, in the Spi-
" ritual Building; *Humility* is that which
" opens the Soil, and it's Office is to dig
" deep into the Earth, to caſt out all that
" is looſe, that is, all the Weakneſs of
" Human Power, as well as Corruptions
" of our Nature," So then you muſt
not lay your Foundation upon your own
Strength ; for this is no better than Sand,
and muſt be thrown out , but denying and
diſtruſting yourſelf, dig on, 'till you come
to the firm Stone, and living Rock ; which
Rock is Chriſt. He indeed is the *principal*
Foundation, whereon the whole Superſtru-
cture is to be raiſed But this is the Foundation which is laid of God, and what we
are therefore *to build upon*. And the
Building which we are to raiſe thereon is
a Holy Life. *Faith* indeed is the Cement
that fixes this Building upon that Rock ;
but *Humility* muſt be the firſt Stone which
we are to lay thereon, and therefore is al-

so called a *Foundation*. He then who by means of *Humility*, will open the Soil well, and dig deep into the *Knowledge of himself*, and cast out all the *Sand of Self-Estimation*, and *Confidence in his own Strength or Merits*, will arrive at that prime *Foundation*, which is *Christ our Lord*, and raise a good and lasting Building, which shall not be thrown down, tho' the Winds blow, and the Floods beat, because it is founded upon the firm Rock. But on the other side, if he build without *Humility*, the Building will instantly sink down, because it is founded upon the Sand.

Moreover they are not true Virtues, but apparent only and false, which are not grounded upon *Humility*.—— St *Augustine* saith, That in those *Romans*, and antient Philosophers, there was no *true Virtue*; not only because they wanted Charity (which gives Life, and Being to every Virtue, and without which no true and perfect Virtue can consist) but principally, because they wanted also the Foundation of *Humility*, and in their *Fortitude, Temperance,* and *Justice,* sought only to be esteemed in Life, and remembred with Veneration when they were dead, their Virtues therefore were but certain empty Things, and without Substance, and indeed but the Shadows, and mere Shews of Virtue. And so, as they were not perfect, and true, but only apparent, *he adds,* that God rewarded the *Romans*

for

for them with the Temporal Bleſſings of Life, which are alſo Bleſſings but of Appearance. If therefore you mean to build up true Virtue in your Souls, take care firſt to lay a deep Foundation of *Humility* therein. "If you deſire (*ſaith he*) to be truly " great, and to erect a high Building of " Virtue in your Hearts, you muſt open " the Ground very low." And again, " The higher a Man means to raiſe this " Building, ſo much the lower muſt he lay " his Foundation." For there is no Height without a ſuitable Depth, and the deeper you lay the Foundation of *Humility*, ſo much the higher in proportion will you be able to raiſe the Tower of Evangelical Perfection, which you have begun. *Aquinas* amongſt other grave Sentences, which are remembered to have been his, was wont to ſay, " He that affects to be honoured, and can- " not bear Contempt, is juſt ſo far from " Perfection, as he courts the one, or " dreads the other ——He may work Mi- " racles, and have *Faith* to remove Moun- " tains, but without *Humility*, his *Virtue* " hath no *Foundation*."

CHAP.

CHAP. III.

Wherein is declared more particularly how Humility is the Foundation of all the Virtues.

THE more clearly to illustrate how true this Sentence of the Saints is, That *Humility is the Foundation of all the Virtues*, and how necessary a Foundation this is for them all, we will briefly discourse upon the chief of them.

[*Note.* As to the *Theological* Virtues we must except them. 1. As they are *Graces* more truly than *Virtues*, and flow solely and immediately from the Gift of the Holy Spirit; so that *Humility*, which is properly a Moral Virtue, must rather spring from them, as an effect from it's Cause, than be to them a Cause or *Foundation*. 2. The *Humility* we are speaking of, being that of Christians, and an Act of the Spiritual Life, owing it's birth to *Faith*, supported by *Hope*, and acted by *Charity*, we cannot so properly say, that these are founded on *Humility*, as that *Humility* is more truly founded upon them. But as to that Branch of Charity, which relates to our Neighbour, and

and is properly the Virtue of *Benevolence*, This, and all the other Moral Virtues do indeed reft upon *Humility* as their proper Bafis, and genuine Foundation. Nor can any Virtue be fincere, which is not fuper-ftructed thereon]

1 As to *Benevolence*, or the Charity of Men towards their Neighbours, it is eafy to be feen, how neceffary it is that it fhould be well grounded in *Humility* For one of thofe things which is moft wont to cool and leffen the Love of Neighbours, is too free-ly cenfuring their Faults, and prying into their Imperfections and Defects. But the *Humble* Man is very far from this; his Eyes are ever caft in upon his *own* Errors, and he never confiders any thing in others, but their Virtues; hence he rather counts other Men Good, himfelf only to be Im-perfect and Faulty, and fcarce worthy to live amongft his Brethren Hence alfo he conceives a high Efteem, Refpect, and Love to all Befides, the Humble Man is never troubled that others are preferred before him, that much account is made of them, while he perhaps is forgotten, or that Things of great moment fhould be re-commended to the Care of others, and the leaft and meaneft to him Befides, *Envy* can have no Place amongft Humble Men, (for Envy fprings from Pride) wherefore if there be *Humility*, there can be no *Envying*

or

or *Contention*, nor any thing that may weaken a Man's Love to his Neighbour.

From *Humility* also grows *Patience*, which in this Life is so necessary to all Men For the *Humble* Man acknowledges his Faults, and Sins, and considers himself as one worthy of Punishment; nor can any Affliction happen, but what he esteems to be less than he deserves; so that he holds his Peace, and knows he has no just Cause to complain; but rather saith with the Prophet *, *I will bear the Indignation of the Lord, because I have sinned against Him*, Whereas the proud Man is ever complaining, and still thinks that Men do him Wrong, tho' they do him Right, and that they treat him not as he deserves, but the Man who is *Humble*, tho' indeed you do him Wrong, minds it not, nor regards the Injury; he is so far from resenting the Offence, that he looks on his greatest Enemy as the Instrument of Heaven, and all that he suffers, to be much less than what he merits from the Hand of God

Humility then is an effectual means for obtaining *Patience* —— For this Reason the *Wise Man* advising his Son how to serve God with Chearfulness and Patience, amidst the many Temptations and Troubles, he is to expect in the Course of his Duty, assigns him for the best means thereof, that

* Micah vii 9

he

he fhould be Humble *My Son, if thou come to ferve the Lord,* faith he, *prepare thy Soul for Temptation. whatfoever is brought upon thee, take cheerfully, and be patient when thou art changed to a low Eftate,* &c. —— And then concludes, *They that fear the Lord, will prepare their Hearts, and* humble *their Souls in his Sight.* Ecclus ii. This is a kind of Armour, which if you put on, you will either not feel Affliction, or if you feel it, will be able to fupport it —— Poffefs then *Humility,* and you fhall have *Patience* therewith.

From *Humility* doth alfo fpring that kind of Peace, which is fo much defired by all, and the moft becoming Badge of all Religious Perfons So faith *Chrift, Learn of me, for I am meek and lowly in heart, and ye fhall find Reft to your Souls.* Be but *humble,* and ye fhall have great Peace, both in yourfelves, and with your Brethren. And as amongft the Proud, there are ever Contentions, Difputes, and Brauls (as the *Wife Man* obferves, *Prov.* xiii. 10); fo amongft the *humble,* there can be no Contention or Strife, except only that Holy Strife and Contention, who fhall be the Inferior, and how to pay all kind of Honour and Refpect to his Neighbour Thefe are pious Contentions, which as they grow from true *Humility,* and Fraternal Charity, fo they alfo ftrengthen and conferve the fame.

That

That *Humility* is alfo neceffary for the preferving of *Chaftity*, we may learn from many Examples, in the Hiftories of the Primitive Times; where we Read of foul, and abominable falls of fome Men, who had Spent many Years in a Religious, Solitary, and Penitential Life : all which proceeded from want of *Humility*, and prefuming too much on their own Strength. This, God is wont to punifh, by permitting Men to fall into fuch fhameful Sins as *thofe*. *Humility* is fo great an *Ornament* likewife to Chaftity, that St *Bernard* faith, " I dare " adventure to fay, that even the Virgi- " nity of the Bleffed Virgin *Mary* would " not have been pleafing to God, without " *Humility* "——Finally, as to the Virtue of *Obedience*, it is an undoubted Truth, that He cannot be truly *obedient*, who is not *humble* ; and that he who is *humble*, cannot but be *obedient*. The *humble* Man may be commanded to do any thing; but fo may not the *proud*. The *humble* Man frames no contrary Judgment, but conforms himfelf in all things to his Superiors, not only in the Work requir'd, but even in the Will and Underftanding alfo · He neither makes any Refiftance, nor any Contradiction

But altho' we may not call *Humility* the *Foundation* of thofe Virtues, which are properly the Acts of the fpiritual Life, and fpring from the Operations of Divine Grace , he should be Humble. *My Son, if thou come to serve the Lord*, saith he, *prepare thy Soul for Temptation whatsoever is brought upon thee, take cheerfully, and be patient when thou art changed to a low Estate*, &c.

—— And then concludes, *They that fear the Lord, will prepare their Hearts, and humble their Souls in his Sight.* Ecclus III. This is a kind of Armour, which if you put on, you will either not feel Affliction, or if you feel it, will be able to support it —— Possess then *Humility*, and you shall have *Patience* therewith.

From *Humility* doth also spring that kind of Peace, which is so much desired by all, and the most becoming Badge of all Religious Persons So saith *Christ, Learn of me, for I am meek and lowly in heart, and ye shall find Rest to your Souls* Be but *humble*, and ye shall have great Peace, both in yourselves, and with your Brethren. And as amongst the Proud, there are ever Contentions, Disputes, and Brauls (as the *Wise Man* observes, *Prov* XIII. 10), so amongst the *humble*, there can be no Contention or Strife, except only that Holy Strife and Contention, who shall be the Inferior, and how to pay all kind of Honour and Respect to his Neighbour These are pious Contentions, which as they grow from true *Humility*, and Fraternal Charity, so they also strengthen and conserve the same.

That

That *Humility* is alfo neceffary for the preferving of *Chaftity*, we may learn from many Examples, in the Hiftories of the Primitive Times; where we Read of foul, and abominable falls of fome Men, who had Spent many Years in a Religious, Solitary, and Penitential Life all which proceeded from want of *Humility*, and prefuming too much on their own Strength. This, God is wont to punifh, by permitting Men to fall into fuch fhameful Sins as *thofe*. *Humility* is fo great an *Ornament* likewife to Chaftity, that St *Bernard* faith, " I dare " adventure to fay, that even the Virgi- " nity of the Bleffed Virgin *Mary* would " not have been pleafing to God, without " *Humility*."——Finally, as to the Virtue of *Obedience*, it is an undoubted Truth, that He cannot be truly *obedient*, who is not *humble* ; and that he who is *humble*, cannot but be *obedient*. The *humble* Man may be commanded to do any thing , but fo may not the *proud*. The *humble* Man frames no contrary Judgment, but conforms himfelf in all things to his Superiors, not only in the Work requir'd, but even in the Will and Underftanding alfo He neither makes any Refiftance, nor any Contradiction

But altho' we may not call *Humility* the *Foundation* of thofe Virtues, which are properly the Acts of the fpiritual Life, and fpring from the Operations of Divine Grace ,

GRACE, such as *Faith, Hope, Charity, Devotion,* &c. Yet we may most certainly affirm, that *Humility* is absolutely necessary to the Performance and Exercise of them. So that without it, they not only degenerate, but cease to Be, or rather are changed into their very contraries —— Faith becomes Infidelity, Hope Presumption, Charity turns into Hatred, and Prayer into an Abomination.

1. *Humility,* tho' not the *Foundation* of *Faith, is yet necessary to the receiving of it.* For Faith supposeth *a submissive and humble Understanding, bringing into Captivity* (as the Apostle speaks) *every Thought to the Obedience of Christ.* On the contrary, a proud Understanding raises Difficulties and Impediments against the Dictates of Faith. Our Redeemer declared as much to the *Pharisees,* when he said, *How can ye believe, who receive Honour one of another, and seek not the Honour that cometh from God only ? John* v. 44. Nor is *Humility* necessary only for the first receiving of Faith, *but for it's Conservation also.* It is the received Opinion of our Doctors and Divines, that Pride is *the beginning of all Heresies* when a Man is so fond of his own Opinion and Judgement, that he prefers it before the *common Voice of the Saints,* and Sense of the Church, the Consequence must needs be Error and Heresy. The Apostle had said 2 *Tim.* iii. *This know also, that in the last Days perillous Times*

fhall come, for Men fhall be lovers of their own felves, covetous, boafters, proud; and St *Auguftine*, in his Expofition on the Place, fhews plainly that the Caufe of all *Herefy* is juftly affignable to Conceitednefs and *Pride*

2. *Hope* alfo is cherifhed and preferved by *Humility.*——The *humble* Man finds, and feels his Infirmity, he knows that of himfelf he can do nothing , and therefore reforts to God the more earneftly, and places all his Truft in Him

3 *Charity*, or the Love of God, is revived and kindled by *Humility* —— The *humble* Man knows, that whatfoever he hath, comes to him from the Hand of God ; that himfelf is very far from deferving it : and this Confideration alone inflames him fo much with the Love of God, that, in a pious Aftonifhment, he cries out with the Holy *Job*, Chap. vii. 17. *What is Man, that thou fhould'ft magnify him, and fet thy Heart upon him ?*—— What is Man, that thou fhouldft vouchfafe him fo many Benefits and Favours ?—— What am I, to be fo wicked towards thee, what art Thou to fo good to me?—I, to be fo ungracious in offending thee, Day by Day ; and thou, in renewing to me thy Mercies every Hour? This is one of the moft affecting Motives, whereby the Saints have ever been wont to inflame their Souls with the Love of God   The more they confidered their own Unworthinefs and Mifery, the
more

more highly they found themfelves in Gratitude obliged to love and to ferve Him,
who difdained not to caft his Eyes upon fo
great Unworthinefs. Even the holy Virgin, whom all Generations fhall call Bleffed, could not forbear crying out in a Rap
ture of Love and Humility, —— *My Soul doth*
magnify the Lord, who hath regarded the Low-
linefs of his Handmaid n !

Laftly, *Prayer*, upon which the very
Effence of a religious, and fpiritual Life
depends, if not accompany d with *Humility*,
is of no worth; whereas *The Prayer of the*
Humble pierceth the Clouds, and 'till it come
nigh, he will not be comforted Ecclus xxxv. 17.
Thus the holy and humble *Judith*, being
fhut up in her Oratory, clad with Sack-
cloth, and covered with Afhes, and pro-
ftrate upon the Earth, cries out in thefe
Words: *The Prayer of the humble, and meek*
of Heart, was ever pleafing to thee, O Lord.
Thus alfo the pious *Pfalmift Lord, thou*
haft heard the Defire of the the Humble. thou
wilt prepare their Heart, thou wilt caufe thine
Ear to hear Pfal. x. 17 ——The *humble* Man
fhall not be fent empty away, nor depart out
of Countenance , *the patient abiding of the*
Meek fhall not perifh for ever Do but confider how highly that humble Prayer of the
Publican in the Gofpel pleafed God ! he pre-
fumed not fo much as to lift up his Eyes to
Heaven, but ftanding a far off, and fmiting
on his Breaft with humble Acknowledg-
ment

ment of his Sins, said ; *Lord, be merciful unto me a Sinner !*—*I tell you* (saith our Redeemer) *this Man went home justified, rather than the other* , rather than that proud *Pharisee,* who held himself for a Saint In like manner might we discourse of the rest of the *Virtues.* If therefore you desire to go the nearest way, for the gaining of them all , if you would learn a short and compendious Rule, for the speedy obtaining of Perfection, this is it, *BE HUMBLE.*

C H A P. IV.

Of the particular Necessity, which they have of this Virtue, *who profess the* Cure of Souls.

THE *Greater thou art, the more humble thy self* (saith the *Wise Man) and thou shall find favour before the Lord.* Ecclus iii 18. We, who make profession of gaining Souls to God, may say with fear and trembling, *who is sufficient for these things?* God hath called us to a very high Station, our Office being to serve the Church in certain Ministries, which are very eminent and sublime, even the same, to which He chose his Apostles; namely, the Preaching of the Gospel, the Administration of

the

the Sacraments, and the difpenfing of
His bleffed Body and Blood; fo that we
may fay with St *Paul*, 2 *Cor* v. 18. *God
hath given to us the Miniftry of Reconciliation.*
He calls the Preaching of the Gofpel, and
Difpenfation of the Sacraments, by which
Grace is communicated, *the Miniftry
of Reconciliation* , God having made us his
Meffengers of Peace, the Minifters and
Embaffadours (as his Apoftles were) of his
Son, that chief Bifhop and Shepherd of our
Souls, *Jefus Chrift*. — made us the Tongues
and Inftruments of the Holy Ghoft, ex-
horting and perfwading Men by us. Our
Lord is pleafed to fpeak to Souls, by our
Tongues, even by thefe Tongues of Flefh
doth he move the Hearts of Men. How
great Need then have we (we of the *Clergy*
above all other Men) of this *Virtue* of *Humility*! becaufe, the higher our Office and
Vocation is, fo much more Hazard than o-
thers, do we run; fo much ftronger is the
Temptation to Vanity and Pride.——The
higheft Hills ftand moft expofed to the higheft Winds   It is certain, the Miniftries we
are employed in, are of very great Dignity,
and generally procure us great Refpect and
Veneration in the World. We are held to
be Saints, and even for other Apoftles upon Earth, that all our Converfation is
Sanctity, (and fo indeed it ought to be,
and woe unto us, if it be not) and that our
whole Study is, to make them Saints alfo,
with

with whom we converfe. The greater need of a deep Foundation of *Humility*, that fo high a Building as this, may not fall to the Ground. It requires no fmall Degree of *Virtue*, to be able to bear the Weight of Honour, with all it's attending Circumftances of Pomp and Splendour, and yet fuffer no Part thereof to faften on the Heart; to afcend to a great Height, and keep a fteddy Brain, is a Tafk that very few are equal to. Alafs! how many have grown giddy, and fallen down from that high Station, to which they were raifed, for want of this Foundation of *Humility?* How many, who feemed Eagles, towring up in the Exercife of feveral Virtues, have thro' Pride, become as blind as Bats, and funk down into Perdition!

For this Reafon we, of all Men, had need to be well eftablifh'd in this Virtue; if we be not, our Heads will turn, we fhall foon grow giddy, and fall into the Sin of Pride, yea into that, which is the greateft of all others, Spiritual Pride. *Bonaventure* fpeaking of this, tells us, *There are two kinds of* Pride, one that refpects Temporal Things, which is called *Carnal* Pride, and another concerning Things Spiritual, which is called *Spiritual* Pride, and this, *faith he*, is the more dangerous Pride, and a far greater Sin than the former. The Reafon hereof is plain; for, as he adds, "The
"proud

" proud Man is a Thief, and a Robber,
" for he runs away with the Goods of ano-
" ther, against the Will of the Owner."
——He steals away that Honour and Glory
which belongs to God, and which God
will not part with to another, but reserves
to himself. *My Glory will, I not give to a-
nother* (saith he by his Prophet. *Isa.* xlii.
8) but this the *proud* Man steals from
Him, he runs away with it, and applies it
to himself. When a Man grows proud
of any *natural* Advantage, as of Nobility,
Beauty, or Strength of Body, of Quick-
ness of Understanding, of Learning, or
the like, this Man is a Robber, but
the Theft is not so great. For tho' it be
true, that all these Blessings are of God,
they are but as the Chaff of His House.
but whoso grows proud of his *Spiritual*
Gifts, namely, of Sanctity, or of that Fruit,
which is gathered by Gaining of Souls, this
is a great Thief, a Robber of the Honour
of God, and steals those Jewels which he
esteems the most Rich, and of the greatest
Price, and Value, and which indeed were
set at so high a Rate, that He thought
His own Blood and Life well laid out upon the Purchase of them For this Reason,
a certain Holy Father, being full of Care
and Fear lest he should fall into Pride,
was wont to say thus to God *O Lord, if
thou give me any thing, keep it for me, who
dare*

dare not truft myfelf with it, for I am no better than a Thief, and am ftill running away with thy Goods. With what Care and Circumfpection ought *we* to walk, who have fo much more reafon to be afraid, and are fo far from being as Humble as he was, that we may not fall into this moft dangerous kind of Pride ; nor run away with thofe Goods of God, which he hath entrufted in our Hands?

———— Let no Part thereof ftick to us ; let us arrogate nothing to ourfelves ; let us return the whole to God. It was not without great Myftery, that Chrift our Saviour, when he appeared to his Difciples upon the Day of his glorious Afcenfion *, *upbraided them* firft *with their Unbelief, and hardnefs of Heart*, and Then commanded them *to go into all the World, and preach the Gofpel to every Creature*, and gave them Power to work many and mighty Miracles. For he gives us thereby to underftand, that he, who is to be exalted to the Honour of doing great Things, hath need to be Humbled firft, to be abafed in himfelf, and to have a true Knowledge of his own Frailties and Miferies ; that fo, tho' he come afterward to great Perfection, he may ftill remain intire in the Knowledge of himfelf, and retain a conftant and lively Senfe of his own Bafenefs, without attributing any other thing to himfelf than Unworthinefs. *Theo-*

* Mark xvi. 14

C

doret

doret to this Purpose notes, that " God re-
" folving to chufe *Mofes* for the Captain
" and Conducter of His People, and to
" work by his Means fuch wonderful Things
" as he refolv'd the World fhould fee,
" thought fit, for the Caufe aforefaid, that
" that very Hand, wherewith he was to di-
" vide the Red-Sea, and effect thofe o-
" ther Miracles, fhould firft be put into
" his Bofom, and then drawn forth full of
" Leprofy, to remind him of his own na-
" tural Impurity and Corruption.

A fecond Reafon, why *we* ftand in more
efpecial need of *Humility*, is, that we may
gather the more Fruit in thofe Miniftries,
wherein we are imploy'd, fo that *Humility*
is neceffary for us, not only in regard of
our own Improvement, left otherwife we
fhould *grow Vain* and *Proud*, and fo become
Caft-aways; but likewife, *for the gaining of
others, and the bringing Forth Fruit in their
Souls.* One of the principal Means for ef-
fecting this End, is *Humility*; to wit, that
we fhould diftruft ourfelves, and not rely
upon our own Induftry, or Prudence, or
Parts, but that we fhould place all our
Confidence in God, and afcribe and refer
all to Him, according to that of the wife
Man; *Truft in the Lord with all thine Heart,
and lean not to thine own Underftanding* *.
And the Reafon hereof is, (as afterwards I

---

* Prov iii 5

fhall

shall declare more at large ,) because, when distrusting ourselves, we place all our Confidence in God, ascribe all to Him, and place the whole to His Account, we thereby engage Him to take the whole Care thereof. As if we should say thus to him, " The Con- " version of Souls, O Lord, is thine alone, " and not ours, —— prosper thou thine own " Work : for what Power have we to save " Souls?"—But alas ! when we are too confident in the Means we use, and the Discourses we hold, we then make ourselves Parties in the Business, and take it out of the Hands of Almighty God ; yea rob Him of the Honour that is due to him alone.——Thus like two Balances, as one rises, the other falls, so what we take to ourselves, we pilfer from God, and run away with that Glory and Honour, which is only His ; hence it comes to pass, that for want of his Blessing, no good Effect is wrought. And this seems to be the true Cause, why oftentimes we do our Neighbours so little Good by our Sermons and Books.

We read of many Preachers in former Days, and remember some of our own Time, who tho' they were not very learned Men, no nor very eloquent, yet by their Preaching, Catechising, and private Communications in an humble and low Way, have converted, quickened, inflamed, and strengthened many of their Flock, and that because they preached not them-

C 2 selves,

felves, but Chrift Jefus the Lord ; *not with
enticing Words of Mens Wifdom, but in
Demonftration of the Spirit and Power,* as
St *Paul* fpeaks †.   In a Word, they were
diftruftful of themfelves, and placed all
their Confidence in God ; and therefore
God gave Strength and Spirit to their
Words, which feem'd even to dart burning
Flames into the Hearts of their Hearers.
But as for *us*, what is the Reafon we produce not at this Day fo great Fruit, but becaufe we ftick too clofe to the Opinion of
our own Parts and Abilities . we reft and
rely fo much upon our own means of Per-
fwafion and Learning, our quaint Difcourfe,
and polite and elegant manner of Expref-
fion, and go on pleafing and delighting
ourfelves much with ourfelves. —— " Well
" then, may God fay, when you conceive
" that you have faid the beft Things, and
" delivered the moft convincing Reafons,
" and reft content and pleafed with Con-
" ceit that you have done great Matters,
" you fhall then effect leaft of all.   That
" fhall be fulfilled in you, which the Pro-
" phet *Hofea* * faid, *give them a mifcarrying
" Womb and dry Breafts* ; you fhall be as a bar-
" ren Mother, have no more than the
" Name , —— I will give you *dry Breafts,*
" fuch as no Child fhall hang upon, nor
" any Word ftick by them which was

† 1 Cor II 4.   * Hof. IX. 14.

" faid;

" said, " ——— for this doth he deferve,
who will needs ufurp the Goods of God, and
attribute that to himfelf, which is proper,
and only due to His divine Majefty. I fay
not, but whatfoever Men fhall preach, ought
to be diligently ftudied and well confider-
ed· but this is not all ; it muft alfo be very
well *wept upon*, and very well recommended to God ; and when you fhall have made
your Head ach with ftudying it, and ru-
minating upon it, you muft fay, " We
" have done but what we ought, we are
" all unprofitable Servants. —— As for me,
" what am I able to effect? I have made
" a little Noife of Words, like a Piece
" which fhoots Powder without a Bullet,
" but if the Heart be wounded, it is thou,
" O Lord, muft do it. *The King's Heart*
" *is in the Hand of the Lord, He turneth it*
" *whitherfoever He will* *.——He alone that
" knows them, can touch and move the
" Hearts of Men Alas ! what are we
" able to do to them? What Proportion
" can our Words, what can any human
" Means, bear to an End fo high, and fo
" fupernatural, as it is to convert Souls ?——
" none in the leaft " How comes it then
to pafs that we are fo Vain, and fo over
pleafed with ourfelves when we think fome
Good is done, and that we have acquitted
ourfelves notably, as if we were the Men

* Prov xxi 1

C 3

who had done the Feat. —— *Shall the Ax* (faith God by his Prophet *) *boaſt itſelf againſt him that heweth therewith ? or ſhall the Saw magnify itſelf againſt him that ſhaketh it ? as if the Rod ſhould ſhake itſelf againſt them that lift it up, or as if the Staff ſhould lift up itſelf, as if it were no Wood.* —— Now altho' we have ſome Concern in the Cure of Souls, we are no more than Inſtruments in the Hand of God, with reſpect to any ſpiritual and ſupernatural End of their Converſion. We are but like ſo many Wands, that cannot once ſtir, if God ſtir us not, and therefore we muſt aſcribe all to Him, as having nothing to boaſt of in ourſelves.

God doth ſo highly eſteem all diffidence in our own Strength, Wit, or Diligence, and that we rely not upon ourſelves, but aſcribe all to Him, and give him the Glory of all, that for this very Reaſon (as St *Paul* acquaints us) Chriſt would not make choice of eloquent and learned Men for the Converſion of the World, by the preaching of the Goſpel, but of poor Fiſhermen, who were ignorant and unlearned ; *not many wiſe Men after the Fleſh,* (faith he) *not many mighty, not many noble are called, but God hath choſen the fooliſh things of the World to confound the Wiſe, and God hath choſen the weak things of the World to confound the things which are Mighty. And*

---

* Iſaiah x 14.

base

bafe things of the World, and things which are de-
fpifed hath God chofen, yea and things which are
not, to bring to naught things which are. But
know you why? hear St *Paul*. —— even to
this End, that *no Flefh fhould glory in his Pre-*
fence, —— that no Man fhould take occafion
of afcribing any thing to himfelf, but give
the Glory of all to God. Had the Preachers
of the Gofpel been rich and powerful, had
they gone about with armed Troops, and a
ftrong Hand to propagate God's Word over
the World, they might have imputed Men's
Converfion to the Force of their Arms:——
Had God chofen the learned Men, or the
moft excellent Orators of the World, who
by their Learning and Eloquence fhould
convince the Philofophers, a Man might
have attributed the Converfion of Mankind
to excellency of Speech, the power of Rhe-
torick, or fubtilty of Argument, in dimi-
nution of the Credit and Reputation of
the Efficacy and Power of Chrift and his
Gofpel. But it muft not be after this manner, faith St *Paul*; God was not pleafed
that this great Bufinefs fhould be effected by
eloquence of Speech, or human Wifdom,
l-ft the Crofs of Chrift fhould be made of none
effect *. St *Auguftine* faith, "our Lord Jefus
" Chrift refolving to humble the Necks of
' the Proud, did not by means of Orators
" gain Fifhermen, but by means of Fifher-

* 1 Cor 1 17

C 4 "men,

" men, gain'd both Orators and Emperors.
" *Cyprian* was a great Orator, but St *Peter*
" the Fisherman was before him, by means
" of whom was converted, not the Orator
" only, but also the Emperor "

The holy Scripture is full of Examples,
to shew that God is wont to chuse abject
Means, and weak Instruments, for the doing
of mighty Things, to teach us this Truth,
and deeply fix it in our Hearts, that we have
nothing whereof to glory, or to ascribe to ourselves, but that we should refer all to God.
This we are taught by the Story of *David's*
Triumph over *Goliath**; this poor Shepherd
and beardless Boy, smote that mighty Giant,
with no other Weapon but his Sling, and his
Scrip, *that all the Earth* (as he said) *may
know, there is a God in Israel*; and that all
Men might understand, that God *saveth not
with Sword and Spear, for the Battle is the
Lord's*, i e " Victory is his Gift; and to
" assure Men hereof, He gives it when, and
" to whom he will, even without Arms "

This was also the mystical Sense of *Gideon's* Victory †, He had drawn together two
and thirty Thousand Men against the *Midianites*, who were more than a Hundred
and thirty Thousand Men; but *the Lord
said unto Gideon, the People that are with thee
are too many for me to give the Midianites into
their Hands.*——Consider what a strange Dif-

---

* 1 Sam xvii. † Judg vii

course

courfe of God this is, "thou fhalt not over-
"come, becaufe *the People with thee are too*
"*many*". If he had faid, "thou canft not
"overcome them, becaufe they are fo
"many, and thou haft fo few," it feems
that the Difcourfe had been rational, but
you are deceived, and underftand not the
Bufinefs; this had been a good Reafon for
Men to allege, but that other was proper for
God.—You cannot overcome, faith God,
becaufe you are many. But why fo?—*left*
Ifrael vaunt themfelves againft me, and fay, mine
own Hand hath faved me; that is, fteal a-
way the Honour of the Victory from me,
and become Vain and Proud, as conceiving
that the Enemy was conquered by their own
Strength.—God therefore ordered the Matter fo, that there only remained three
Hundred Men with *Gideon*; then commanded that he fhould offer Battle to the Enemy,
and by them gave He *Gideon* the Victory.
—Yea, and Thefe had not fo much as
need to put themfelves in Arms, or even
to take their Swords in their Hands, but
only with the Sound of the Trumpets,
which they carried in one of their Hands,
and the Noife of breaking certain Pots, and
with the Brightnefs of flaming Torches,
which they carried in the other, God ftruck
the Enemy with fuch Terror and Amazement, that they overthrew and killed one
another, and the reft betook themfelves to
Flight, as thinking the whole World was

in Arms against them. So then, here was no Room or Pretence for the *Israelites* to say, that they had overcome by their own Strength.——And this was that, which God desired, namely, that they should be compelled to acknowledge Him the only Giver of Victory If then, even in temporal and human Things, wherein our own Diligence and Means bear some kind of Proportion to the End, as our Arms and Forces do towards the obtaining of Victory, God will not permit, that we attribute any thing to ourselves, but must ascribe the Success of a Battle, and indeed of all Affairs to Him ;——if even in natural Things, neither he who plants, nor he who waters, is any thing ; that it is not the Gardener, who can make any Plant to grow, nor any Tree give Fruit, but only God ; what shall we say of spiritual and supernatural Things, of the Conversion of Souls, of a Man's own progress and increase in *Virtue*, wherein our Means, Endeavours, and Diligence fall so short, and come so far behind, that they bear no proportion at all to so high an End? The Apostle St *Paul* saith *I have planted, Apollos watered but God gave the Encrease. So then, neither is he that planteth any thing, neither he that watereth, but God, that giveth the Encrease* * It is God alone that can give the spiritual Fruit and Growth ; God

* 1 Cor iii 6, 7.

alone

alone can ftrike the Hearts of Men with A-
mazement and mighty Fear; God alone
can make Men abhor Sin, and forfake a
wicked Life. As for us, we can only make
a faint Sound with the Trumpet of the Gofpel, and tho' we break thefe earthen Pitchers
of our Bodies with Mortification, fo that
Men may fee the Light of a very exem-
plary Life fhining in us, we fhall indeed
have done our Parts, but yet ftill it is only
God, who muft blefs our Labours, and
crown them with Succefs.

There are two Things we may gather
from hence, of great Ufe in the Exercife of
our Functions with Comfort, and to the
fpiritual Advantage both of ourfelves and
our Neighbours; the firft is, that, *diftrufting ourfelves, and placing all our Confidence
in God, attributing the whole Fruit and good
Succefs of all Things to him* ; we fhall the
better obferve the Rule which we are taught
by the Apoftle St *Peter, if any Man fpeak,
let him fpeak as the Oracles of God, if any
Man minifter, let him do it as of the Ability
which God giveth, that God in all things may
be glorified* ‖, that is, He that fpeaks fhould
be perfwaded, that it is God put thofe Words
into his Mouth, he that works, fhould
think it is God that worketh by him, and
fo attribute the whole Glory and Praife of
all to Him, *through Jefus Chrift, to whom*

* Hon 38 ad Pop Ant ‖ 1 Pet iv. 11.

be

be Glory and Dominion for ever and ever Never afcribing any thing to ourfelves, as of ourfelves; never giving way to high Thoughts, nor taking any vain Contentment in the Act, be it never fo holy: —— But as the fame Apoftle advifes, *ver.* 10. —— *as every Man hath received the Gift, even fo minifter the fame one to another, as good Stewards of the manifold Grace of God.*

The fecond thing we may draw from hence, is, that we fhall not be difcouraged or dejected, when we look upon our own Wretchednefs and Mifery.——Of this we have alfo great need, for who that feeth himfelf called to fo high an Office, fo fupernatural an End, as it is to convert Souls, to draw Men out of Sin, out of Herefy, out of Infidelity; who, I fay, confidering this, will not faint under the Thought, and fay, O Jefu ! how great a Difproportion is this ? Who is *fufficient for thefe Things ?* Who am I to undertake them ? Such an Imployment fuits not well with me, who am the moft unworthy and moft miferable Creature of all others ——But in this you are deceived ; for even for this very Reafon, this enterprize is fit for you; *Mofes* could not believe, that he was ever to perform fo great a Work, as to bring forth the People of *Ifrael* out of *Egypt* †, and he excufed himfelf thus to God, who was defirous to fend him . *What am I that*

---

† Exod iii.

I fhould

I fhould go unto Pharaoh, and that I fhould bring forth the Children of Ifrael out of Egypt? and he faid, O my Lord, fend I pray thee by the Hand of him whom thou wilt fend. —— And the Reafon he gives, is, *I am not Eloquent, neither heretofore, nor fince thou haft fpoken unto thy Servant, But I am flow of Speech, and of a flow Tongue* ‖ But what faid God in anfwer to him? *Who hath made Man's Mouth? or who maketh the Dumb or Deaf, or the Seeing or the Blind? have not I the Lord? Now therefore go, and I will be with thy Mouth, and teach thee what thou fhalt fay.* The fame happened alfo to the Prophet *Jeremiah,* ch. i. whom God fent to prophefy to the *Jews,* but he began to excufe himfelf thus, *Ah! Lord God, behold, I cannot fpeak, for I am a Child* —— " Hŏw " unfit then for fo great an Undertaking!" But the Lord faid unto him, *fay not I am a Child, for thou fhalt go to all that I fhall fend thee, and whatfoever I command thee thou fhalt fpeak.* —— As if he had faid, " Thou " art the Man I want, and for this very " Reafon I fhall employ thee, becaufe " thou art fo unfit." Had he been endued with great Parts, He had not been fo proper for God's Purpofe, but now he could have no colour to fteal the Praife, and attribute any thing to himfelf, and it is by

‖ Exod iv 10.

fuch

such weak Instruments that God most commonly effects the greatest things.

The holy Evangelist tells us, that the seventy Disciples returning from executing their Mission, and our Lord observing the Fruit which they had gather'd, and the wonderful things they had done, *did highly rejoice in Spirit, and said, I thank thee, O Father, Lord of Heaven and Earth, that thou hast hid these things from the Wife and Prudent, and hast revealed them unto Babes. even so, Father, for so it seemed good in thy Sight* †. O happy little ones, happy humble Souls! for these are they whom God exalts; these are they by whom he works Wonders, and whom he takes for his Instruments in doing great Things, in working great Conversions, and gathering great Fruit of Souls, therefore let no Man be discouraged or dismaid. *Fear not, little Flock* ‖ Be not dejected, or put out of Heart, because thou seest thyself very little, and least of all others, *for it is your Father's good Pleasure to give you the Kingdom;* yea to give you Power over the Hearts and Souls of Men, *I will be with you* (saith Christ,) I will assist you, *unto the End of the World.* Let us then believe for certain, that Jesus will ever be our Succour, as himself promised to our Fathers the blessed Apostles, and that we shall ever have Him for our Conducter and

† Lu'e x 21.   ‖ Luke xii 32

Head;

Head , and therefore let us not grow weary, or be difcouraged in this fo great Affair of helping and faving Souls, to which God hath called us.

C H A P. V.

Of the firft Degree of Humility, *which con-fifts in* a Man's thinking meanly of him-felf.

L*aurentius Juftinianus* faith, " that no " Man knows well what *Humility* is, " but he that hath received the Gift of be- " ing humble from God." It is indeed a very hard thing to be known " A Man, " faith he, deceives himfelf in nothing " more, than in thinking that he knows " what true *Humility* is." Do you think it confifts in faying, *I am a miferable finful Creature, I am Proud,* &c. If it confifted in this, the thing were eafy enough, and we fhould all be humble, for we all fay of ourfelves, we are this, and we are that, and I would to God that we all thought as we fpeak, and that we did not fay it with the Mouth alone, and meerly by way of Form, or pretended Refpect to others. Do you think that *Humility* confifts *in wearing*

poor

poor and mean Cloaths, or *imploying ourselves about mean Objects and contemptible things?* It consists not in this, for herein may be *much Pride,* and a Man may desire to be much esteemed and valued even for this, and so hold himself to be better, and more humble than others, which is the very *heighth of Pride.* It is true, these exterior Things may serve as Means for acquiring *Humility,* if they be used as they ought, (whereof I shall say more afterwards,) but *Humility* itself doth not consist in this. St *Hierome* saith, " many follow the Appearance and " Shadow of *Humility,* few the Truth." An easy thing it is, to carry the Head bowed down, the Eyes lowly, the Speech submiss and soft, to sigh often, and at every Word to be calling themselves miserable and sinful Creatures, but yet if you touch these very Men with any little Word, though never so lightly, you shall instantly see how far they are from true *Humility.* Away then with all Hypocrisy and Counterfeit shew; the true *humble* Man, (saith he) " is shewed by his *Suffering* and *Patience.* " This is the *Touch-stone,* whereby true *Humility* is proved "

St *Bernard* descends more particularly to declare, wherein this *Virtue* consists, and gives us this Definition thereof. " *Humility* is a Virtue, whereby a Man most " truly discerns and observes his own De-" fects and Miseries, and holds himself in " small

" fmall Account   *Humility* confifts not in any outward Things or Words, but in the very Root of the Heart, in a Man's thinking moft lowly of himfelf, and not feeking to be efteemed by others ; but this can only fpring from a moft profound Knowledge of himfelf.

To explain, and as it were anatomife this Truth, the antient Fathers fet down many Degrees of *Humility*. *Aquinas* affigns Twelve ; St *Anfelm* fpeaks of Seven , *Bonaventure* reduces them to Three ——We will follow this laft, both for Brevity's fake, and to the end, that reftraining this Doctrine to fewer Points, we may the more eafily keep them in view, and fo proceed to put them in Execution

The firft Degree then of *Humility*, (faith he) is, " that a Man think meanly of " himfelf, and have himfelf in fmall ac-" count," and the neceffary and only Means to this, is the *knowledge of a Man's felf*. Thefe two Things be they, which St *Bernard*'s Definition of *Humility* comprehends, and fo it belongs only to the firft Degree ; namely, that *Humility* is a Virtue, whereby a Man holds himfelf in mean account

This is then the firft Degree , and this, faith St *Bernard*, " is wrought in Man " by his having a true knowledge of " himfelf, and of his Miferies and Defects " For this Caufe, fome are wont to put the

know-

knowledge of a Man's self, for the first Degree of *Humility*; and not without Reason. But for as much as we reduce all the Degrees to Three, with *Bonaventure*, and place for the first Degree, the holding of a Man's self in small account; the knowledge of a Man's self we make to be the one only necessary Means, whereby to attain this Degree of *Humility*; but in Substance and Effect it comes to the same Thing. We all agree in this, that the *knowledge of a Man's self*, is the Beginning and Foundation whereby *Humility* is to be obtained, and the way to judge of ourselves as we really are. For how can we make a right Judgment of any Man's State or Character, if we know him not? —— It cannot be; —— it is therefore necessary, first that we know what *any Man is*, and then we may esteem or honour him more or less, according to his Merit In like manner you must first know yourself, and what you are, and then make your Estimate accordingly; if you esteem of yourself as you deserve to be esteemed, you cannot but *be very humble*, for you will value yourself but very little. But if you esteem yourself more than you deserve, you fall into *Pride* St *Isdore* saith, *Superbus dictus est, quia super vult videri. quam est.* " A Man is therefore " called *Proud*, because he affects to be " thought above what he really is;" and this is one of the Reasons, as some say,

why

why God loves *Humility* fo much, becaufe he is a great lover of *Truth*; and *Humility* is *Truth* · but Pride is a Deceit, and a mere Lie; for you are not what you take yourfelf to be, and what you defire others fhould think of you If therefore you refolve to walk in Truth, walk in *Humility*, and you will efteem yourfelf but what you are Methinks I afk no great matter of you, in defiring that you will efteem yourfelf but *what you are*, and not *what you are not* For it is a very unreafonable thing for any Man to conceit himfelf to be better than he is. It is likewife not only a great, but a moft fatal and dangerous Deceit, for Man to be fo miftaken in his own Cafe, as to efteem himfelf for other than in truth he is.

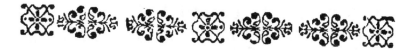

C H A P. VI.

Of the Knowledge of our felves, *which is the firft Step, and neceffary Means for obtaining of* Humility.

LET us then begin to found, and defcend deep into ourfelves, that is, into the Knowledge of our Weaknefs and Mifery, that fo we may difcover this rich Mine, For, as St *Jerome* faith, " In the " very Dung-hill of our Bafenefs, our In- " firmities, and Sins, fhall we find the " precious Pearl of *Humility*."

Begin we with this Body of ours, let that be the firft preffing of the Spade.—St *Bernard* advifes, " Set thefe three things ever before " thine Eyes, *faith he*, what thou wert, " what thou art, and what thou art to be. " What waft thou before thou wert ingen- " dred?——nothing. What art thou now? " ——a mere Veffel full of Dung, a thing fo " filthy, that we may not give it the true " Name What art thou to be fhortly? " —— the Food of Worms" We have here Matter enough to meditate upon, and Work enough for the Spade " O bafe " and vile Condition of human Nature! " *faid a Holy Father,* Look upon the

" Trees

" Trees and Plants, and thou wilt find
" they yield beautiful Leaves, fweet
" Flowers, and fair Fruits; but Man pro-
" duces out of himfelf, Nits, Lice, and
" Worms. The Plants and Trees yield
" out of themfelves Oil and Balfam, fra-
" grant Odours, and rich Wines: but the
" Body of Man is moft impure, vile,
" and offenfive. —— In fine, fuch as the
" Tree is, fuch is the Fruit: *a corrupt Tree*
" *cannot bring forth good Fruit.*

With much Reafon therefore, and with
great Propriety, is the Body of Man compared to a Dunghil overcaft with Snow, on
the outfide appearing beautiful and fair, but
within full of Filth and Uncleannefs. " If
" you but confider, *faid St* Bernard, what
" you vent by your *Eyes*, your *Ears*, your
" *Mouth*, your *Noftrils*, and the other
" Sinks of your Body, there is not in the
" World, a Dunghil that throws out fuch
" Stench and Ordure as this." How well
then might Holy *Job* * compare Man to
Rottennefs itfelf, and a very Fountain of
Worms; *I have faid to Corruption, thou art*
my Father, to the Worms, thou art my Mother
and my Sifter. Such a thing as this is Man,
a very running Stream of Rottennefs, a
wide Sack full of Worms. Of what then
fhould we glory? — *Shall Duft and Afhes be*
proud? — From this Confideration of our

* *Job* xvii 14.

bodily

bodily Frame surely there can arise no colour for being proud, but more than enough for Humiliation and Self-contempt, this made St *Gregory* say, " The Remembrance of our " own Deformity is the best Preservative of " Humility. it will keep safe under these " Ashes."

Let us now pass further on, and thrust the Spade yet lower into the Ground,—— *Consider what you were before God created you*, and you shall find that you were just *nothing*, and that you could never have been delivered out of that dark abyss of Non-entity, if God of His great Mercy and Goodness had not taken you out from thence, and placed you amongst *His Creatures*, giving you that real and true Being, which you now enjoy So that, with respect to ourselves, *we are still nothing*, and are to hold ourselves but equal to those things which *are not*; what Advantage soever we have above them now, we must wholly ascribe it to God. This is that which St *Paul* saith, *If a Man think himself to be something, when he is nothing, he deceiveth himself* *. Here then we have discovered a deep and noble Mine, from whence we may enrich ourselves with *Humility*. But this Thought may be still further improved, if we consider that even since we were Created, and have received our

* Gal vi 3

Being,

Being, it is not we who uphold it, or can retain it of ourselves. When the Architect hath built an House, it sustains itself when he leaves it, without needing his Support who made it. But it is not so in our Case; but now that we are made, we have still as great need of God, in every Moment of our Lives, for preserving the Being he gave, as we had whilst we were nothing, that we might Be. He is ever sustaining, and holding us up, with the Power of His Hand, that so we may not again fall back into that profound Pit of *Nothing*, out of which He took us before. So *David* · *Thou Lord hast fashioned me behind and before, and laid thine Hand upon me* *. And this Hand of thine, O Lord, still holds me fast, still preserves me, that I relapse not again to my former *Nothing*. We so continually depend upon this Divine Support, that if once it fail us, and He should take off His Hand, but for a Moment, in that very Moment we perish, this curious Frame of our Body is dissolved, and reverts into it's primitive *Nothing*. ——— This made the Prophet say, † *All Nations before Him are as nothing, and they are counted to him less than nothing, and Vanity*

This also is what we all say, and have continually in our Mouths, that *we are nothing*, but I doubt we only say it with our

---

* Psalm cxxxix. † Isaiah lx. 17.

Lips

Lips, and underſtand not what we ſay. For did we underſtand it, as the Prophet underſtood, and felt it, we ſhould from our Hearts ſay with him, *O Lord, we are as nothing in thy Sight.* For indeed what are we but a mere Nothing; for once I had no Being; and this Being which now I have, was not of myſelf; Thou, O Lord, didſt give it me, to thee muſt I aſcribe it all, and what have I whereof to brag, or glory in myſelf, who had nothing at all to do therein? It is Thou, Lord, alſo art ever preſerving me in being, ſupporting ſtill, and ſtill giving me Strength wherewith to work, all Being, all Strength, all Power comes from Thy Hand; without Thee we can do nothing, of ourſelves are nothing worth, becauſe in truth we are Nothing. What then have we to be proud of but of the Nothing, which we ſay we have? We ſaid before, *Shall Duſt and Aſhes be proud?* but now we may ſay, wilt thou, who art *Nothing,* which is leſs than Duſt and Aſhes, *be proud?* What Pretence then, what Colour can a Thing of *Nothing* take, for looking big, and growing proud, and holding itſelf in any Account? —— certainly none at all.

C H A P.

⁂⁂⁂⁂⁂⁂⁂⁂

C H A P. VII.

*That the principal Means for a Man's know-
ing himself, and obtaining* Humility, *is the
Consideration of his* Sins.

TO proceed; Once more let us take
the Spade in Hand, and dig,
and sink deeper into the Knowledge of
ourselves. But is there any thing yet
deeper? can any thing lie lower than Nothing? yes there doth; the Sin which you
have added to it, lieth much lower. Sin is
a Pit much deeper than Nothing, for Sinning is much worse than not Being, and
it were better for a Man not to Be, than
to have sinned; so our Lord affirms in the
Case of the Traytor *Judas, It had been better for him, that he had not been born.* There
is not a Place so low, so distant, so despised in the Eyes of God, amongst all
those things, which either are, or are not,
as that Man who *Lives in Sin, without Repentance.* he is disinherited of Heaven,
he is the Enemy of God, and under the
Sentence of Eternal Condemnation. Altho'
for the present, your Conscience may not
stand Charged with the Guilt of any known,
or voluntary Sin; yet, as for gaining the

Knowledge

Knowledge and Difcovery of our Nothing,
we looked back, and called to mind that
time wherein we had no Exiftence, fo for
the better apprehending of our Bafenefs
and Mifery, let us now call that time to
mind, when we lived *in Sin.* Confider in
how wretched a State you were, when
in the Sight of God, you were Ungracious, Deformed, his Enemy, the Child
of Wrath, obnoxious to Eternal Torment, and then defpife yourfelf throughly, and abafe yourfelf to the loweft and
profoundeft Degree that poffibly you can;
for you may fafely believe, that how much
foever you humble, and defpife yourfelf,
you will never defcend low enough, never
reach that Depth of Contempt, which he
deferves, who hath offended againft that
infinite Goodnefs, which God is. *The*
Abyfs of Sin hath no Bottom at all, it is a
moft profound, an infinite Depth, for 'till
we fhall be able to fee in Heaven, how
good God is, we fhall never be able to
know perfectly, how great the Evil of Sin
is, which is committed againft God, and
how great a Punifhment he deferves, who
commits it.

O that we would in earneft purfue this
Meditation, and dig on, and ftill found
deeper and deeper into this Mine of our
Sins and Miferies, how humble fhould we
then be! in how fmall Account fhould we
hold ourfelves! and how patiently fhould
we

we submit to the Dif-efteem and Contempt of others! He that hath been a Traytor to God, what Contempt will he not be willing to endure in Atonement for his Crime? He, who gave God away for a Fancy, a Toy, a momentary Pleafure; He who offended his Creator, and his Lord, and for it deferved to remain for ever in Hell; what Difhonours, what Affronts, or Injuries will he not think himfelf worthy to receive; yea accept them as gentle Chaftifements for thofe Offences, which he hath committed againft the Majefty of God? — *Before I was troubled,* faid the penitent Pfalmift, *I went wrong, but now have I kept thy* Word. —— Which is as much as to fay; " Before ever the " Trouble came to humble and afflict me, " I was gone aftray; I had already finned, " and for this Reafon I am filent, I dare not " complain. All is lefs than my Sins deferve, " my Punifhment is far fhort of my Of- " fence." Whatfoever we can poffibly fuffer in this Life, is meerly nothing in comparifon of what any One of our Sins hath deferved. Can it be conceived, that he deferves not to be difhonoured and defpifed, who hath *difhonoured and defpifed God?* Is it not ftrictly juft, that he be lightly efteemed, who hath fet light by God? Will you not confefs, that, that Will, which durft refift

---

* Pfalm cxix.

it's

it's Creator, fhould never from thence-forward be gratified in any one thing, which it affects or defires, as a juft Punifhment of fo great a Prefumption?

This Confideration [*of our Sins*] carries alfo this particular and very alarming Circumftance along with it, that altho' we may rely on the Mercy of God for the pardon of our Sins, yet can we not be abfolutely fure of it. *No Man knoweth either Love or Hatred*, faith the *Wife Man*, *by all that is before them*. (Ecclef. ix. 1.) And an Apoftle hath faid, *I know nothing by myfelf, yet am I not hereby juftified*. (1 Cor. iv. 4) And yet, wo unto me if I am not. — Little will it profit me, if I profefs Religion, and turn others to God, *if I fpeak with the Tongues of Men and of Angels, and have the Gift of Prophecy, and underftand all Myfteries, and all Knowledge, and tho' I beftow all my Goods to feed the Poor*, and fhould convert the whole World, *and have not Charity, I am nothing*. All would profit me nothing —— How powerful a Motive to Humility muft it then be, how juft a Ground of Self-abafement, to live in Uncertainty as to our State of Grace or Sin! —— That I have offended God, I cannot but know: that he hath forgiven me that Offence I cannot be pofitively fure Who then may prefume to lift up his Head, and fay, *I am clean from my Sin?* —— Who but muft ftand confufed, and be humbled to the very Earth with a Senfe of

his

his Guilt? For this Reason, faith St *Gregory*, *doth God hide Grace from us, that we may have one certain Grace, namely, Humility.* And altho' this Fear and Uncertainty, wherein God leaves us with respect to our State of Grace, may seem to be painful and uneasy, to wit, that we can have no express Assurance whether we be in his Favour or no; yet is it no inconsiderable Mark of his Favour and Mercy towards us, forasmuch as it greatly conduces to the gaining and preserving *Humility*; and likewise serves to keep us from despising others for the Faults they commit, be they never so great, or so many. Alas! wilt thou say, he may have committed more Sins than I, but he may also have obtained Pardon, and is forgiven. —— He is in Peace with God, —— whether I am so or no, is more than I can tell —— Furthermore, let this be a Spur to every good Work, to cast off all Sloth, and with Fear and Trembling to walk before God, with earnest and diligent Prayer imploring his Mercy and Forgiveness, according to that of *the Wise Man, Happy is the Man that feareth alway* *. And, *Concerning Propitiation be not without Fear* † This Consideration of our past Sins, is a most efficacious Means to keep us from thinking *more highly of ourselves, than we ought to think, but to think*

---

* Prov xxviii 14 † Ecclus v 5

soberly

soberly, and to hide ourselves as it were under Ground, for under this Earth there is room for a profound Descent.

Besides this, if we attentively consider the Defects and Wounds, which *Original Sin* hath caused in us, how copious Matter, how large a Field will this afford for our Humiliation? How perverted is our Nature! how corrupted by Sin! As a Stone is inclined by it's own natural Weight to fall downward, so by the Corruption of *Original Sin*, we have a most strong Propensity to the things of this World, it's Honours, it's Riches, and it's Pleasures: a Sense extreamly quick and wakeful to all the Temporal Things, which concern us; but stark dead toward those which are Spiritual and Divine. That Part of us Commands and Reigns, which, in all Reason, ought to obey; and that is Enslaved, which should of right bear Rule, and Command. To conclude, under the Out-side and Appearance of Men, the Appetites of Beasts lie concealed; and we have Hearts, which as naturally as theirs tend grovelling towards the Ground; —— *The Heart of Man is deceitful above all Things, and desperately wicked, who can know it* *? Wherefore the further we dig thro' this Wall, the greater Abominations shall we discover: what was shewed in a Figure to *Ezekiel* ‖, is verified in us

* Jer. xviii. 9   ‖ Chap. viii. 8, 9

If

If next we apply ourselves to the Consideration and Recollection of our *Actual Sins* and *Defects,* we shall find ourselves full of them; for these grow out of our own Store; they are the Product of our own Crop How slippery are our Tongues, how ill guarded our Hearts! How inconstant are we in our good Purposes, and how eager for our worldly Interests and Pursuits! How desirous are we to gratify our Appetites! How full of Self-love! How vehement in the abetting of our Humours and Will! How lively do we still find our Passions! How unmortified our bad Inclinations! And how easily do we suffer ourselves to be transported by them! St *Gregory* descants very well upon those Words of *Job, Wilt thou break a Leaf driven to and fro? Chap.* xiii 25. " With " much Reason is Man compared to the " *Leaf of a Tree*; for as a Leaf is moved " and shaken with every Wind, so is Man " by the Blasts of Passions and Tempta- " tions " — Sometimes he is transported with Anger, sometimes he is puffed up with vain Glory; now he is hurried by the Love of Money; now of Honours, now of Pleasure, one while he is hoisted up by Pride, and soon again cast down by inordinate Fear. So that in us is fulfilled what was said by the Prophet, * *We all do*

* Isa lxiv 6.

D. 4

fade

fade as a Leaf, and our Iniquities, like the Wind, have taken us away. For as Leaves are tossed to and fro, and made the Sport of Winds, so are we assaulted and shaken by Temptations: — we have no Stability in Virtue, no Firmness in executing our good Purposes, no Strength in withstanding bad ones. And is not this Matter sufficient for Self-Confusion; when not only the Sense of our wretched Condition, and real Faults, but the very best of our Actions, if strictly examined into, afford such ample Cause for mortifying our Pride? —The many Defects and Imperfections, wherewith our Virtues are blended and depraved, cannot but be a most humbling Consideration.——According to that of the same Prophet; *We are all as an unclean Thing, and all our Righteousnesses are as filthy Rags* * But of this we have amply spoken † elsewhere, so there is the less Occasion to enlarge upon it here.

* Isa lxiv 6.　　† *In his Treatise against Vain Glory.*

C H A P.

CHAP. VIII.

How to exercise ourselves in the Knowledge of what we are, that we may not be dejected or dismaid.

SO great is our Misery, so much Reason have we to humble ourselves, and such hourly Experience have we of our Frailty, that we seem to stand in more need of being *animated* and *encouraged*, that we be not *dejected* and *dismaid*, with the View of our *Faults* and *Imperfections*, than to be thus urged to the Consideration of them. —— This seems so true, that the Writers and Instructors in the way of Holiness, teach us, that we must indeed penetrate into the Knowledge of our *Miseries* and *Frailties*; but yet in such wise, as not to stop there, lest the Soul should sink down into Despair, when we see so great Misery in ourselves, and such Inconstancy in our good Purposes; but that from hence we should pass on, to the Knowledge of *the Goodness of God*, and place our whole Confidence in him: That so our Grief for having sinned, may not prove too hard for our Faith, and drive us into Dejection and Despair, that

D 5

we may not, as St. *Paul* speaks, *be swallowed up with over-much Sorrow* *. Penitential Grief must be a well tempered Sorrow, ever mingled with the Hope of Pardon, having an Eye to the Mercy of God in Christ Jesus, not fixing them wholly upon the Contemplation of our Misery, and the Deformity and Heinousness of Sin. We are not therefore to dwell so long upon the Consideration of our Poverty and Weakness, 'till we faint and be dismaid, but so far only, as to learn to distrust ourselves, and be convinced that on our Part we have no leaning Place whereon to rest : then instantly to look up to God, and put our Trust in him. Thus shall we not only not be discouraged, but rather be animated, and revived thereby ; because that which inclines us to distrust, while we behold ourselves, will serve to strengthen our Hope, when we look up to God. The more we know of our own Weakness, and the more distrustful we be of ourselves ; by looking up to God, relying on Him, and placing all our Confidence in Him, the more Strength shall we receive, the fuller of Courage shall we be in all Things.

For this Reason the Fathers do here Advertise us of a Point, which imports us very much, namely, that as we must not dwell too long upon the Knowledge of our Infirmities

---

* 2 Cor. i. 7.

and

and Miseries, least we fall into Distrust and Despair; but pass on to a View of the Goodness, and Mercy of God in Christ, and place our whole Confidence in Him; so also must we rest as little a while here, but quickly turn our Eyes in again upon ourselves, and upon our own Miseries and Defects. For if we fix our Thoughts wholly on the Goodness, the Mercy, and Free Grace of God, and forget what we are in ourselves: we shall run great hazard of Presumption and Pride, be apt to grow too secure of ourselves, too bold, and less Humble and careful than we ought to be, which is a dangerous Course, and hath proved the unhappy Cause of many fearful and great Falls. —— How many Men, who were very Spiritual, and who seemed to be exalted as high as Heaven in the Exercise of Prayer and Contemplation, have been cast down headlong by this Precipice! How many, who seemed to be Saints, have come by this Means to most shameful Downfalls, because they forgot themselves; because they made themselves too sure thro' the Abundance of the Favours, which they had received from God! —— They grew secure and full of Confidence, as if they were quite out of the Reach of Danger; and this was the Cause of so deplorable a Ruine.

Our

Our Histories abound with Relations of such unhappy Falls. St *Basil* saith, the Cause of that miserable Fall of King *David*, both into Adultery and Murther, was the Presumption which once he had, when visited with abundance of Consolation, that he was safe and out of all Danger; —— *I said in my Prosperity, I shall never be removed* *. —— Well, stay but a while; God will soon remove His Support; those extraordinary Favours and Graces shall be withdrawn, —— and when that happen'd, hear how he then complains,—*Thou turnedst away thy Face from me, and I was troubled.* If God forsake you in your Poverty, and leave you then to yourself; you shall soon know to your cost, when you are fallen, what you would not know, whilst you were upheld and favoured by the Almighty. The same St *Basil* saith also, that the Cause of St *Peter*'s Fall and Denial was the confiding and *presuming vainly in himself.* He had said with Arrogancy and Presumption, That tho' all Men should be offended at Christ, yet would not he be offended: *Tho he should die with him, yet would he not deny him.* For this Cause did God permit him to Fall, that, seeing his own Insufficiency, he might *be humbled, and know himself* We must never let our Eyes wander long from ourselves, nor ever be se-

* Psalm xxx.

cure

cure in this Life; but have a continual guard on our Hearts, confidering not only how frail, but even how treacherous we are to ourfelves, carrying ftill an Enemy about us, which is ever throwing fome Snare in our Way, to caufe us to fall.

As then we muft not dwell too long upon the Knowledge of our own Mifery and Weaknefs, but pafs on from thence to the Knowledge of the Goodnefs of God, left we fhould defpair; fo neither muft we ftay upon the Knowledge of God, and His Mercies and Favours, but return with fpeed again, to caft our Eyes down upon ourfelves, that fo we may not Prefume   This is that *Jacob*'s Ladder, whereof one end is faftned to the Earth, in the Knowledge of ourfelves, and the other reaches up to the very Height of Heaven by the Knowledge of God.   By this Ladder muft you afcend and defcend, as the Angels afcended and defcended by that other. Be raifed up by the Contemplation of the Goodnefs of God, yet not too high, left we forget ourfelves: defcend again to the Knowledge of ourfelves; yet not too low, left we forget that God is Gracious, and fo fink into Diftruft of his Mercy.

In fine, this Afcending and Defcending, that is, fuch frequent and alternate Acts of Faith and Humility are the beft Counterpoize to each other, and the only Security from any dangerous Extreams.

We

We read of a certain Devout Woman that did ufe this Exercife, to free herfelf from feveral Temptations, which the Devil affaulted her with: when he tempted her to Defpair, by fuggefting that her whole Life was nothing but Sin, Error, and Corruption, then fhe would raife herfelf up, but yet ftill with *Humility*, by the Confideration of the Mercies of God; and would be faying to this Effect, " *I confefs, O my* " *Creator, that my whole Life hath been led* " *in Darknefs, but yet I will hide myfelf in* " *the Wounds of Chrift Jefus Crucified, and* " *I will Bathe myfelf in His Blood, and fo* " *my Wickednefs fhall be cleanfed away; I* " *will Rejoice in my Creator, and my Lord* " *Thou fhalt Wafh me, and I fhall be Whiter* " *than Snow.*" Again; when the Devil ftrove to puff her up with Pride, by Temptations of another kind, fuggefting to her thoughts, that fhe was Perfect, and in high Favour with God, that there was no caufe, why fhe fhould any longer afflict herfelf, and lament her Sins; then would fhe *humble* herfelf the more, and make the following Anfwer; " *Wretch-* " *ed Creature that I am! St* John *Baptift* " *was Sanctified in his Mother's Womb, and* " *yet, notwithftanding all that, was continu-* " *ally exercifed about Repentance.* —— *But* " *I am guilty of infinite Defects, yet have not* " *lamented them, no nor even confidered them* " *as they deferved.*" With this the Devil

not

not enduring so great *Humility* on the one hand, nor so great Confidence on the other, said thus (as we may imagine) to her, " *Cursed be thou, and cursed be that taught thee* " *this, for I know not how to make Entrance* " *here: if I abase thee by Confusion, thou* " *raisest thyself up as high as Heaven, by the* " *Consideration of the Mercy of God: And* " *if I raise thee up towards Presumption,* " *thou abasest thyself as low as Hell, by* " *way of* Humility." Upon this he gave over a Temptation, which turned so much to his own Disadvantage, and her greater Benefit.

After this very manner are we to use this Exercise, and so shall we on the one hand be full of Circumspection, and holy Fear ; and on the other, full of Courage and spiritual Joy. Fearful, in regard to ourselves; and Joyful, thro' our Hope in God. These are those two Lessons which God gives daily to his Elect, the one to make them sensible of their Defects, and the other to let them see the Goodness of God ; that so the Knowledge of their Sin may make them abhor it, and the Sense of his Goodness may lead them to Repentance.

CHAP.

C H A P. IX.

*Of the great Benefit and Profit arifing from this
Exercife of* Self-Knowledge.

THAT we may be ftill the more
excited to the Attainment and Exercife of *Self-Knowledge*, it will be of ufe to
enlarge on the great Benefits and Advantages which attend it.   One of the chief
thereof hath been fhewed already, (*Chap.
vi.*) namely, that this is the Foundation
and Root of *Humility*, at leaft one of the
moft neceffary Steps both to obtain and to
preferve it.   One of the antient Fathers being afked, which was the beft way to obtain *Humility*, made anfwer, " If a Man
" confider only his own Sins, not ano-
" thers : if he turn his Eyes from others
" Faults, and fix them on his own." Even
this alone were fufficient to engage us wholly in this Exercife, that it contributes fo
effectually to the Attainment of *Humility*

But the Holy Fathers proceed further,
and fay, that the *humble Knowledge of ourfelves* is a more certain way towards the
Knowledge of God, than the profoundeft Study of all other Sciences.   'Tis for this Reafon

fon St *Bernard* calls this the higheft Science of all, and of the greateft Benefit, becaufe by this a Man comes to the Knowledge of God. The fame is intimated to us, as *Bonaventure* faith, " By the myftical Senfe of " that miraculous Cure, which Chrift " wrought upon the Man who was born " Blind *. For by laying Duft upon his " Eyes, he gave him both Corporeal Sight " wherewith to *fee himfelf*, and Spiritual " Sight alfo, wherewith *to know*, and *adore* " God So, faith he, to us, who are by " Nature born Blind, through Ignorance " both of God and of ourfelves, God gi- " veth Sight by laying Dirt upon our " Eyes, that is, caufing us to reflect on " our Original Duft, whereof we were " made, to the end, that knowing our- " felves to be but Men, and the Offspring " of Earth, we may receive that Sight " whereby, firft, we may fee our own " Vilenefs, and from thence be led to " know God" —— The more any Man knows his own Bafenefs, the more fhall he difcern the Greatnefs and Majefty of God. For one Contrary, and one Extream, il- luftrates the other, and ferves to make it the more Confpicuous. White upon Black appears the more frefh and clear So Man's Bafenefs, and the High Excellence of God, are oppofite Extreams, and fo very

* John ix.

Contrary,

contrary, that the more he knows himself, his Misery, his Sins, and want of Goodness, the more sensibly, he apprehends and feels the Goodness, the Mercy, and free Grace of God, who vouchsafes to Love, and, as it were, to converse with, such vile and worthless Creatures as we are.

From hence the Soul cannot but be greatly kindled and inflamed with the Love of God, for it never gives over Marvelling, and Giving Thanks to God, for that, Man being so miserable, and so wicked, yet God endures him upon the Earth, and daily also doth him many Favours. For the Sense of our own Unworthiness is sometimes so strong upon us, that we cannot so much as endure ourselves, and yet the Goodness and Mercy of God towards us is such, that not He only endures us, but is pleased to say, *My Delight is to be with the Sons of Men* "Ah Lord! What "dost thou find in the Sons of Men, that "thou shouldest say, My Delights are to "converse with them."

For this Cause it was, that the Saints were so frequent in the Exercise of the *Knowledge of themselves*, that thereby they might acquire a greater Knowledge of God, and a greater Love to His Divine Majesty. This was the Reason of that Prayer, which St *Augustin* was wont to use, *O my God, which art the same, and never changest, let me know myself: let me know thee.* And

this

this was the Prayer of another, who spent whole Days and Nights in saying only this, *Lord, who art Thou? who am I?* By this way it was that the Saints arrived to a very high Knowledge of God, and it is a very plain and certain way: the deeper you descend into the Knowledge of yourself, the higher shall you rise, and the more shall you increase in the Knowledge of God, and of His infinite Mercy and Goodness. On the other side, the higher you rise, and the more you increase in the Knowledge of God, the lower will you descend, and the more you will profit in the Knowledge of yourself. For the Light which comes from Heaven, will shew you such Defilement in your Souls, as will make you ashamed of that, which in the Eyes of the World may perhaps seem very fair and good. *Bonaventure* saith, " That as " when the Sun-Beams enter into a Room, " every Mote of the Air will shew itself; " so the Soul being enlightened by the " Knowledge of God, and the Beams of " the true Sun of Righteousness, discerns " instantly the very least Defects in itself," and so comes to hold that for faulty, which he, who enjoys not so great Light, will esteem to be innocent and good.

This is the Reason why all Holy Men are so *humble*, and so little in their own Eyes: and the more Holy and Perfect, so much the more Humble and Lowly they are.

For

For ftill, in proportion to the Light they receive, the greater will be their Knowledge both of God, and of themfelves. And how well foever they know themfelves, and how many Faults foever they fee in their own Souls, they ftill believe, that there are many more which they fee not, and that what they do fee, is the leaft part of their failings. — After this rate do they efteem themfelves —— As they believe that God is more good, than they are able to comprehend, fo alfo do they believe that they themfelves are more wicked, than they can conceive. And as how much foever we conceive, or know of God, we cannot perfectly comprehend him, but ftill there will be more, much more, to be conceiv'd and known; fo how much foever we know ourfelves, and how much foever we humble and defpife ourfelves, we fhall never be able to defcend low enough to reach the Depth of our Mifery Nor is this a mere Hyperbole, or Exaggeration of the Cafe, but the very Truth. For fince Man hath nought of his own Store, but Nothing, and Sin, who will ever be able to humble and abafe himfelf fo low, as thofe two Titles deferve?

We read of a devout Woman, who defired Light of God to know herfelf, and fhe difcerned fo much Deformity, and Mifery in her Condition, that fhe was not able to endure it, and then fhe prayed

thus

thus to God. *O Lord not so much, for I shall faint under the Burden.* —— Of a Man also, who begged of God many times, that He would make him see, and know himself. —— God opened his Eyes a little, and it had like to have cost him dear. For he saw himself so hideous, and so abominable, that he uttered loud Cries, and said. *Lord, I beseech thee, even for thy Mercies sake, to take away this Spectacle from before mine Eyes, for I can no longer bear this horrible Figure of myself*

From hence grows also, that Holy kind of Hatred, and Detestation of themselves, which we sometimes observe in the Servants of God. The more they know the immense Goodness and Love of God, so much the more do they abhor themselves, as having been sworn Enemies and Rebels against Him, according to that of *Job. Why hast thou set me as a Mark against thee, so that I am a Burden to myself,* Chap vii. 20 They see that in themselves they have the Root of all Evil, which is the wicked and perverse Inclination of the Flesh, and upon this Knowledge, they stir themselves up against, and abhor, themselves For why? Do you not think it just to abhor him, who made you forsake, and sell so great a Good as God is, for a little vain Contentment, or carnal Delight? Do you not think it reasonable to hate him, who makes you lose eternal Glory, and deserve Hell

Hell for ever? Him, who wrought you
fo much Hurt, and ftill perfifts in doing
it, do you not think you have Caufe to
deteft? And who is this Perfon? this Traytor to God? this fworn Enemy to your
Salvation? Who, but your own felf?

CHAP. X.

That the Knowledge of one's felf *doth not difmay, but rather gives Courage and Strength.*

THERE is another great Benefit,
which flows from the Exercife of
knowing a Man's felf; and that is, it not
only caufes no Difmay, or bafe Fear, as
fome perhaps might apprehend, but rather
infpires a great Heart and Courage towards
every good Work. And the Reafon is,
that when a Man *knows himfelf*, he fees
there is no Colour or Pretence, why he
fhould rely upon himfelf, but rather that
diftrufting himfelf, he fhould place all his
Confidence in God, in whom he finds himfelf ftrong and able *to do all things thro'
Chrift that ftrengtheneth him.* Hence it is,
that thefe are the Men, who are the apteft
to attempt and undertake great Things;
thefe are they, who go thro' with them.
For

For whereas they afcribe all to God, and nothing to themfelves, God takes the Bufinefs in Hand, makes it His own, and holds it upon His own Account; and then it is, that He is wont to do mighty Things, and even Wonders, by the Means of weak Inftruments. And the weaker thefe are, the more they commend the Riches and Treafures of Divine Goodnefs, as well as Power: the meaner the Veffels of his Mercy, the brighter will His Glory fhine. This is that, which God faid to St *Paul,* when being even tired with Temptations, he cryed out, and befought the Lord thrice, that he might be delivered from them; God made him this anfwer, *My Grace is fufficient for thee** Then doth the Power of God approve itfelf to be moft Strong and Perfect, when the Weaknefs and Infirmity of a Man is moft apparent. For as the Phyfitian gains more Honour, when the Sicknefs he cures, is moft dangerous; fo the greater our Weaknefs is, the greater will the Glory be to the Divine Arm and Goodnefs for our Deliverance, fo both St *Auguftin,* and St *Ambrofe* expound that Place —— When a Man knows and diftrufts himfelf, and puts all his Confidence in God, then doth His Mercy interpofe and help, but when, on the other fide, a Man puts Confidence in himfelf,

* 2 Cor XII

and

and in his own Diligence and Means, he is forsaken of Almighty God. *This, saith St Basil, is the Cause, why on particular high Festivals, and certain solemn Occasions, when we expect and desire to have most Devotion, it often falls out that we have less; because we place too great Confidence in the Means we use, and in our own Diligence and Preparations At other times, we are prevented with great Benedictions and Sweetness, when we least look for them; to the end, we may know, that this is purely an Effect of the Free Grace and Mercy of our Lord, not of any Effort or Merit of ours.* So that a Man's knowing his Misery or Frailty, causes no Cowardice or Dismay, but rather animates him, and gives the greater Courage and Strength, in regard that it makes him distrust himself, and place all his Confidence in God. This is also the Apostle's Meaning, when he saith, *When I am weak, then am I strong* *. That is, as both St *Augustine* and St *Ambrose* expound it, " When I am humbled and " cast down with a Sense and Conviction " of my own Weakness, then am I exalted " and raised up   The more I know and " see my Infirmity and Misery, the more " I depend upon God, and from him de- " rive new Strength, and new Courage, " for He is all my Confidence, and all my

* 2 Cor. XII 10.

" Strength "

" Strength, according to that of *Jeremiah*,
" *the Lord shall be his Confidence* †.

Hence you may understand, that it is
not *Humility*, nor any thing which springs
from thence, when we fall sometimes into excessive Dejections and Despondency
concerning our little Progress in Grace ;
when we fear we shall never obtain such or
such a *Virtue* ; never overcome such an ill
Habit or Inclination ; or that we shall not be
fit for this or that Office, or Business, in
which we are, or may be, imploy'd This
may look like *Humility*, but many times it
is not so, but rather springs from Pride.
For such a one so considers himself, as if by
his *Own* Strength and Diligence, he were to
accomplish the Affair , whereas he ought
to cast up his Eyes to God, in whom alone
we are to place our Confidence and our
Courage, and say with the Psalmist, *The
Lord is my Light and my Salvation, whom
then shall I fear? the Lord is the Strength of
my Life, of whom then shall I be afraid? Tho'
an Host of Men were laid against me, yet shall
not my Heart be afraid, and tho' there rose up
War against me, yet will I put my trust in
him* ‖ *Yea tho' I walk thro' the Valley of the
Shadow of Death, I will fear no Evil, for
thou art with me, thy Rod and thy Staff comfort me* *. With what variety of Words,

doth the Holy Prophet exprefs the felf fame thing! and indeed his Pfalms are full of fuch Expreffions, as teftify the abundance of pious Affections, and of that Confidence he had, and which we ought to have in God. *Thro' the help of my God, I fhall leap over the Wall,* how high foever it may be. Nothing fhall be able to fet itfelf between me and Home. God can conquer Giants by Grafhoppers. *In my God, I will tread Lions and Dragons under my Feet.* By the Grace and Favour of our Lord, we fhall be Strong. *He teacheth my Hands to Fight, and mine Arms fhall break even a Bow of Steel.*

CHAP.

CHAP. XI.

Of other great Benefits and Advantages, arifing from the Exercife of a Man's Knowledge of himfelf.

AMONG all the Means, which, on our part, we are able to ufe, for engaging the Divine Favour, and procuring the extraordinary Graces and Gifts of God, the very chief is, the humbling ourfelves before him, and a through Senfe of our own Frailty and Mifery. To this Effect is that of the Apoftle St *Paul, moft gladly will I rather glory in mine Infirmities, that the Power of Chrift may reft upon me* †. And St *Ambrofe* upon thofe Words, [*I take pleafure in Infirmities,*] faith, " If a Chriftian " glory at all, it muft be in his *Humiliation ;* " by this he may grow and profper in the " Sight of God " St *Auguftin* brings that of the Pfalmift to this Purpofe *Thou, O God, fenteft a gracious Rain upon thine Inheritance, and refrefhedft it when it was weary* ‖. " When think you that God will give the

" sweet and refreshing Rain, of his Gifts
" and Graces to his Inheritance, which is
" the Soul of Man? *Answer*. When the
" same Soul shall understand her own In-
" firmity and Misery, then will He perfect
" it, and send a plentiful Shower of His
" Gifts and Graces upon it." As here a-
mongst us, the more our Poor Beggars
discover their Misery, and their Sores,
to rich and charitable Men, the more they
move them to Pity, and receive the larger
Alms at their Hands; so the more a Man
humbles himself, and acknowledges his
Wretchedness, the more doth he invite and
incline the Mercy of God, to take Pity and
Compassion on him, and to communicate
the Gifts of His Grace with the greater A-
bundance. For *He giveth Power to the Faint,
and to them that have no Might, He encreaseth
Strength* †

To comprize in few Words, the great Benefit and Advantage of this Exercise, I may
truly say, that " *the Knowledge of a Man's
" self,* is the universal Remedy of all the
" Errors in Life." It serves also in general
to solve all Questions, which in spiritual
Conferences are wont to be asked. Suppose
the Enquiry were, whence such or such an
Evil proceeds, and what may be the Remedy thereof, the ready Answer is this,
it proceeds from the want of a Man's know-

† Isa. xl 29

ing

ing himself; and that the Remedy, is to know, and humble himself as he ought If you ask, whence it comes that we judge rashly of our Brethren? it comes from the want of knowing ourselves Did we diligently watch over ourselves, and duly examine our own Hearts, we should find so much to do, and so many Miseries to bewail, that we should not censure the *Faults of others* If you ask, whence comes it, that sometimes we speak sharp, and unmortify'd Words to our Brethren? this also grows from the want of knowing ourselves For did we know ourselves well, and were lowly in our own Eyes, so as to look upon other Men as our Betters, we should not presume to use such passionate Language. If it be asked from whence grow those Excuses, those Complaints, and those Murmurings, such as " why do they not give me this or that, " or why do they treat me after such a " manner?" it is plain that it springs from the same Root If you ask, from whence it happens, that a Man is so much troubled and dejected, when he finds himself molested by variety of Temptations, or grows Melancholy, and is discouraged, when he often falls into the same Defect; why, this also grows from the want of a *Man's knowing himself* For, were we truly humble, and considered well the Malice of our Hearts, we should not faint or be dismaid at this, but rather wonder, that we commit

E 3

no worfe things, and have not more dangerous Falls, we fhould be giving great Thanks
and Praife to God, for holding us fo faft
in his Hand, that we fall not into thofe
things, which infallibly we fhould have fallen
into, if He had not held us up   For from
a very fource and fink of Vice, what Sin is it
that will not flow? From fuch a filthy Dunghil what can we expect, but an odious and
abominable Stench, and from fuch a Tree,
what but fuch Fruit? Upon thofe Words
of the Royal Prophet; *He remembreth that
we are but Duft* †, St *Anfelm* faith, "What
"wonder is it, if Duft be blown away by
"Wind?"   In a Word, if you enquire
which way brotherly Charity, ready Obedience, chearful Patience, a Life of Pe-
nitence and Mortification may be obtained?
The Anfwer is fhort; Learn to *Know yourfelf*, that is a prefent and immediate Remedy of every Evil.

† Pfal. c111.

CHAP.

❧❧❧❧❧❧❧❧❧❧❧❧❧❧❧❧❧❧

CHAP. XII.

How much it behoveth us to be continually exercised in the Knowledge of ourselves.

FROM what hath been said it will appear, how neceſſary it is for us to be well exerciſed in the Knowledge of ourſelves. *Thales* the *Mileſian*, one of the ſeven wiſe Men of *Greece*, being aſk'd, which of all natural Things, was the hardeſt to be known, made this Anſwer, "a Man's ſelf" Becauſe the Love which a Man bears himſelf, is ſo ſtrong, that it obſtructs and hinders this Knowledge. And from hence grew that ſaying, ſo much celebrated amongſt the Antients, *Noſce Teipſum,* know thyſelf. And that of another, *Tecum habita,* dwell with thyſelf. But let us leave theſe Strangers, and come home to others of our own Communion, who are better Maſters of this Science. The bleſſed St *Auguſtin,* and St *Bernard* ſay, that the Science of a *Man's ſelf,* is the moſt profitable, and moſt ſublime of any that ever was found out. "Men, ſaith St *Auguſtin,* are wont to be
" highly delighted with the Knowledge of
" the Heavens, and of the Earth, which
E 4. they

" thy learn by Aftronomy and Geography,
" and to underftand the Motions of the
" Heavens, and the Courfe of the Planets ;
" with their Properties, and Influences·
" but yet the *Knowledge of a Man's felf*, is
" the higheft, and moft profitable Science
" of them all." Other *Knowledge puffeth
up*, but we are humbled and edified by this.
Hence the Fathers, and all fpiritual Guides
ftrictly charge us, to employ ourfelves much
in this Exercife, and they reprove the Error of thofe, who dwell chiefly upon thofe
acts of Religion, which afford them a fenfible Pleafure and Confolation , but fhun,
or too lightly pafs over the Confideration of
their Defects and Faults, becaufe they find
no Pleafure in looking into *themfelves*, in
this they are like to fuch as are deformed,
who, becaufe they are fo, care not to look
upon themfelves *in a Glafs*.

St *Bernard*, fpeaking to a Man in the
Perfon of God, faith thus ── " O Man,
" didft thou but fee and know thyfelf, thou
" wouldeft be lefs pleafing to thyfelf, and
" more pleafing to me But now, becaufe
" thou doft not fee and know thyfelf, thou
" art pleafing to thyfelf, but greatly dif-
" pleafing to me. ─── Take heed there
" come not a Time, when thou fhalt
" neither be pleafing to God, nor to thy-
" felf not to God, becaufe thou haft Sin-
" ned ; not to thyfelf, becaufe thou wilt
" be Self-condemn'd for ever."

St

St *Gregory*, treating of this, faith; " there
" are some, who as soon as they begin a
" Course of Virtue and Religion, think
" presently, that they are Holy and Good ;
" and do so set their Eyes upon the good
" they do, that they forget the Sins of their
" Lives past, yea and sometimes, their
" present Sins also ; for so very intent are
" they upon the Good they do, that they
" neither attend to, or see the Ill which
" sometimes they commit." But such as
are truly Good, Holy, and Sincere, proceed after a very different Manner For
albeit they are full of Virtue and good
Works, they are yet ever looking upon
the Evil they do, ever considering their
Imperfections, and jealous of their Defects.
——Time will quickly shew what becomes of
both these kinds of Men —— They who
have the most tender Sense of their Sins,
secure their good Actions, and conserve the
great Virtues which they possess, by remaining ever in *Humility*, on the contrary,
those, who look with such Complacence
upon their good Deeds, lose them, because
they grow *Vain* and *Proud* thereof. So that
good Men often serve themselves of their
very Sins, and draw good and spiritual Profit from thence ; whereas ill Men draw Hurt
and Loss, even from their good Deeds, because they make an ill use thereof. As it
happens in the Case of corporal Food , tho'
in itself it be healthful and good, yet if a

Man

Man eat of it without Rule or Meafure, it
will make him fick: So on the other fide,
the very Poifon of a Viper, if taken with
a certain Compofition, and due Proportion,
will become a Treacle, and give him Health.
When therefore the good Things, you
have done, occur to your Memory, and you
find yourfelf tempted to efteem and value
yourfelf for them, do as St *Gregory* advifes;
" oppofe your ill Deeds againft them,
" and call your former Sins to Mind." So
did St *Paul*, to the end, that his great Virtues might not puff him up, nor his having
been caught up into the third Heaven, and
admitted to thofe high Revelations, which
were imparted to him, exalt him *above meafure*. Alas! faith he, *I have been a Blafphemer, and a Perfecutor of the Servants of
God, and of the Name of Chrift; I am not
worthy to be called an Apoftle, becaufe I perfe-
cuted the Church of God.* This is a very good
Counterpoife, and a moft ufeful Defenfative
againft this Temptation.

Upon thofe Words, which the Archangel
Gabriel fpake to the Prophet *Daniel* *, *Underftand, O Son of Man*, &c. St *Jerom* faith,
that " thofe holy Prophets, *Daniel, Ezekiel*,
" and *Zechariah*, thro' the high and conti-
" nual Revelations, which they had, feem-
" ed already, as it were, to converfe a-
" mongft the *Quires of Angels*, but to the end,

* Dan. viii. 17.

" they

" they might not exalt themfelves above
" themfelves, and grow Vain and Proud up-
" on that Occafion, through a Conceit that
" they were advanc'd to a kind of fuperior
" and angelical Nature, the Angel, on
" the part of God, reminds them of their
" human Nature and Frailty ; often ftiling
" them *Sons of Men*, that they might *Know*
" *themfelves to be but Men*, frail and mifer-
" able Creatures like the reft , and fo con-
" tinue humble, and *not think of themfelves*
" *more highly than they ought to think.*" We
have many Examples in Hiftory, both Ec-
clefiaftical and Prophane, of Saints, and o-
ther illuftrious Perfons, Kings, Emperors,
and Prelates, who ufed this Means , and
ever kept fome about them, who might
admonifh them from time to time, that they
were but Men ; in order to keep them in
Humility, and prevent their growing Vain
and Proud.

It is recounted of *Francis Borgia*, that
while he was Duke of *Candia*, an holy Man
gave him this Counfel, That if he defired
to profit much in the Service of God, he
fhould let no Day pafs, without thinking
ferioufly of fomewhat, which might give
him Confufion, and a low Opinion of
himfelf. He fo ftrictly obferved this Counfel, that from that time, ufing himfelf to
the *Exercife of mental Prayer*, he employed
the two firft Hours of every Day, upon

E 6 this

Man eat of it without Rule or Meafure, it will make him fick: So on the other fide, the very Poifon of a Viper, if taken with a certain Compofition, and due Proportion, will become a Treacle, and give him Health. When therefore the good Things, you have done, occur to your Memory, and you find yourfelf tempted to efteem and value yourfelf for them, do as St *Gregory* advifes; " oppofe your ill Deeds againft them, " and call your former Sins to Mind." So did St *Paul*, to the end, that his great Virtues might not puff him up, nor his having been caught up into the third Heaven, and admitted to thofe high Revelations, which were imparted to him, exalt him *above meafure. Alas!* faith he, *I have been a Blafphemer, and a Perfecutor of the Servants of God, and of the Name of Chrift; I am not worthy to be called an Apoftle, becaufe I perfecuted the Church of God.* This is a very good Counterpoife, and a moft ufeful Defenfative againft this Temptation.

Upon thofe Words, which the Archangel *Gabriel* fpake to the Prophet *Daniel* *, *Underftand, O Son of Man,* &c St *Jerom* faith, that " thofe holy Prophets, *Daniel, Ezekiel,* " and *Zechariah,* thro' the high and conti- " nual Revelations, which they had, feem- " ed already, as it were, to converfe a- " mongft the *Quires of Angels;* but to the end,

* Dan. viii 17.

" they

" they might not exalt themſelves above
" themſelves, and grow Vain and Proud up-
" on that Occaſion, through a Conceit that
" they were advanc'd to a kind of ſuperior
" and angelical Nature, the Angel, on
" the part of God, reminds them of their
" human Nature and Frailty ; often ſtiling
" them *Sons of Men*, that they might *Know*
" *themſelves to be but Men*, frail and miſer-
" able Creatures like the reſt ; and ſo con-
" tinue humble, and *not think of themſelves*
" *more highly than they ought to think.*" We
have many Examples in Hiſtory, both Ec-
cleſiaſtical and Prophane, of Saints, and o-
ther illuſtrious Perſons, Kings, Emperors,
and Prelates, who uſed this Means ; and
ever kept ſome about them, who might
admoniſh them from time to time, that they
were but Men ; in order to keep them in
Humility, and prevent their growing Vain
and Pioud.

It is recounted of *Francis Borgia*, that
while he was Duke of *Candia*, an holy Man
gave him this Counſel, That if he deſired
to profit much in the Service of God, he
ſhould let no Day paſs, without thinking.
ſeriouſly of ſomewhat, which might give
him Confuſion, and a low Opinion of
himſelf. He ſo ſtrictly obſerved this Counſel, that from that time, uſing himſelf to
the *Exerciſe of mental Prayer*, he employed
the two firſt Hours of every Day, upon

this

the Knowledge and Contempt of himſelf. Moreover, whatſoever he heard, or read, or ſaw, he turned it all to ſerve this Deſign of Humiliation and Self-abaſement. Let Us obſerve this Counſel, and do likewiſe: not letting a Day paſs, without ſpending ſome Time in Prayer, and ſome Thoughts on ourſelves, which may mortify our Pride. Nor let us grow weary, or give over this Exerciſe, till we find our Soul hath gotten the better of every Symptom of Vain glory, and we feel ourſelves greatly aſhamed, to appear with ſo much Baſeneſs and Miſery as ours is, before the high Preſence and Majeſty of almighty God.

And great need have we all of this; for ſo great is our Pride, ſo ſtrong our Inclination, to be honour'd and eſteem'd, that if we walk not continually in this Exerciſe, we ſhall find ourſelves every Hour to be lifted up above ourſelves, as a Cork ſwimming upon the Water; yea no Cork is ſo light and vain as we. We muſt ever therefore be repreſſing and beating down that *ſwelling of Pride* which heaves us up; we muſt often look down on the Feet † of our Deformity and Baſeneſs, that ſo the gaiety of our Plumes may not puff up the Mind to Levity and Folly Often think of the Parable of the Fig-tree, mentioned in the Holy Goſpel,

---

† *Alluding to the Fable of the Swan, which has gay Plumes, and black Feet.*

which

which the Owner had a mind to pluck up by the Roots, becaufe in three Years it had born no Fruit, but the Gardener moved that it might be fuffered to grow a Year longer, faying, *he would dig about it, and dung it, that if then it bare no Fruit, it might afterwards be cut down.* Dig you in like manner, about the dry and barren Fig-tree of your Souls, and let the Dung and Miferies of your Sins be caft round about it, feeing you have fuch ftore thereof, fo fhall you alfo be fertile and bear Fruit.

To animate us the more to ufe this Exercife, and that no Man may take occafion thro' any Mif-apprehenfions to give it over, we are to underftand two Things, *Firft,* That no Man fhould think this Exercife belongs only to Beginners,——*it concerns the greateft Proficients, and the moft perfect Men;* for we fee that fuch, and even St *Paul* himfelf, did ufe it.——*In the fecond Place,* It is neceffary for us to underftand, that this Exercife is no afflictive, or melancholy Thing, no caufe of Trouble or Difquiet, but rather brings with it great Peace and Reft, yea, great Contentment and Joy, for a Man to have a right Knowledge of himfelf Notwithftanding the Defects or Faults he commits, yea, notwithftanding he perfectly underftands that becaufe of fuch Defects, he deferves of all Men to be hated and defpifed. For when this Knowledge of ourfelves grows from true *Humility,* the
very

very Concern it gives, comes accompanied with a certain kind of Suavity and Contentment, that a Man would be forry to be without it. Other Pains and Troubles which fome feel, when they confider their Faults and Imperfections, are Temptations of the Devil, either to make them think they are truly Humble, when they are not fo, or elfe to make them diftruft the Goodnefs of God, and be difheartened in His Service.

Were we indeed continually to dwell upon the Senfe of our own Mifery and Weaknefs, we fhould have occafion enough to be Afflicted and Sad, yea, to be quite Difcourag'd and Difmay'd, but we muft not ftay there, but pafs on to the confideration of the Goodnefs and Mercy of God, how much He loves us, what He fuffered for us, and therein place all our Hopes. So fhall that which would otherwife be an ocafion of Dejection and Sorrow, ferve to animate and incourage us, and prove an occafion of greater Comfort and Joy, when we lift up our Eyes to God. A Man beholds *himfelf,* and fees nothing there, but caufe of Grief, but looking up to God, he fees fo much Goodnefs and Love, as cafts out every Fear, notwithftanding all the Faults, Imperfections, and Miferies, which he difcerns in himfelf. For the Goodnefs and Mercy of God, doth infinitely exceed and out ftrip all that can be evil in us. And this Confideration, being rooted in the very

Ground

Ground of the Heart, unties a Man from himfelf, as from fome broken Reed, and cafts him wholly upon God, as a firm Support, and a fure Refting-place ; fo that confiding in him, and not in ourfelves, we may fay with the holy Prophet *Daniel*, *We have finned, we have done wickedly,*———*but, O Lord, hear,* &c. *for we do not prefent our Supplication before thee, for our Righteoufneffes, but for thy great Mercies* *.

* Dan ix

CHAP. XIII.

Of the fecond Degree *of* Humility, *and wherein this Degree confifts.*

THE fecond Degree of *Humility*, is, when a Man is contented *to be held by others in fmall account.* This part of *Humility* is of a paffive Nature, having a Reference to our Neighbour alfo, and is that Effect of it, which is contrary to *Vain-glory* For as the former Degree confifts in the *Knowledge*, and of courfe in the *Contempt, of ourfelves* ; this fecond Degree fubmits chearfully to be flighted and defpifed by *others* And if we be well grounded in the firft Degree of *Humility*, we fhall have made a confiderable

able Advance in our Way towards the fecond.—— Did we indeed think meanly of
ourfelves, it would feem no unreafonable
Thing, much lefs hard or unjuft, that o-
thers alfo fhould efteem as lightly of us,
yea I had almoft faid, we would be glad
thereof *.

St

* *According to former Editions, the Author defines
this fecond Degree of* Humility, *to confift in a* Defire *to
be defpifed and meanly efteemed yea to* love *and be glad
of* Contempt *This he grounds on a Saying of* Bonaventure's *— Ama nefcui & pro nihilo reputari —* " Love to
" live unknown, and to be no long accounted of "——
*But this is one of thofe Points, which this Author, and
other* Popifh *Divines carry to too rigid an Extream,
further indeed than* Bonaventure's *Words can ftrictly
bear I have therefore taken the Liberty to exprefs this
fecond Degree of* Humility *in a more qualify'd Senfe, as
more agreeable both to Reafon and true Religion and
I may add, even to the Author's own Sentiments, as will
appear by fome other Paffages, particularly the Conclufion
of his fifteenth Chapter, (which in Juftice to the Author, as well as the Reader, and it's foundnefs of Doctrine, and intrinfick Excellence, is there replaced out
of the* Latin *Edition)—— Neverthelefs I beg leave in
this place to add the following Animadverfion, as a neceffary Caution againft that Enthufiaftic Extream in
Humility, which is recommended by fome, of feeking and
defiring Contempt In the firft place it is a Violation
of the Law of Nature, to defire a real Evil, and love
and covet Shame for it's own fake ——Contrary alfo to
the Rule of Charity, to rejoice, and be pleafed at another
Man's Sin, who certainly commits a great one, if he defpife his weaker Brother and is a flat Contradiction to
our daily Prayer, —— not to be led into Temptation,
(for what greater Temptation than Contempt !) but to be
delivered from Evil —— The looking on our own Frailties
and Imperfections, muft neceffarily give us Pain, and Contempt*

St *Gregory* upon thefe Words in *Job*, (according to the vulgar *Latin*) *I have finned and tranfgreffed indeed ; and have not received as I was worthy* †, makes this Remark, many with their Tongues fpeak ill of themfelves, and fay they are this, and that, but they think not as they fpeak, for when others fay the fame, yea, and lefs than this, they cannot bear it. Such Men when they fpeak ill of themfelves are not in earneft, they feel it not fo in their Hearts, as the Penitent in *Job* is fuppofed to do, when he faid, " *I have finned, and perverted that* " *which was right, and God hath not punifh-* " *ed me, according to my Defert.*" This Confeffion came from the Heart, but thefe Men do but humble themfelves in Appearance, and in Word only, whereas in their Heart they have no *Humility.* They would feem to be Humble, but they have no Mind to be fo indeed. If in earneft they

---

tempt of ourfelves ——— How is it poffible the like Contempt from others, for the fame Failings, fhould afford any Pleafure or Delight? ——— This may be a Stoical Bravado, but is far from a Chriftian Duty, or any part of true Humility The utmoft therefore that this fecond Degree of Humility requires, is, that a Man bear with Patience, if others think as meanly of him, as he doth of Himfelf, and is not offended or difpleafed with them, if they do, I have therefore given that turn to the Doctrine contained in this Chapter, and in the fifteenth endeavour'd to explain, how, and on what Occafions, we may rejoice in Contempt, and be glad thereof.

† Job xxxiii 27

defire

defire it, they would not be fo much offended, when they are reproved, and admonifhed of any Fault by others ; they would not fo paffionately excufe, or vindicate themfelves ; they would not be fo troubled and jealous of their Honour, as we fee they are

Caffanus relates, that a certain Monk came once to vifit a devout Father, *Serapion*, who in Habit, Gefture, and Words, feemed to have great *Humility*, and Self-contempt, his whole Difcourfe was fpeaking ill of himfelf, often faying, he was fo great a Sinner, fo wicked a Man, that he was not worthy to breathe the common Air, nor to tread upon the Earth ; much lefs would he confent, they fhould wafh his Feet, or do him any Service, neither would he accept of any Seat, but upon the bare Ground. After Dinner, wife *Serapion* began to treat of fome fpiritual Matters, as he had been accuftomed, and taking occafion to apply fome part of the Difcourfe to his Gueft, he gave him this good Advice with great Mildnefs and Love, that, as he was young and ftrong, he fhould rather keep at Home, and labour with his Hands for his Living, according to the Rule of St *Paul*, and not go idly up and down to the Houfes of others The young Man was fo nettled at this Admonition and Advice, that he could not diffemble his Refentment : the Change of his Countenance and Behaviour betrayed the Diforder of his Mind.

Then

Then said *Serapion*, " what is this, my Son,
" that till now you have been speaking so
" freely of your Faults, and treated your-
" self with so much Contempt, yet now,
" upon an Admonition so gentle as this,
" which contains no Injury, or Affront at
" all, no, nor so much as the least harsh
" Word, but rather much Love and Cha-
" rity, you appear so highly Offended,
" that you cannot conceal it? Did you
" hope perhaps, by speaking all this Ill of
" yourself, to hear that Sentence of the
" wise Man out of my Mouth, *This is a good*
" *Man; he first accuses himself* * ? —— Did
" you intend we should praise you, and
" take you for a Saint?——

This praise of Men is what we too often
aim at by dispraising ourselves, but such a
kind of *Humility* is in truth the rankest Pride.
And to humble ourselves for the sake of
being counted *Humble* and *Good*, is the vilest
Hypocrisy. If you will not grant me this,
give me leave to ask you, why you say that of
yourself, which you will not have others to believe? If you be in earnest, and speak it from
your Heart, you must intend that others
should believe it too, and hold you for such
as you say you are, if you mean not this,
you shew plainly that all your *Humility* is only a Net of Vanity, and a mere Design to

---

* Prov xviii 17 *according to the Vulgar* Latin, Ju-
stus prior est accusator sui.

be valued and esteemed. What is this, but acting the Part, which the wise Man describes *There is a wicked Man that hangeth down his Head sadly, but inwardly he is full of Deceit* ‖ For what greater Deceit can there be, than by means of *Humility*, to court the Honour and Praise of Men ; and what greater Pride, than to affect to be thought Humble? ——— "To aim at the "Praise of *Humility*, is not (saith St *Bernard*) the *Virtue* of *Humility*, but the very "Reverse, and a perverse Abuse thereof" For what more perverse, what more unreasonable can there be than this, to desire to be esteemed the better Man, for feigning yourself to be a bad one ? How unworthy and absurd is it, to desire and expect Applause, for even the bad Character you bestow upon yourself? St *Ambrose* reprehending this piece of Folly, as well as Sin, "Many, *saith he*, have the Appearance, "but few the *Virtue* of *Humility*, many "profess it outwardly, but inwardly they "reject and hate it."

And yet, alas! this Pride, and vain Inclination of ours to be esteemed and valued, is so great, that we use a thousand Inventions and Ways how to compass it. Sometimes we do it directly, sometimes indirectly, but are ever contriving to bring the Water to this Mill. St *Gregory* Saith, " it

‖ Ecclus xix 26.

"is

" is the property of proud Men, when they
" conceive they have faid or done any thing
" well, to defire fuch as faw or heard it,
" to tell them the Faults, but this is no
" more than begging a Compliment "
They feem indeed to humble themfelves ex-
ternally, by defiring others to tell them
their Faults, but this Condefcenfion is no
Humility, but mere Pride, their only Defign being to traffick for Praife ; like the
Merchant, to make a Gain by what they
part with, and to profit by their Lofs. At o-
ther Times you fhall have a Man fpeak ill
of fomewhat he hath done, and declare he
is not pleafed with it, that fo he may come
to know what the other thinks, and have
the vain Pleafure to hear himfelf contra-
dicted with a, —" no certainly, it was very
" well faid or done, and you have no reafon
" at all to be difpleafed with yourfelf, upon
" that Account" A certain grave *Father*,
who was a very fpiritual Man, was wont to
call this, a Pride *by hook or by crook* , becaufe
by this Device or Engine, one Man fetches
Praife out of the Mouth of another A Man
makes an end of his Sermon, and is much
pleafed and fatisfied with himfelf, but in-
treats another to tell him the Faults ——
Now to what End ferves this Hypocrify
and Pretence? you believe not there were
any Faults, what you want is a Compliment on your Performance —to have your
Sermon commended, and your Ear tickled
with

with Praife, is all you intend or defire But if he be fo free, as to find any Fault, you are fo far from being pleafed, that you rather defend it, yea fometimes it happens, that you will defpife the Perfon who told you of it, as one of little Underftanding, and weak Judgment, in things of that Natnre, becaufe he taxed that as a Fault, which you conceive to have been well faid. All this is Pride and a downright Vanity, which you intend to gratify, by this pretended *Humility*. At other times, when we cannot conceal the Fault, we confefs it very freely, to the End, that fince we have loft a Point of Honour by making a wrong Step, we may recover it again, by confeffing it in a frank and humble Manner " At other times, faith " *Bernard*, we exaggerate our Faults, and " fay more of ourfelves than is true, to " the End, that others feeing us fo much " harder on our Faults, than is either pof- " fible or credible to be true, may think " there was no Fault at all, and fo charge " the Accufation to the Account of our " *Humility* " By fuch Aggravation and owning more than is true, we hope to conceal or extenuate the Fault ―――This was in truth the very thing we defign'd ――― And thus by a thoufand Artifices and Tricks, we endeavour to palliate and difguife our Pride, under the Cloak of *Humility*.

By the way, you fee, as the fame mellifluous Doctor goes on, *how pretious a thing* Humility,

Humility, *and how bafe and hateful Pride is.*
—How fublime and glorious a Thing muft
Humility be, fince even Pride defires to
ferve itfelf thereof, and to be cloathed therewith, that fo it may not be defpifed! On
the other hand, how bafe and fhameful a
thing is Pride, fince it dares not fo much as
appear with the Face uncovered, but is
mafqued and difguifed with the Veil of *Humility!* You would be extreamly Afhamed,
and much out of Countenance, fhould your
Vanity be difcover'd, and that all you aim
at is Praife and Efteem ——Pride is too confcious of it's own Deformity, to ftand fuch
a Difcovery, and appear in it's proper Character: and this is the Reafon why you
ftrive to cover your Pride, with the more
fpecious Appearance of *Humility* But now,
why will you indeed be that, which you are
fo afhamed to be thought? If you would
Blufh at another's knowing that you defire
to be Honoured and Praifed, why are you
not much more afhamed to defire it? For
the Defect and Evil thereof, confifts in
the thing itfelf, in the act of your defiring
it, and not in another's knowing you defire
it ——And if you be afhamed that Men
fhould know it, why are you not much
more afhamed that it fhould be feen and
known of God, *whofe Eyes did fee our Subftance, yet being unperfect* ‖. *Neither is there*

‖ Pfal. cxxxix 16.

any

any Creature that is not manifest in his Sight, but all things are naked and open unto the Eyes of him, with whom we have to do †.

And all this happens for want of being well rooted in the first Degree of *Humility*, the *Knowledge of Ourselves* ;——this is it which keeps us far from the second, to wit, the *meek enduring of Contempt.* And this is a Degree we can never attain to, without a thorough Skill and Experience in the First ——We must therefore have recourse to the Spring Head, begin our Work there, and be well grounded in the Knowledge and Sense of our own Misery, our real Nothing, that so we may be led to a mean Opinion and hearty Contempt, that is a true knowledge, of ourselves, which is the first Degree of *Humility* ——From thence only can we ascend to the Second So that it is not sufficient to condemn and speak ill of yourself, even tho' you speak it sincerely, and from your Heart, but you are to proceed still farther, even to bear without the least Impatience or Uneasiness, that others think of you, as you think and know of yourself, and not resent it, if they disesteem and despise you

St *John Climacus* saith, " He is no hum-
" ble Man who thinks meanly of himself,
" (for what Man is he, who can in Reason
" think otherwise?) but that Man is hum-
" ble, who can easily submit to be ill treated

† Heb iv 13

" and

" and defpifed by others." It is but meet and right that a Man fhould condemn himfelf, and ever be ready to confefs that he is proud, and flothful, and impatient, and the like, but how much better were it that he kept his Temper, when he is told as much by others. If you can patiently bear, that others think fo of you, and hold you in no greater Eftimation, or account, than you do your felf, and are neither grieved or angry at the Contempt you receive, and juftly deferve, this indeed is true *Humility.*

CHAP. XIV.

Of fome Steps, whereby a Man may rife to the Perfection of this fecond Degree *of* Humility.

IN regard that this fecond Degree of *Humility* is the more practic and difficult Part of that *Virtue,* we will divide it, as fome have done before us, into four Afcents or Steps, that fo by little and little, and as it were by meafured Paces, we may rife up to that higheft Pitch and Perfection of *Humility,* which this fecond Degree leads to.

The firft is, *not to defire to be Honoured,* nor to love the Praife of Men, but rather

F   to

to fly from all Affectation of Efteem and Applaufe. Our Books are full of the Examples of Saints, who were fo far from loving to have the Pre-eminence, or courting the Honours and Dignities of the World, that they ftudioufly avoided all thofe Occafions which might tend to them, as the moft capital Enemy, they could have.

The firft Example of this Kind was given us by Chrift our Redeemer and Mafter *. The *Jews* having feen that furprizing Miracle of feeding five Thoufand Men, with five Loves and two Fifhes, intended to have made Him a King; but He, to avoid the Honour defign'd, immediately convey'd himfelf out of the Place. He (we are fure) ran no Hazard of forfeiting his *Humility* in any State of Life, how high foever it might be: He only did it by way of Enfample. For the fame Reafon alfo, when He was pleafed to manifeft the Glory of His moft facred Body to His three Difciples, in His admirable Transfiguration ||, He commanded them *not to fpeak of it to any*, till after his Death, and glorious Refurrection †. In like manner, when He had given Sight to fome Blind Men, and done other Miracles, He commanded them to be filent, and *not to tell any Man*. All which was done to fet us a Pattern of flying from Honour, and all popular Efteem, in regard of the

---

* John vi. 16. || Matth. xvii.   † Ver 9.

great

great Danger we incur of growing Vain, and perishing thereby.

Gerson accommodates to this purpose, what the Poets feign of the Giant *Antêus*, Son of the Earth; who fighting with *Hercules*, recovered new Strength, every time he was cast down to the Ground, and could not be overcome: *Hercules* observing this, lifted him up on high, and then cut of his Head. This, saith *Gerson*, is what the Devil seeks to do to us; He strives to hoise us up with Honour and Praise, that so he may slay our Souls, and then cast us down more low than ever we rose high. For this Reason the true humble Man casts *Himself* down to the Earth, in a profound Knowledge of himself, and fears and flies from every thing, that is likely to puff him up.

The second Degree, as St *Anselm* saith, is this, *To suffer Contempt with Patience, wherever the Occasion presents, and to bear it well.* We do not *here* say, that you should *desire* Injuries and Affronts, that you should go in search of them, or rejoice therein, when you find them: That is a Point too high for your present Condition; ——nor is this the proper Place to treat thereof. What we now say is, that, when any thing shall offer itself, which may seemingly, or really, tend to your Disparagement, you bear it at least with Patience, if you cannot yet do it with Joy. According to that of the wise Man. *All that is brought*

F 2

upon thee, [how difagreeable foever to Flefh and Blood,] *accept, and in Grief fuftain it; and in thy* Humility *have Patience**. This is one of the beft Means both for the obtainment of *Humility*, and the preferving it. For as Honour, and the high Efteem of Men, proves a means to make us Proud, and Vain, (which made the Saints fly fo far from it;) fo all, that tends to our Difefteem and Contempt, is a very great means both for the gaining of *Humility*, and encreafing in it. For this Reafon *Laurentius Juftinianus* was wont to fay, *That* Humility *is like a Stream or Brook, which in Winter carries much Water, and little in Summer*. For fo, this Virtue grows lefs in Profperity, and greater in Adverfity

Many and daily are the Occafions for the Exercife of *Humility*, if we would embrace and improve the Opportunities of profiting thereby. We may inftance in the Words of *Kempis* ‖, " What pleafes others, fhall " be done, that which thou haft fet thy " Heart upon, fhall not fpeed what others " fay, fhall be heard, what thou fayft fhall be " nothing regarded. Others fhall afk and " receive; thou fhalt beg and not obtain " others fhall be great in the Mouths of " Men, none fhall make account of thee. " great Affairs fhall be communicated to " others; thou fhalt be held unfit to know

---

* Ecclus i 4 Vulg. Tranf.   ‖ l 3, 49

" them.

" them. For this, Nature will sometimes
" Repine, and undergo no small Conflict;
" but great is the Benefit will arise hence,
" if thou bear it all with Silence and Sub-
" mission." Let every Man therefore examine himself, and consider well those particular Occasions, which may, or do offer themselves, and observe how he behaves
therein Observe how you take it, when
another commands you in a resolute and
imperious Manner. Observe how you like
it, when they admonish you, or reprove
you, for any Fault. Observe what you
think, when you conceive that a Supe-
riour treats you with an Air of Distance,
and looks upon you with a kind of wary
or jealous Eye St *Dorotheus* advises, when
ever any such Occasion happens, to receive it
as a Remedy and a Medicine, for the cure
and healing of our Pride; and to pray
God for him, who ministers the Occasion,
as for the Physician of our Souls, and,
lastly, to be fully perswaded, that whosoever abhors these Things, abhors *Humility*
itself.

The third Step is, *that we rejoice not in*
the Praises we receive, nor take Complacence
in the Esteem of Men. This is a Step more
difficult to attain than the former; so St *Au-*
gustin observes. " To bear the want of
" Praise when it is not given, is no hard
" Matter; but not to be pleased with being
" Esteemed, nor carried away with a secret

F 3 " Delight,

" Delight, when one hears himself com-
" mended, is very hard." St *Gregory* handles
this Point very well, in his Comment on thofe
Words of *Job.* *If I beheld the Sun when it*
fhined, or the Moon walking in Brightnefs,
and my Heart hath been fecretly enticed, &c. *
——" *Job,* faith he, fpake thus, to intimate
" by that Emblem, that he did not joy,
" or take vain Satisfaction in the Praife of
" Men. For to *behold the Sun when it*
" *Shines, and the Moon when it is Bright*, is
" for a Man to reflect on the good Opi-
" nion and Fame, which he hath amongft
" Men, with too much Pleafure and De-
" light, and fecretly to pride himfelf there-
" in."

He further faith, " there is this Diffe-
" rence between the Humble and the
" Proud; the Proud love to be praifed,
" altho' they deferve it not; they gape for
" Applaufe, and are tickled with every
" vain and idle Compliment, without con-
" fidering what they are in themfelves, or
" what in the Sight of God; their fole Am-
" bition is to be honoured and efteemed of
" Men. If they can carry this Point, they
" think themfelves happy, and look big
" upon it, as Men who have gain'd their
" End. But the truly humble Man of Heart,
" is the very Reverfe to this; when he
" finds that Men efteem and praife, and

* Job xxxi 26.

" fpeak

" fpeak well of him, he is fo far from ta-
" king Delight in the Refpect juftly paid
" him, that he rather fhrinks from it, and
" is the more confounded in himfelf, ac-
" cording to that of the Pfalmift. *When I*
" *was exalted, then did I humble myfelf the*
" *more* || ;" *i. e.* walked with the greater
Lowlinefs and Fear. And that with Reafon.
For he fears left he fhould be the more
fharply corrected by almighty God, for
wanting that very thing, for which he is praifed; or if it happens that he want it not, ftill
he fears left thefe Praifes fhould provoke God
to take away thofe Graces, for which he is
commended, and fo beguile him of his Reward ; or leaft it fhould hereafter be faid unto him, thou haft received thy Reward already.

So that, whereas the Proud take occafion to fwell and grow vain upon the Praifes
of Men, the Humble, on the contrary, take
occafion from thence to abafe and confound
themfelves fo much the more. And this,
faith St *Gregory*, is what the wife Man affirms ; *as the Fining Pot for Silver, and the*
Furnace for Gold, fo is a Man tried by the
Mouth of him that praifeth him †. As Gold
and Silver are tried by the Fire, whether
Pure or Adulterate, fo a Man is proved by
Praife ; it foon appearing what he is, by

|| Pfal lxxxviii. 17, *according to the Vulgar* Latin.
† Prov xxvii 21, *according to the Vulgar* Latin Sic
probatur homo ore laudantis

the

the Temper, wherewith he bears any great Commendation or Applause. For if, when a Man is esteemed and praised, he exalt himself, and grow Vain and Proud thereof, it is plain, his Gold and his Silver is but Dross, because the Furnace of the Tongue hath consumed it. But he who can hear his own Praises, and take occasion from thence to be the more Confounded and Humbled, is pure Sterling, because the Fire of Praise did not waste or consume it; but rather purify'd and refin'd it the more; that is, the Man was the more confirmed in his *Humility.* Take you therefore this for a *certain* Sign, whether you be a Proficient in that Virtue or no; seeing the Holy Ghost delivers it for such. Observe whether you be uneasy at Commendations and Praise, or rather, whether you be not pleased and highly delighted therewith. By this you may judge, whether your Gold be Standard or no, whether your Virtue be Genuine, or of the false and spurious Kind.

We read of *Francis de Borgia,* that no one thing troubled him so much, as when he found himself to be honoured for a Saint And being ask'd once, why he afflicted himself so much for this, (himself not desiring, nor procuring it) he made answer, *That he feared the Account which he was to give to God, finding himself to be so far short of what he was conceived to be.* This is what

we

we said before out of St *Gregory* ; and after this Manner ought we to be very deeply grounded in the *Knowledge of ourselves,*
that so the vain Wind of Praise, and E-
steem of Men, may not puff us up, and
make us forget what we are. We should
rather be the more ashamed of such Praises,
and confounded thereby, considering how
false they are; at least that we have no such
Virtue in us, as to deserve them ; neither
are we such as the World conceives and
reports of us, and as indeed we ought to
be.

C H A P. XV.

Of the fourth Step, which is, to rejoice in
Contempt, *and to be* glad thereof.

THE fourth and last Degree, by which
we may arrive to the Perfection of
this second Branch of *Humility,* is not only
to shun the Praise of Men, but *to take Plea-*
sure in Dishonour and Contempt.

[But then to render both these safe and
secure Steps towards the Virtue of *Humi-*
lity, 'tis necessary for us to be apprized,
that altho' the Degrees be different, the
Ground on which both are fix'd, must be

F 5   the

the fame; and that is, that the thing in itfelf be *Right*, and a real point of *Duty*. *Blef-fed are they*, faith our Lord, *who are perfe-cuted for Righteoufnefs Sake.*——But, *what Glory is it, if, when ye be buffeted for your Faults, ye take it patiently.* If ye decline the Praife that is undeferved, or meet with juft Contempt for what is wrong, and bear it, *what thanks have ye?*——It is fo far from being the *Perfection* of *Humility*, that it fcarcely deferves to be called a *Virtue*. But when the Difgrace we receive is indeed in God's Caufe, and *for Righteoufnefs fake*, then to accept it, not only with Patience and Meeknefs, but with Joy and Gladnefs of Heart; this is indeed thank worthy, and the Perfection of this fecond Degree of *Hu-mility.*——So our Lord places this kind of Perfecution, as the *laft* and *chief* of all his Beatitudes, and not only pronounces thofe *Bleffed*, who are Perfecuted and Reviled for his Name's fake, but bids them for this very Reafon, becaufe fuch Revilings were falfe and undeferved, to *rejoice* and *be exceeding glad*, for great is your Reward in Heaven. ——Hence, the Apoftles *rejoiced that they were counted worthy to fuffer Shame for His Sake* *. But the Contempt and Igno-miny, which ufually accompanies the Crofs of Chrift, is not to be defired or fought after *for it's own Sake*, but for the Glory

* Acts v.

which

which it leads to, and as it is a real Honour to suffer in so good a Cause.——We may then *rejoice in Contempt* ; not that we suffer Shame, but that by suffering thereof we do God Honour, and promote our own Salvation.

A carnal Eye may look on this Degree of *Humility*, which we say has such respect to the Recompence of Reward, as too interested and selfish to deserve the Rank we have assign'd it, of the *last and highest Degree* of that Virtue. But whoso has spiritual Light sufficient to discern, that a noble and generous Faith, with a lively and ardent Love towards God, is the true Spring of that Contempt of worldly Honour, and of that laudable Ambition of the Honour which cometh from God, wherein this fourth Degree of *Humility* doth consist, must be convinced that it is truly Excellent and Sublime.——It is a Degree none but a Christian is capable of attaining to.——Nature and Philosophy may reach the other three ; Grace only can ascend to this.

To explain this still more clearly, we may note with St *Bernard**, that of this kind of *Humility*, there are two Sorts ; one of which he calls, *of the Understanding*, when a Man, considering Himself, and conscious of his own Defects, is convinced in his Judgment of his own Misery and Baseness,

* Pag 694.

and

and holds himfelf in no Efteem, but judges himfelf *worthy* to be Defpifed of God and Man.—— The other is *of the Heart and Will*, when we not only fubmit to the Shame we deferve, but rejoice in that, we deferve not; efpecially when it happens in the Caufe, and for the Sake of God. The former *Humility*, namely, that *of the Underftanding*, was not in Chrift our Lord, for it was not poffible for Him to think, that He *deferved* to be held in mean Account, much lefs to be Difhonoured and Defpifed; yea He blames the *Jews* ‖ for that they *Difhonoured him*; becaufe, as He faith elfewhere, *He knew whence He came*; He underftood per-fectly His own Dignity, that he was truly God, as well as a moft innocent Man.—— But the fecond Kind of *Humility* was in Him, namely, *that of the Will*; for in regard to the great Love which he bare us, He empty'd Himfelf of His Glory, He made Himfelf of no Reputation, He was pleafed to feem Vile and Contemptible in the Eyes of Men;——and this His *choice* of Contempt being for fo great, fo gracious a Defign, we are to underftand the Leffons of *Humility*, which He has both by Precept and Ex-ample given us, of this *Humility* of *the Will* and *Affections*. —— *Learn of me*, faith He, *for I am Meek and Lowly in* HEART.—But altho' this kind of *Humility* be the moft Per-

---

‖ John viii. 49.

fect, and peculiarly exhibited in our Lord's Example, yet for us, we ought to have both these kinds of *Humility.* The latter without the First, is too high to be attained, the Former without the Second, is too low and weak to be Sincere.——He that can delight in Contempt from others, without a real Sense of his own Baseness, is in danger of falling into the worst kind of Pride, Presumption and Arrogance.——He that despises and abhors himself for his own Wretchedness, yet dreads the Contempt of others, is in danger of falling into that *False Humility,* which leads to Despair.——Both these kinds of *Humility* therefore must go together; and, to render them genuine and compleat, must be such as St *Bernard* describes them. ——Like the *Spikenard, which sendeth forth the Smell thereof* ||; i. e. both *low* and *sweet,* like that odoriferous Shrub, and sending forth it's Perfume *when the King sitteth at his Table.* 1. Must be *low,* in the Knowledge of ourselves, and so have *Truth.* 2. It must diffuse it's sweetness to others, and so have *Charity.* For as he goes on, " If thou be- " hold and judge thyself, without Flattery, " by the Light of Truth, thou canst not " but be abased in thine own Eyes.—— " Yet, perhaps, mayst not bear to appear " so in the Eyes of others.——But if *Cha-* " *rity* add Life and Warmth to that Light,

|| Cant 1 12.

and

" and true Knowledge of thyſelf, there will
" be no Difficulty, but much Eaſe and Plea-
" ſure, in bearing Shame and Diſhonour
" for the Sake of God; and perfect Meek-
" neſs and Patience, in ſubmitting to the
" contemptuous or malicious Treatment of
" injurious Men " ———— This is what we
chiefly learn from the Example of our
Lord, who conſtantly joined Meekneſs of
Suffering, with Lowlineſs of Heart;——
and this in ſo high and perfect a Degree,
that He ſeemed to long for, and earneſtly
deſire, the Day of his Paſſion, when he was
to be loaded with Shame and Sufferings.
——*I have a Baptiſm to be Baptiſed with, and
how am I ſtreightened, till it be accompliſh'd* †.
The Deſire He had to endure Affronts, and
Scorn, and Reproach for the Love of us,
and the Honour of God, was ſo great, that
He thought the Time long, and had a kind
of holy Impatience, to be ſuffering thoſe
Indignities for our Sakes. He knew that
they would ſpit in His Face as a Blaſphemer,
cloath Him with white as a Fool, with
purple as a Mock-king, ſell Him as a Slave,
ſcourge Him as a Malefactor, deride Him
as an Impoſtor, revile Him as the worſt
of Men, and at laſt, not only torment Him
on the Croſs, which was then the moſt ignominious and ſhameful Death in the World,
but join Him with Thieves and Murtherers,

† Luke xii. 50.

to enhance the Scandal of Crucifixion. ——
Yet this is what our blessed Redeemer so
eagerly desired to be *accomplished*, and afterwards so meekly endured. But still we
must keep our former Caution in View ——
It was not the *Sufferings themselves* He affected or desired, (for against this unnatural
Desire he plainly enough declares by those
Words——*Now is my Soul troubled, and what
shall I say, Father save me from this Hour?*
&c. ||) but it was the infinite Advantage
which Man was to receive, and the great
Glory which God should have thereby, that
He so earnestly desired: and hence it is
that He immediately adds, to the Question
his Humanity had put,——*but for this Cause
came I unto this Hour.* As if he had said,
" Shall I pray against my Sufferings? No;
" —— 'tis for this very End and Design
" that I came into the World, that I might
" suffer for Mankind, and thereby glorify
" my Father."]

If then the Son of God desired Dishonour
and Contempt, with so great Appetite, and
received them with so much Content, and
Joy for the Love of us; He, who had no way
deserved them; methinks it should be no such
strange thing for us, who have so well deserved all kind of Dishonour and Contempt, to
desire for the Love of Him, to be held for
no other than what we really are, and to

|| John xii. 27.

rejoice

rejoice in suffering those Disgraces and Affronts, which we justly deserve. —— It was the Sense of this, as well as the Example of his Saviour, which made St *Paul* say, *I rejoice in my Infirmities*; that made him *joy in Tribulations*, in Injuries, and Affronts, in Necessities, and Persecutions and all kind of Difficulties, for Christ our Lord. But then he adds the Benefits of those Sufferings, to teach us the proper Cause of that Joy, where he saith, *we rejoice in Hope of the Glory of God*; *and not only so, but we glory in Tribulations also, knowing that Tribulation worketh Patience, and Patience Experience, and Experience Hope, and Hope maketh not ashamed, because the Love of God is shed abroad in our Hearts.* And writing to the *Philippians*, and treating of his Imprisonment, he desires them to bear him company in the Joy he had, and to congratulate the Chains he wore for Christ our Lord. He had such abundance of Joy in the Persecutions, and Afflictions which he suffered, that he had to spare for his Friends; and therefore he invited them to partake thereof and rejoice with him * This is that Milk, which the blessed Apostles suck'd from the Breast of Christ. For so we read of them, *They departed from the Presence of the Council rejoicing, that they were counted worthy to suffer Shame for his Name.* And herein they were imitated by other Saints, who trod in their Steps, particularly the holy *Ignatius*, who, as they were carry-

* Phil ii 17, 8.

ing

ing him to be martyred at *Rome*, and treated him with great Indignity and Reproach, was so full of Rapture and spiritual Joy, that he often cried out, and said.——*It is now that I begin to be a Disciple of Christ.*

The following Rule, which a certain Founder of a religious Order instituted for that Society, is full of excellent Advice to this Purpose. —— " Let all who are newly " admitted, as well as every other Member " belonging to this Foundation, consider, " and seriously lay to Heart, as in the Pre- " sence of God, that, in order to a Pro- " ficiency in the spiritual Life, they are " bound in the strictest manner, and not " in part only, to renounce all human At- " tachments, all that the World loves and " esteems, and turn the whole bent of their " Passions and Desires to those things, " which our Lord Jesus Christ delighted " in, and pursued while He was upon " Earth ——As carnal Men set their Affe- " ctions on the things of the World, ex- " erting all their Diligence in quest of it's " Honours, it's Applause, and it's Fa- " vours, and have so been taught ; those " on the contrary, who walk in the Spi- " rit, and follow in earnest the Lord " Christ, should with like Ardour, at least, " love and affect the things which are op- " posite to those worldly Pursuits · So as at " all times to wear the Badge and Livery " of their Lord and Master, for the Love

" and

" and Veneration, which they bear to him.
" Infomuch, that, provided it can be done
" without giving Offence to his divine Ma-
" jefty, or involving their Neighbour in
" Sin, they fhould be glad to fuffer all
" manner of Shame, falfe Teftimony, and
" Reproach; yea be willing to pafs for
" Ideots and Fools. So as neverthelefs
" they give no juft Occafion for fuch In-
" dignities, but regulate their whole Be-
" haviour in fuch a manner, as may moft
" effectually conform them to the Image
" and Imitation of our Lord and Saviour
" Jefus Chrift."

This Rule contains in it a fhort Compen-
dium of all that can be faid upon *Humility.*
——This is all that is meant by forfaking
the World, it's Pomps, and it's Vanities.
——This is to be dead to the World, and
to be crucify'd to all it's Affections and
Lufts.——This is the true Imitation of *Je-*
fus.——He only leads the Life of *Jefus,*
who fhuns the Love, as well as Corruptions
of the World ——— He wears his Livery,
who bears it's Contempt, as well as it's Injuries, with Meeknefs and Peace. —— But
he is moft like his Saviour, (becaufe moft
Humble) who endures fuch Indignities, not
only with Patience, but Joy.

Pf 1 2.

CHAP.

CHAP. XVI.

That the Perfection of Humility, *and of all other Virtues, consists in performing the Acts thereof, with* Delight *and* Chearfulness; *and how much this contributes to our perseverance in Virtue.*

IT is the common Doctrine of the Philosophers, *that the Perfection of Virtue consists in performing the Acts thereof, with Delight and Chearfulness.* For treating of the Signs, whereby it may be known, whether a Man hath obtained the Habit of any Virtue; they say they are these; when a Man acts according to that Virtue *promptè, faciliter, & delectabiliter*; with Promptitude or Readiness, with Ease and Delight. He who hath acquired the Habit of any Art or Science, performs the Acts thereof with the greatest Readiness and Ease; as for Instance, he that is skillful in any musical Instrument, and hath gained the Habit thereof, plays most readily and easily upon it; and hath no need to prepare himself, nor to think much of the Matter; for even tho' he think of other things, he will play well for all that. Now he, who hath acquired
the

the Habit of *Virtue*, performs the Acts thereof, after the very same Manner. If therefore you will know, whether you have gotten the *Virtue of Humility*, look first whether you perform the Works thereof with Promptitude, and Facility; for if you find Difficulty or Repugnance, in the Occasions which present themselves, it is a sign you have not yet acquired the Perfection of that *Virtue*. And if, for acquitting yourself well upon such Occasions, you have need of Preventions and Considerations, I confess they are good Means for improving you in that *Virtue*, but still it is a sign you have not yet attained to a Perfection in it. As he who is to play upon the Lute, if he think where to place one Finger, and where another, and call to mind the Rules, which he was taught, doth well towards his learning to play; but withall, it is a sign that as yet, he hath not gotten the Habit of that Instrument; for whoso hath gotten it, needs not call this or that to mind, in order to play well. And so said *Aristotle. Ars perfecta non deliberat,* &c. *i. e.* " He that " hath perfectly acquired the Habit of any " Art, finds it so easy to perform the Acts " thereof, that he hath no need of Deliberation how to do them well." Hence also came that saying of the Philosophers, *that the* Virtue *of a Man is known by his sudden and unpremeditate Acts* A Man's *Virtue* is less known by the Acts, which he performeth,

formeth, upon great Deliberation, than by such as come from him at unawares.

Yea, the Philosophers give us some further Marks. *Plutarch* treating how a Man may be sensible of his Progress in Virtue, gives twelve Signs thereof, *one* of which (as he quotes it from *Zeno*) is by *his Dreams.* " If even in your Dreams, and when you " are sleeping, you have no ill Impulses, " or unclean Imaginations; or, if you have " such, and take no Delight, or Compla- " cence in them, but on. the contrary, re- " sist the Temptation and Delight thereof, " in your very Dreams, as if you were a- " wake, this is a Sign that Virtue is well " rooted in your Soul, and not only your " Will is subject to Reason, but even your " sensual Appetite and Imagination As " when Coach-Horses are well managed, " tho' the Coachman lay the Reins on their " Necks, and perhaps sleep himself, yet " they go readily on their way. So, adds the Philosopher, -" They, who have per- " fectly obtained any Virtue, and have to- " tally subdued the Causes, and brutish Ap- " petites which oppose it, go on in the right " way, even when they sleep" St *Augustin* teacheth also the same *Some Servants of God bear so great an Affection to* Virtue, *by keeping of God's Commandments, and so great Detestation of Sin; and are so accustomed, and inured to the Resistance of Temptations when they are awake, that they resist them also even when*

when they sleep. In this Sense some interpret that Place of St *Paul, Whether we wake or sleep we should live together with him* *. Which imports not only that both *living* and *dying,* we must ever live with CHRIST, which is the common Exposition ; but moreover, that the zealous Servants of God, must continually live with CHRIST, and that not only *waking,* but also *sleeping* and *dreaming.*

The third Sign, to know if a Man have perfectly obtained any *Virtue,* is, when he performs the Works thereof *with Delight* ; this indeed is the most certain Indication to prove the Perfection of any Virtue. If then you desire to know, whether you have obtained the *Virtue* of *Humility,* examine your self by that Rule, which we delivered in the last Chapter ; and see whether you be as glad of Dishonour and Affront, for the sake of CHRIST, as worldly Men use to be of Honour and Estimation.

Besides, 'till we have attained to this Degree of performing all Acts of Duty with Delight and Joy, it will be a hard thing to persevere and continue in *Virtue.* Some ancient Fathers were wont to say, *That whatsoever was not performed with Alacrity and a Sense of Joy, could not last long.* It may be for some time (as in a Fit) you will live modestly, and recollected ; but 'till this flow from the bottom of your Heart, and

---

* 1 Thess v 11.

by

by Cuftom you make it natural to you, and
peform it with Sweetnefs and Delight, you
are not like to continue long therein, but it
will pafs away, and come to an End, as
every thing that is conftrained and forc'd is
wont to do; for " Nothing forc'd or vio-
" lent, can laft long." For this Reafon
it is of vaft Confequence, and Importance,
to exercife the Acts of any *Virtue* with Con-
ftancy. This by degrees will fo root it in
the Soul, and grow into fo confirm'd a Habit, that the Mind will fall as it were of it
felf upon the *Virtue*, and the Acts thereof
will feem to be Acts of our own Nature;
fo that we fhall perform them with Joy and
Delight, and by thefe means be in a manner affured that we fhall continue and per-
fevere therein. This is that which the
Royal Prophet faith, *Bleffed is the Man,
whofe Delight is in the Law of the Lord, and
in his Law doth he meditate day and night;* *
for that Man will yield the *Fruit* of good
Works, *in his Seafon, like a Tree which is
planted by the River fide.*

C H A P.

CHAP. XVII.

Some Means are propos'd for the obtaining of this second *Degree of Humility, and particularly the Example of* CHRIST *our Lord.*

FOR the acquiring of Moral Virtues, two kinds of Ways or Means are wont to be prescribed. First, Reasons and Considerations, which may convince, and then animate us thereto ; Secondly, Exercise of the Acts of the *Virtue* we are aspiring after, in order to gain the Habit of it

To begin with the First ; One of the principal and most effectual Considerations, whereby we may attain to the Virtue of *Humility*, or rather the very chief of all, is the Example of CHRIST our Lord and Redeemer, whereof though we have already said somewhat before, there will ever be enough to add. The whole Life of CHRIST our Lord, was a most perfect Pattern of *Humility*, from the very time of His Birth, to His expiring upon the Cross. But yet to this Purpose, St *Augustin* * doth particularly single out the Example which he set us, by Washing the Feet of His Dis-

* De Virginit.

ciples; " After his laſt Supper with them
" was ended, and he was now entring upon
" the laſt Stage of His Sufferings, Chriſt
" our Lord, ſaith he, was not content with
" having given them the Example of His
" whole Life paſt, nor yet with that In-
" ſtance of Condeſcention He was ſhortly
" to give them in his Paſſion, altho' the
" ſame were then ſo near at Hand, and
" He was to appear, according to the Pro-
" phet *Iſaiah, without Form or Comelineſs;*
" as the very laſt, or loweſt of Men · Or,
" according to the Royal Prophet, *as a*
" *Worm and no Man, the very Scorn of*
" *Men, and the Outcaſt of the People:*
" Yet our Lord Jeſus knowing *that his*
" *Hour was come, that he ſhould depart*
" *out of this World, unto the Father, ha-*
" *ving loved his own, which were in the*
" *World,* and reſolving to expreſs it now in
" a more ſignal Manner towards the end
" of His Life, when Supper was ended,
" He riſes from the Table, He laid aſide
" His Garments, He took a Towel and
" girded Himſelf; He poureth Water in-
" to a Baſon, He proſtrates Himſelf at the
" Feet of His Diſciples, yea, and of *Judas*
" too, and waſhes them with his own Di-
" vine Hands, and Wipes them with the
" Towel, wherewith He was girded O
" unſpeakable Myſtery! What is this, O
" Lord, which thou art doing? Well might
" St *Peter* ſay with a holy Surpriſe ——

G   " *Lord,*

"*Lord, doest thou wash my Feet?* He could
" not then apprehend the Meaning. *What*
" *I do,* faith Chrift, *thou knoweft not now,*
" *but thou fhalt know hereafter.* He then
" returns to the Table, and declares the
" Myftery at large. *You call me Mafter,*
" *and Lord, and ye fay well, for fo I am.*
" *If I then, your Lord and Mafter, have*
" *wafhed your Feet, ye ought alfo to wafh*
" *one anothers Feet. I have given you an*
" *Example, that ye fhould do, as I have done*
" *to you.*" That fo you may learn to
humble yourfelves, even as I have *humbled*
Myfelf.

The Importance of this *Virtue* of *Humili-*
ty is fo great on the one Hand, and fo difficult on the other, that our Lord was not
content with the many Examples he had
already given us, and was within fuch a
little while to give; but, as one who well
knew our Weaknefs, and who perfectly
underftood the Malignity of that Peccant
Humour, whereof our Nature was fick,
He was pleafed to give us this ftrong Phyfic againft it, and to put it amongft the
chief Legacies of His laft Will and Teftament, that fo it might remain the more
deeply imprinted in all our Hearts.

Upon thofe fore-recited Words of Chrift
our Lord, *Learn of me, for I am meek and low-*
ly in Heart. St *Auguftin* exclaims thus, " O
" Doctrine moft Salutary! O thou Sove-
" reign Lord and Teacher of us poor
" Mortals,

" Mortals, who firſt imbibed Death from
" the poiſonous Cup of *Pride*, What is it
" thou wilt have us come, and learn of
" thee? —— *That I am meek, and lowly in*
" *Heart This is the Leſſon you are to learn*
" *of me.* — Are then (as that Saint goes
" on) all the Treaſures of the Wiſdom,
" and Knowledge of the Father, which
" have been hidden in thee, reduced to
" this ſmall Point, as the higheſt Pitch
" of Learning, that we muſt come and
" learn of thee, to be *meek and lowly in*
" *Heart?* Is it ſo great a thing for a Man
" to become little, that except thou, who
" art ſo great, hadſt made thyſelf little,
" it could not poſſibly have been learnt?
" Yea, ſaith the ſame Father in another
" Place, ſo great, and ſo hard a thing it
" is for a Man to be humble, and to
" make himſelf little, that had not God
" humbled Himſelf, and become little,
" Men would never have been brought
" to humble themſelves. There is nothing
" ſo deeply rooted in our very Nature, and
" ſo incorporated, as it were, into our
" Hearts, as this Deſire of being honour-
" ed and eſteemed ; and therefore was all
' this neceſſary, in order to reduce the
" Tumour of our Hearts, and to conſtrain
" us to be humble ſuch Phyſic did the
" Infirmity of our Pride require; and ſuch
" a Wound, ſuch a Cure. But if (as he
" goes on) the Humiliation of God made

" Man,

" Man, his Cloathing Himſelf with our
" Fleſh, and enduring the Pain and Ignomi-
" ny of the Croſs for our ſakes, be not a *Re-*
" *cipe* ſufficient to recover us, and cure our
" Pride, *I know not what will* " Holy *Gue-*
ricus being amazed at this ſtrange Example
of our Lord's *Humility*, cries out with great
Vehemence, (as all of us ought to do), *Thou*
haſt overcome, O Lord, thou haſt overcome
my Pride, thine Example hath bound me
Hand and Foot. Behold I ſurrender, and yield
up myſelf into thy Hands for an Everlaſting
Slave

It is alſo admirable what St *Bernard*
brings to this Purpoſe, * " The Son of
" God (ſaith he) ſaw two Creatures, both
" Excellent, Noble, and capable of con-
" tinuing in that bleſſed State, wherein
" they had been created by Almighty
" God; but both had loſt themſelves, be-
" cauſe they would needs be like Him.
" —— He Created the Angels, and in-
" ſtantly *Lucifer* had a Mind to be like
" Almighty God, and drew others after
" him, but God caſt them inſtantly down
" to Hell, and ſo of Angels they became
" Devils God alſo Created Man, and
" inſtantly the Devil ſtruck him with his
" own Leproſy, and Poiſon of Pride, ——
" *Ye ſhall be as Gods* —— They greedily
" ſwallowed the Temptation he propoſed,

* 1 Serm in Advent

" broke

" broke the Divine Commandment thro'
" Ambition to be *like unto God,* and so
" became like the Devil —— The Prophet
" *Elisha* said to his Servant *Gehazi,* * after
" he had taken the Presents of *Naaman,*
" *The Leprosy of Naaman shall cleave unto*
" *thee, and to thy Seed for ever* Such was
" the Judgment of God against Man, that
" since he would needs have the Riches
" of *Lucifer,* which was his *Pride,* he
" should have his *Leprosy* also, which was
" the Punishment thereof.

" You see then that Man was undone,
" and made like the Devil, because he af-
" fected to be like unto God. And now,
" what became the Son of God to do, to
" vindicate and secure that Honour,
" whereof his Eternal Father is so jealous,
" and so careful to maintain? *I see,* saith he,
" *that on my Account, and a perverse Emu la-*
" *tion of me, my Father loseth His Creatures*
" *The Angels would needs be as I am, and so*
" *they overthrew themselves. Man wou'd*
" *be so too, and he is like one overthrown.*
" *They all envy me, and would fain be such*
" *as I am* —— *Well then, behold,* saith the
' Son of God, *I will assume such a Form,*
" *that whosoever will from hen eforth become*
" *like me, shall not lose, but gain* And this
" was the Cause why the Son of God came
" down from Heaven, and made himself

* 2 Kings v 27

G 3 " Man.

" Man. —— O Bleſſed be the Bounty
" and Mercy of God! for ever Bleſſed,
" and Praiſed, and Glorified, be the
" Goodneſs which moved our Gracious
" Redeemer to condeſcend to that Deſire
" we had to be like him! Now we may
" be as God indeed, not in a falſe and
" impracticable Manner, as the Devil had
" ſuggeſted, but according to Truth; not
" aſpiring thereto thro' Pride, and Malice,
" but with much Sanctity, and *Humility* "
Upon thoſe Words, *Unto us a Child is
Born*, the ſame Saint ſaith, * " Since God,
" who is ſo great, hath made Himſelf
" little for us, let us be ſure to humble
" ourſelves, and make ourſelves like that
" little one. Let us learn this of him, who
" was Meek and Lowly; that ſo it may
" not prove in Vain, and to no Purpoſe,
" that the Great God did ſo leſſen Him-
" ſelf, as to become a Child for us: Be-
" cauſe if you become not *like* This *little
" Child, you ſhall not enter into the Kingdom
" of Heaven* †.

* Serm. iii.   † Matth xviii 3

C H A P.

C H A P. XVIII.

Of some Human *Reasons and Considerations,
whereby we may be incited to the Pursuit
of* Humility.

WE have from the Beginning of this
Treatise, produced divers Motives
and Considerations, whereby we may be excited to cultivate this excellent Virtue of
Humility: We have shewed, that it is the
Root and Foundation of the Virtues, the surest
Way to get them, the best Means to keep
them; and that if we possess this, we shall
soon be Masters of them all   But having
urged this Duty by Spiritual Reasons, it
will not be amiss to offer some *Human* In-
ducements, that so being convinced not
only by Arguments and Motives drawn
from Divinity, but even from natural Reason also, which is more proportionable
and connatural to our Weakness, we may
be the more animated to the Contempt of
Honour, and the Esteem of the World;
and encouraged to proceed in the Way of
Humility: All this will be needful, for obtaining of a Thing so hard as this, and our

own

own moſt ſtrenuous Endeavours muſt not be wanting, to ſecond the Motions of Grace, if ever we hope to ſucceed.

First then, let us conſider, and examine with Attention, what this Honour and popular Eſteem is, which makes this continual War againſt us, and gives us all ſo much Trouble. Let us ſee what Weight and Bulk it hath, that ſo eſteeming it no better than it deſerves, we may prevail with ourſelves to deſpiſe it. *Seneca* ſaid well, " *There are many Things which we hold to be* " *great, not becauſe they are ſo indeed, but* " *becauſe our Wretchedneſs is ſuch, that the* " *ſmalleſt Things ſeem great to us, and the little,* " *much.*" He illuſtrates this by the Example of that Burthen which is ordinarily carried by Ants. In reſpect of their Bodies it is very great, but in itſelf exceeding ſmall Juſt ſo it is with the Honour and Eſtimation of the World : —— If they commend you, what are you the better ? If they deſpiſe you, what are you the worſe ? According to that Maxim of St *Auguſtin, Neither is the ill Man's Conſcience healed of it's Wound by Praiſe and Eſteem, nor the good Man's hurt, by being Diſcommended and Reproached.* And in another Place, " *Think* " of Auguſtin *what thou wilt, ſo my Con-* " *ſcience reproach me not in the Sight of God* " This, and this only, is a Matter of Importance , the reſt is mere Foolery, for it neither gives, nor takes away : " What (ſaith
                                    the

" the pious *Kempis* *) is any Man the bet-
" ter for being thought Great by another?
" — As any Man is in the Sight of God,
" such indeed he is, and no more." Which
is to the same Purpose with that of St *Paul*;
Not he that commendeth himself is approved,
but whom the Lord commendeth, 2 Cor. x. 18.

St *Augustin* brings a good Comparison
to this Purpose, *Pride and Esteem of the*
World, is not Greatness, but Swelling, and
Wind. When any Part is swelled, it seems
to be, but is not truly great So proud Men,
when they are esteemed by the World,
seem as if they were great, but really are
not so; their fancied Greatness is but
a Tumour. Some sick Men are thought
to be upon Recovery, when they look fat
and well, but such Fatness is not sound
and good, it is rather a Swelling and
Symptom of Sickness *Such is the Applause*
and Estimation of the World; it may puff up,
but it cannot make you great. If this then
be so, that the Opinion and Vogue of the
World is not any thing of real Greatness,
but rather a Distemper and Cause of
Swelling, why do we go up and down
like Cameleons, sucking in Wind with our
Mouths open, that so we may be the more
Swollen, and consequently more Sick? It
is better for a Man to be in Health, tho'
he seem sick, than to be sick indeed, and

---

* Lib ii. Chap 50

appear

appear found; fo alfo is it better to be good, tho' you feem wicked, than to be wicked indeed, and be held for good. For what Benefit can it do you to be accounted virtuous and fpiritual, if indeed you be not fo. St *Jerom* faith upon thefe Words, *Her Works fhall praife her in the Gates,* "It is "not the vain Praifes of Men, but your "good Works, which muft defend and "praife you, when you appear in Judg- "ment before Almighty God."

St *Gregory* relates of a Monk in a Monaftery of *Iconium,* who was generally efteemed a Saint, and efpecially for being very abftinent, full of Penance, and extreamly Mortified But the Hour of Death approaching, he defired that all the Monks might be called to him ——— For their Parts they were very glad, conceiving they were to hear from him, fome Matter of much Edification, but he, trembling and full of Anguifh, found himfelf compelled from within, to declare his true State to them, letting them know that he was Damned, becaufe his whole Life had been a continual Hypocrify   For when they thought he fafted, and did Penance, he eat fecretly; and for this, faith he, am I now delivered over to a terrible and furious Beaft, whofe Tail hath wreathed itfelf about, and tied my Feet; and his Head is juft now entring into my Mouth to fetch out, and carry away my Soul with

him

him for ever. With thefe Words he expired, to the great Amazement of them all. —— And now, what was this miferable Man the better, for having been reputed a Saint?

St *Anfelm* compares proud Men, who go in fearch of Honour, to Children hunting Butterflies. Others compare them to Spiders, who deftroy and wear out themfelves with making Webbs, for the catching of Flies, according to that of *Ifaiah, They weave the Spiders Webb,* Chap lix. 5. For fo the proud Man is coutinually fpending and wafting his very Heart and Bowels, to obtain a little human Praife. We read in the Life of a certain holy Man, that he ever fhewed a moft particular Deteftation againft all popular Applaufe, and the Praife of the World ; for he faid, *That it was the Caufe of great Mifchief, and the Impediment of many Bleffings.* And he was often heard to cry out, with much Earneftnefs, O Opinion, Opinion, and vain Efteem of the World ! *How many Mifchiefs haft thou wrought already ! How many workeft thou now ! And how many wilt thou work hereafter !*

CHAP

C H A P. XIX.

Of other Human *Reasons, for promoting of*
Humility.

ST *Chrysostom* upon those Words of St
*Paul, Not to think of himself more high-
ly than he ought to think, but to think soberly,
Rom.* xii. 3. plainly proves that the proud
and arrogant Person, is not only wicked
and sinful, but a meer Fool   To confirm
this, he brings that of *Isaiah, (Chap.* xxxii
6. according to the LXX) *The foolish Man
will speak foolish Things.* By the foolish
Things he utters, you shall understand
how silly he is.   For Instance, let us observe the Follies, which are acted by the
arrogant and proud Man, and we shall
quickly see what a Fool he is   The first
proud Creature was *Lucifer,* and what said
he ? *I will ascend into Heaven, I will exalt
my Throne above the Stars of God, I will ascend
above the Heights of the Clouds, I will be like
the Most High**. What could be more vainly
and more foolishly devised? And in the *tenth
Chapter,* the Prophet sets down the very

* Isaiah xiv. 13, 14

arrogant

arrogant and foolifh Words of the King of *Affyria*, wherein he boafted, that with His powerful Hand, He had conquered and fubdued all the Kings of the Earth. *By the Strength of my Hand have I done it, and by my Wifdom; for I am prudent; and I have removed the Bounds of the People, and have robbed their Treafures, and I have put down the Inhabitants like a valiant Man; and my Hand hath found as a Neft the Riches of the People; and as one gathereth Eggs that are left, have I gathered all the Earth, and there was none that moved the Wing, or open'd the Mouth, or peeped.* —— And what greater Folly could there be than this? faith St *Chryfoftom.* —— The fame Father brings in divers other Speeches of proud Men, which difcover fufficiently what Fools they be; fo that if you hear, and mark their Words, you will fcarce difcern whether they be the Words of a proud Man, or of fome one, who is a meer Sot, fo abfurd and incoherent they are.

And as we daily fee that Fools move us to Laughter, with what they fay and do; fo do alfo *proud* Men in their Converfation, by the arrogant Words which they utter, redounding to their own Praife, and by the affected Geftures which they ufe, and the State and foolifh Gravity of their Gait and Mein, by the great Deference which, forfooth, they expect Men fhould pay both to their Perfons, and all
that

that is theirs ; and by the high Value they
set upon themselves. To this St *Chrysostom*
adds, *That the Folly of proud Men is worse,
and more reproachful than that which is Natural, for this carries no Fault or Sin with
it, but the other doth* Hence also follows another Difference between these two Follies,
that they, who are *natural* Fools, move all
Mens Concern and Compassion for their
Misery , Whereas the Folly of *proud* Men
moves not others so much to Pity, or Concern, as to Laughter and Scorn.

Proud Men therefore are meer Sots, and
so must we deal with them   For as we
condescend, and seem to like what Fools
say, that we may keep Peace with them,
be the Thing never so silly, yet we con-
tradict them not, because in *fine* they are
Fools, and understand no better , just so
we proceed with proud Men And indeed
this Humour and Madness reigns so much
in the World, that now-a-days we can
hardly converse with Men, but we must
be fain to sooth them, and to say what is
not fact, nor so conceived by us, meerly
to keep them quiet and content them , there
being no other Way to oblige either a
proud Man, or a *Fool*, and to gain his good
Will, but by praising him And this is one
of the Vanities and Follies which the *Wise
Man* saith, he saw in the World, *I saw the
Wicked buried, who while they lived were in
the Holy Place, and they were praised in the
City*

City (fo the Vulgar Latin hath it) as for Righteous Works; this alfo is Vanity *.

What greater Vanity or Folly can there be imagined than to be praifed of Men, who think the very Reverfe of what they fay, who condemn and defpife in their Hearts, what in Words they commend. But fo little Sincerity is there to be met with in the World, that thofe who Flatter you to your Face, to gratify your foolifh Pride, never ftick to make a Jeft of you and your Failings behind your Back. —— Indeed Pride is fo unhappy it cannot bear the Truth; fo that to keep it in Humour you muft treat it like a Child, either fpeak downright Lies in commending what is fimple and wrong, or feek out fome by-way to evade the Truth, that fo you may feem to like, what you do not at all approve. —— This Condefcention may be thought Complaifance, and good Breeding, but in reality is ufing a Man as a meer Child or Fool. —— And Pride has made fuch Delufion not only Common and Fafhionable, but even Reciprocal, fo that Men take a Pleafure in Deceiving and being Deceiv'd The Perfon who delights to be flatter'd himfelf, and takes all, that is faid in his own Favour, for Truth, yet fees his Friend's Blind-fide, and pays him again in his own Coin, conceiving it to be

* Ecclef. viii 10,

not only a Piece of Civility, but the beft
Entertainment he can give him, to treat
him juft after the fame Manner, that he likes
to be treated himfelf. Thus Pride makes
Fools of both each knows he Deceives,
yet neither thinks himfelf Deceived. And
by this mutual Impofition the great End
and Ufe of Converfation is defeated, all
Society depraved, and Friendfhip turned
into Hypocrify and Grimace: and not only fo, but it betrays us into Miftakes of the
moft dangerous Confequence; for whoever
has any knavifh Defign on a proud Man,
'tis but wheedling of him, and foothing his
Vanity, he may eafily gain his Ends, and
even deceive him to his Ruin, at leaft
make him more and more Ridiculous, by
encouraging him to repeat his Follies, and
expofe himfelf to Contempt. Befides Men
dare not now-a-days fpeak what they think,
becaufe they know that Truth is difagreeable *Veritas odium parit*, —— Nothing is
more ungrateful to a proud Man, than to
tell him the Truth. As he who is mad and
frantic, refufes to take Phyfic, and fpits in
the Doctor's Face, when he defires to cure
him, fo doth the proud Man reject Admonition, and refent all Reproof, and therefore Men are afraid to tell fuch a one what
will difcontent him; they think it a fafer,
as well as fhorter way, to make him think
they like that, which yet indeed they mif-
like; while the other believes all, and is
well

well pleafed. By this we may alfo fee, how great a Vanity, and Madnefs it is, to make any Account of the Praifes of Men, fince we fee that in this Age, nothing is to be met with, but Compliment, Deceit, Flattery, and Lies. So that it is not without Reafon, that one has given for a Definition of what we call Breeding or good Manners, as they are commonly practifed, that they are a fafhionable Habit of concealing our own Pride with Dexterity, and flattering that of others.

To this we may add, what St *Chryfoftom* further remarks, that proud Men are abhorred by all. In the firft Place they are hateful to God: fo the *Wife Man* faith, *Every one that is proud in Heart, is an Abomination to the Lord. Prov.* xvi. 5 And of *feven* Things which God abhors, he places a *proud Look* in the Front, *Chap* vi 17. Nor are the Proud odious to God only, but to Men alfo, for fo the Son of *Sirach, Eccl* x. 7 *Pride is hateful before God and Man* And again, *As fumeth unfavoury Breath from a foul Stomach, So is the Heart of the Proud, Chap* xi. 32. *fec. Vulg.* So that even this World, which they take fo much Pains to pleafe, pays them often the due Reward of their Pride, mulcting and punifhing them with the Lofs of the very Thing they fo paffionately purfue. Hence it comes to pafs, that Pride never attains the End it feeks, but generally meets with
it's

it's Difappointment as well as Punifhment in all it's Attempts Honour and Efteem is what it eagerly hunts after, yet never finds ought but Shame and Difgrace, *for when cometh Pride, then cometh alfo Contempt.* To *be beloved of all* is the great Ambition of the Proud, but none are more *hated by all* than they ; —— By their Betters, becaufe they make themfelves their Equals, —— By their Equals, becaufe they make themfelves their Betters ; —— By their Inferiors, becaufe they deprefs them more than they fhould. Even his domeftic Servants fpeak ill of their proud Mafter, and indure him not. Whereas the *humble* Man is valued and efteemed, affected and beloved by all. " As Children for their " Goodnefs, their Innocency, their Simplicity of Heart are beloved, fo, faith " St *Gregory*, are the *humble*." For the Ingenuity and Plainnefs of their Speech, their honeft unaffected Simplicity without Guile, robs Men of their very Hearts. Humility *is a Loadftone*, which draws all Mens Affections to it. And in return all Men if they could, would take the humble Man, and put him in their Hearts.

To conclude this Argument, whereby we have endeavoured to evince the extream Folly of courting the Praife and Efteem of Men, I fhall crown all with that invincible Dilemma of St *Bernard*, " Either " it was Madnefs in the Son of God to " abafe

" abafe and empty himfelf fo far, as to
" make Contempt and Difhonour his
" Choice, or elfe it is extream Madnefs
" in us, to be fo very defirous of the
" Honour and Efteem of the World " But
it was not Folly or Madnefs in the Son of
God, neither could it be, tho' the World
might think it fo, for as St *Paul* faith,
tho' Chrift Crucified, was unto the Jews a
ftumbling Block, and to the Greeks Foolifhnefs;
yet unto them which are called, both Jews, and
Greeks, Chrift is the Power of God, and the
Wifdom of God 1 *Cor* 1 23 24. Now if His
Humility and Condefcention were infinite
Wifdom, it follows that our courting, as
we do, the Efteem and Honour of the
World, muft be the moft extravagant Folly.

C H A P.

C H A P. XX.

*The true Way to be Valued and Esteemed by
Men, is to addict ourselves to the Study of
Virtue, especially the Virtue of Humility.*

IF all we have said, will not abate the
Edge of your Defire for Honour and
Efteem, but you will ftill be faying, it is
a great Point of Wifdom to fecure a good
Opinion and Reputation among Men, and
that this is of great Importance, to promote even the Edification of your Neighbour, and ferves to many other good
Ends that the *Wife Man* alfo counfels us
to *have a Care of our good Name* * I anfwer, be it fo, that you have a Care to
keep the good Name you have But yet
be affured, that if you eagerly defire it,
as you feem to do, and are follicitous for
it, you err, even tho' it be in order to the
obtaining thofe good Ends, for which you
defire it, nor fhall you ever obtain thofe
Ends by this Means, but rather the contrary.

The only fafe and certain way, whereby
you fhall come to be Valued and Efteem-

* Ecclus xli 15 *fec Vulg*

ed

ed by Men, is the Way of *Virtue* and
Humility So St *Chryfoftom*, "Let every
"one of you, in particular, take care to
"be indeed a good and religious Man, to
"be indeed the lowlieft and humbleft of
"all, and appear fo to be by your manner
"of Living, and upon all Occafions; fo
"fhall you be Valued and Efteemed by all
"Men" This Contempt of Honour is
the only true Honour of a religious Man,
who hath forfaken the World, and profeffeth himfelf to be a Citizen of Heaven.
On the contrary, for fuch a one to defire to
be Valued and Efteemed by Men, is in
truth a real Difhonour to him, for which
he juftly deferves to be defpifed. For fuch
worldly Honour properly belongs to the
Men of the World, but you profeffedly
renounced it, as one of the Pomps and Vanities thereof, when you made the Holy
Vow at your Baptifm

To convince you more clearly how
fhameful and reproachful a Thing it is,
for a Chriftian to affect the Efteem of the
World, who profeffeth to afpire towards
Perfection; Let fuch a Defire but once
come fo to Light, that others may difcern it,
and you will quickly find yourfelf confounded, and out of Countenance, that any
fuch Thing fhould be known of you.

We have a very remarkable Example
of this, in the Gofpel. The Evange-
lift,

relates, That as our Lord was on his Journey from *Galilee*, the Disciples being at some Distance from him, far enough as they thought to be out of Hearing, fellupon a Discourse about Precedency, and disputed with some Warmth, *which of them should be the greatest Man When he came to Capernaum, and being in the House, He asked them, what was it that ye disputed among yourselves by the way?* The holy Gospel adds, *That they held their Peace* the poor Men were so ashamed, and out of Conntenance to see their Vanity and Ambition discovered, they had not one Word to say *For by the Way they had disputed among themselves, who should be the greatest.* But then did the Saviour of the World call them to him, and told them, that worldly Men indeed, and the Great Ones of the Earth, exercise Authority over their Inferiors, but it should not be so in his School. That there, *If any Man desire to be First, the same shall be Last of all, and Servant of all. And then he took a Child, and set him in the midst of them.* By these Words, and this Emblem, he gave a home Rebuke to their Pride, letting them understand, that even a *Child* might teach them more Wit, as well as greater *Humility*, nothing contributing more effectually to defeat a vain Ambition, of the Honour and Greatness it desires, than the very desire itself, when ever it

* Mark ix.

came

came to be known :—aiming to be firft, is ever the way to be laft —— That worldly Honour is at beft but a Toy, yea fo vain and defpicable a Toy, that even Children themfelves are not tempted with it.

To this purpofe St *John Climacus* obferves very well, " That Vain-Glory hath many " times proved an occafion of Ignominy to " it's Followers, for it hath made them " fet about things, whereby they have be- " tray'd their Vanity and Folly, and fo " funk into Infamy and Contempt" For fo fimple is the proud Man, that he has not the Senfe to fee his own weak Side the very things he fays or does to fet himfelf off, ferve only to make him the more defpifed : his Paffion for Praife turn him and his Pride into Ridicule. the higher he raifes himfelf in his own conceit, the lower he falls in that of others.

Bonaventure adds, " That Pride blinds " the Underftanding in fuch Sort, that " many times the more Pride you have, " the lefs you know it, hence the proud " Man faith, and doth fuch Things, as " could he but fee and reflect on them, " he would not for the World either fay, " or do, even tho' there were no fuch " thing as God, or Virtue, but meerly " for that Reputation and Honour's Sake, " which he fo eagerly purfues." How many times doth it happen, that a Man is troubled, and complains of ill Treatment,

ment, want of that Refpect that was due to his Quality, Merit, or Pretenfions, that others have been preferr'd before him on fuch or fuch an Occafion, or in fuch, or fuch a Bufinefs: that the Affront reflects on his Honour, leffens his Credit, and expofes him to Contempt. By fuch peevifh Exceptions, and the immoderate Concern he fhews for his Honour, 'tis plain his Heart is full of Pride, he is noted for a vain haughty Man, and acquires a Character the moft odious, and abominable that can be, to every humble and good Chriftian. Whereas had he paffed it over without Refentment, made light of the Neglect or Difappointment he received, and patiently fubmitted thereto, he might have been highly efteemed, and gained more Honour than he loft.

So that altho' there were no fuch Thing as a Spiritual way of Life, but that Men were only to live according to the Dictates of natural Prudence, and Difcretion, yea in Conformity to the Rules of good Breeding, and the very Laws of the World, 'tis certain, the moft effectual way for a Man to be Valued and Efteemed, Affected and Beloved by Men, is to addict himfelf ferioufly to *Virtue* and *Humility*. Hence even among the *Gentiles*, we find it related of *Agefilaus*, King of *Lacedemon*, and accounted one of their *Wife Men*, that being afked by *Socrates*, what a Man fhould

do

do, to gain the Esteem and good Will of o-
thers, made this Answer: *Be such indeed, as
you would seem to be.* Being again asked
by another concerning the same thing, he
answered thus, *Speak always what is Best;
do always what is Just and Honest.* Another
Philosopher being told by his Friend, that
he owed him much, because he had taken
all occasions to praise him, and extol his
Virtue; he returned him this Answer, *I pay
you well for your Pains, by living so, that you
may not be found a Liar in any thing, you
have said of me.*

Howbeit, we say not that we are therefore to addict ourselves to *Virtue* and *Humility,* that we may be valued and esteemed
of Men; for that were Pride and a perverse Error. What we say is this, that if
we endeavour to be humble in deed, and
in Heart, we shall be valued and esteemed much, whether we will or no · Nay,
the more we fly from Esteem, it will follow us the faster. St *Jerome,* in the Life
of the devout Matron *Paula,* saith. *Fugi-
endo gloriam, gloriam merebatur, &c.* " The
" more she fled from Honour, the more
" it still pursued her; for Honour is Vir-
" tue's Shadow, and the Reflection of true
" Merit, which ever shuns its Pursuers, and
" pursues its Contemners." Whilst a Man
flies from his Shadow, it follows him on
the contrary, if he follows it, it flies from

H

him ,

him; and the fafter he runs, the fafter it flies, fo that he can never overtake it such is the Cafe of Honour and worldly Eftimation.

This our Lord hath taught us in the Gofpel, by the Advice he gives, concerning the Conduct Men fhould obferve at a public Entertainment *When thou art bidden of any Man to a Wedding, fit not down in the higheft Room, left a more honourable Man than thou be bidden of him; and he that bode thee and him, come and fay to thee, Give this Man place; and thou begin with fhame to take the loweft Room But when thou art bidden, go and fit down in the loweft Room, that when he that bade thee, cometh, he may fay unto thee, Friend, go up higher. then fhalt thou have Worfhip in the prefence of them that fit at meat with thee**. Which in fubftance is the fame with what the Holy Ghoft had fpoken before by the Mouth of the wife Man **, *Put not forth thyfelf in the prefence of the King, and ftand not in the Place of great Men For better it is that it be faid unto thee, come up hither, than that thou fhouldeft be put lower in the prefence of the Prince, when thine Eyes have feen.* For this Reafon our Lord concludes his Parable thus, *Whofoever exalteth himfelf fhall be abafed, and he that humbleth himfelf, fhall be exalted.* Hence

* Luke xiv 8, &c.   ** Prov xxv. 6, 7

you fee how the *Humble* Man, who chufes the lowest and meaneft Place, is valued and esteemed, not only in the fight of God, but before Men alfo . on the other Hand, that the *Proud* Man, who feeks the best, and higheft Seat, is undervalued, and defpifed. Well therefore might St *Auguftin* cry out, and fay, *O boly* Humility, *how unlike art thou to Pride* ! Pride caft Lucifer *down out of Heaven,* But Humility *made the Son of God to become Man* Pride caft Adam *out of Paradife ;* But Humility *carried the good Thief thither* Pride *divided and confounded the Tongues of the Giants ;* But Humility *hath united all that were divid'd :* Pride *transformed* Nebuchadnezzar *into a Beaft ;* But Humility *made* Joſeph *Lord of* Egypt, *and Prince of the People of* Iſrael : Pride *drowned* Pharaoh ; *But* Humility *raiſed and exalted* Moſes.

CHAP.

CHAP. XXI.

That by Humility *is obtained true Peace of Mind, and cannot be had without it.*

LEARN *of me, faith our Lord, for I am meek and lowly in Heart, and you shall find REST unto your Souls* ‖ One of the Chief, and moſt weighty Reaſons that can be urged for deſpiſing worldly Honour, and learning to be Humble, is by our Redeemer propounded to us, in theſe Words, namely, that it is a moſt excellent Means, for the obtaining of internal Quietneſs, and Peace of Mind ; a thing ſo much deſired by all Spiritual Men, and which St *Paul* ſets down for one of the Fruits of the Holy Ghoſt *. *But the fruit of the Spirit is* Love, Joy, Peace, &c.—That we may the better underſtand what this *Reſt* and *Peace* is, which the Humble Man enjoys, it will be convenient for us to conſider the Diſquiet and Reſtleſſneſs which the *proud* Man ever carries in his Heart, *For one Contrary is beſt illuſtrated and known by another.*

‖ Matth xi. 29   Gal. v 22.

Pride

Pride in itfelf is a moft reftlefs Paffion, ever purfuing with moft anxious Defire what it never can obtain. the Honour it feeks, flies ever from it ; the fhame it obhors, is ever at its Heels, fo that it cannot poffibly have either Eafe, or Reft. And the Holy Scriptures are full of fentences, which declare, that wicked Men have no Peace. *There is no peace, faith the Lord, unto the wicked,* Ifai. xlviii. 22. *They are like the troubled Sea, when it cannot Reft* —Then he repeats it again ; *There is no Peace, faith my God, to the wicked.* Chap. lvii 20, 21. again (Ch lix. 7, 8.) *Wafting and Deftruction are in their Paths. The way of Peace they know not* —— They know not what Peace is ; and though fometimes they may feem outwardly to have Peace, yet that is not true Peace ; They fay, *Peace, Peace, when there is no Peace ·* for within, in their very Hearts they have a War, which their confcience is ever raifing againft them. So that we may well apply to them, what, the mourning *Hezekiah* faith of himfelf ; *Behold for Peace I had great bitternefs,* Ifaiah xxxviii 17. —— Thus all wicked Men ever live with bitternefs and fadnefs of Heart ; but more efpecially the *Proud,* who are fubject after a particular manner, to continual unquietnefs, and want of Peace.

The Reafon hereof we may collect out of St *Auguftin,* who faith, that, " *Envy*

H 3

" is the Daughter of *Pride*; that *Pride*, who
" begets her, is never to be found without
" the company of this her hateful, but
" genuine Issue . and that these are the two
" Sins which make the Devil to be that
" very Devil he is " By this then we may
understand what mischief these two Sins are
like to work in the Heart of Man ; seeing
they are bad enough to make the Devil a
Devil. He, who on the one side, is puffed
up with Pride, and Vain-Glory, and sees that
things succeed not according to his wish
on the other Hand, is full of Envy, to
see others more esteemed, and preferred before him, cannot but be full also of
bitterness, and restlessness; For nothing
wounds a proud Heart, like such things
as these.

The holy Scripture paints this to the life,
in the Person and Character of proud *Haman* , He was the Favourite of King *Aba-
fuerus*, advanced above all the Princes and
Grandees of his Dominions , he had abundance of Temporal Goods and Riches, and
was so highly revered and courted by all,
that nothing more seemed wanting for him
to desire. Nevertheless, one petty slight
from a single Man, and he a mean Person,
who usually sat at the Gate of the Palace,
troubled him so greatly, that he lost all re
lish and enjoyment of his Grandeur and
Prosperity. This he himself confessed, by

way

way of complaint to his Wife and Friends, whilst he was speaking to them of his extraordinary Honours, and great Interest with the King *Yet all this availeth me nothing, so long as I see* Mordecai *the Jew sitting at the King's Gate* †. Thus we see the restless and unquiet Condition of a proud Man. his Passions are in perpetual Agitation ; as raging Waves and furious Storms , they continually toss his Heart,—— *like the troubled Sea, whose Waters cast up Mire and Dirt.* Now so great was the rage of *Haman* upon this occasion, that he disdained to lay hold upon *Mordecai* alone, who was but a poor private Man, too mean to bear the whole Weight of his Resentment , he determines to sacrifice a whole Nation to his Fury , and therefore, knowing him to be a Jew, he procures warrants from the King, for putting to the Sword, and utterly destroying all the race of *Jews*, who were to be found in his Dominions. He commanded also a very high Gibbet to be erected in the Court of his own House, whereon he meant that *Mordecai* should be Hanged. But the Issue of his wicked Scheme fell out far otherwise than he had designed in the Event, the *Jews* proved to be the Men, who executed upon their Enemies, the Sentence, which had passed against

† Esther v 13

themselves

themfelves; and *Haman* himfelf was Hanged upon the very Gallows, which he had prepared for *Mordecai.*

But firft, there happened a notable Mortification to him, and it was this; going one Morning very early to the Court in order to gratify his deteftable Malice, and to obtain a Warrant from the King for putting the fame in Execution, it happened that the Night before, the King not being able to Sleep, had commanded them to bring the Hiftory, and Chronicles of his own times, and to read them to him. When they came to the Relation of what *Mordecai* had done for the fervice of his Majefty, by difcovery of a certain Treafon, which fome of his own fervants had plotted againft him; he enquired what reward had been given that Man for fo extraordinary a fervice: they told him; none at all. The King then afked, who was without, and whether any of his Nobles were yet come to Court. They Anfwered that *Haman* was there. When he came into the Prefence, the King put this Queftion to him? *What fhall be done unto the Man, whom the King delighteth to Honour?* —— *Haman* conceiving that himfelf was the Man, to whom that Honour was defigned, made this Anfwer: *For the Man whom the King delighteth to Honour, let the Royal Apparel be brought, which the King ufeth to wear, and the Horfe that the King ri-*

deth

deth upon, and the Crown Royal, which is set npon his Head. And let this Apparel and Horse be delivered to the Hand of one of the King's most noble Princes, that they may array the Man withal, whom the King delighteth to honour, and bring him on Horseback thro' the Streets of the City and Proclaim before him, thus shall it be done to the Man, whom the King delighteth to honour. Then the King said to Haman, *make hast and take the Apparel and the Horse, as thou hast said, and do even so to* Mordecai *the Jew, that sitteth at the King's Gate, let nothing fail of all that thou hast spoken.* —— Think now what Anguish that wicked and proud Heart must feel ! Yet durst he not fail to execute the Order in every particular Circumstance. It seems indeed beyond the Power of imagination, to think of a greater Mortification to a haughty Spirit than this ; yet soon after followed that other far greater, of his being Hanged upon the very Gibbet, which he had caused to be provided for *Mordecai.*—— Such are the Wages of *Pride,* this is the Pay, it gives to all, that serve it —— And now whence did all this sad Catastrophe proceed? Why forsooth, because *Mordecai bowed not to him, nor did him Reverence*

Such a Trifle, even one such small Matter as this, is enough to make a proud Man unquiet and restless ; to wound his Peace, and make him sad at Heart. We see the

H 5 same.

fame at this Day in all worldly Men; and
fo much the more may we fee it, as they
are the more eminent in Rank and Degree.
Their Hearts are as bitter as Gall, they e-
ver walk up and down the World, like
the proud Enemy of God and Man, with
perpetual Unquietnefs, and want of Reft.

Hence we may alfo account for that Melancholy, and thofe fits of Spleen, which
we often obferve in fome Perfons. it is not
fo much the Humour of Melancholy, any
corporeal or complexional Infirmity, as the
Humour of Pride, and ficknefs of the Soul.
You are Melancholy and Sad, becaufe
you performed not fuch, or fuch a
Thing with fo much Applaufe, and Reputation, as you hoped for and expected,
you conceive that you have fuffered in your
Credit; that you are flighted or forgotten,
and laid afide. The bufinefs fucceeded not
as you defire : That Sermon, that Difpu-
tation, thofe Conclufions, you fear have
loft you fome fhare of Reputation, and
therefore you are Melancholy and Sad. At
another time you are to perform fome
of thefe public Exercifes, or other things
wherein your Credit is concerned, and the
fear of Succefs makes you afflicted and
grieved. But the Root of this immoderate Concern for your Credit is Pride, for
the fear of Shame is ever fure to make the
proud Man Melancholy and Sad. But the
Humble

Humble Man of Heart, who affects no Honour or Efteem, but contents himfelf with a mean Place, is free from all this reftleffnefs and difquiet, and enjoys great Peace of mind; according to thofe Words of Chrift our Lord, which we have fo often cited from, *Matth.*xi and from whence that holy Man *Kempis,* took this faying of his : " If there be fuch a thing as Peace in this " World, the humble of Heart poffeffes " it". And therefore tho' *Humility* were no Duty; and fetting afide the Virtue and Perfection of it , yet for our own Intereft, and the keeping our Hearts in Peace and Quietnefs, for this, I fay, were there nothing elfe to move us; we ought to learn it. —— To lead our Life by her Rules, is indeed to live; whereas the contrary, at beft, is but a dying Life.

St *Auftin* *, to this Purpofe, relates a Story of himfelf, — whereby, thro' Divine Grace he came to underftand the Blindnefs and Mifery wherein he then was . " As I " went along one day (faith he) full of " Thought about an Oration, which I had " prepared to fpeak before the Emperor in " his Praife, the greateft part of which was " Flattery and Lies , yet I myfelf expected " to be Applauded and Careffed for thofe " very Lies, even by them who knew them " to be fo But fo great was the Fear

* Conf Lib 6. C. 6

" and Concern I felt for the Succefs of
" my Speech, that it put me into an A-
" gony of Trembling, and threw my Spi-
" rits into a perfect Fevour of confum
" ing Thoughts, left I fhould not come off
" with Honour and Applaufe. Paffing,
" I fay, thro' one of the Streets of *Milan*, I
" happened to fee a poor Beggar, who
" having, as I fuppofed, gotten his bellyful
" of Meat and Drink, was very Jovial and
" Merry, and playing a Thoufand antick
" Tricks to divert himfelf and the Croud
" When I faw this, I could not forbear
" fighing, and from hence took occafion
" to obferve to my Friends that were with
" me, how very fhort we came of that
" poor Fellow's Happinefs. All we got
" by playing the Fool, was Mifery and
" Sorrow (and I myfelf was at that time a
" prefent Inftance of it.) We aimed in-
" deed by all our Exploits at fuch a fettled
" State of Peace and Quietnefs, as might
" be out of the reach of Trouble or Difcon-
" tent ; but herein that poor Beggar had
" far out-ftripped us already, and perhaps
" we fhould never be able to overtake
" him. No Man could be happier than
" he for the time · While his Skin was
" full of Wine, his Heart was full of Joy,
" and a few pence had purchafed all this
" Felicity. The happinefs, I fought, was
" the fame in Kind, with what this Beggar
                              " already

" already enjoy'd ; nothing lefs than a fort
" of Anodyne, an immediate Cure and
" general Releafe from all Sorrow and Care
" Yet with all my Labours, I could never
" attain to it ; and the very fearch, inftead
" of gaining my end, did but remove me ftifl
" further off to a greater Diftance from it.
" It may be faid indeed, the poor Man
" was Merry, but could not be faid to
" have true Joy. I grant ye, he was not
" *truly* Happy, but yet he was happier
" than I. And the very Good, I was in
" queft of, was of a Kind more falfe and
" precarious than his. —— In fhort, he
" was Merry, I fad ; he was fecure and
" quiet, I full of Cares and Fear ——
Then he goes on. —— " If any Man fhould
" afk me now, whether I had rather be
" glad or grieved, I fhould quickly make
" Anfwer, I had rather be glad · fhould
" he ask me yet again, whether I had ra-
" ther be that Beggar, or myfelf, I fhould
" chufe to keep to my own Condition,
" though then fo full of Affliction ; yet for
" ought I know, I fhould have no Reafon
" for making fuch a Choice. For my be-
" ing more Learned, made me not the
" more contented, but only intoxicated
" me with a vain Ambition of pleafing
" others by my Knowledge, and that
" too not with the View of inftructing
" them, but foothing my own Vanity
" But

" But befides all this, without doubt, (adds
" he) that poor Man was much happier
" than I, not only becaufe he was Merry
" and Jolly, and I was full of Anguifh and
" Care; But becaufe he had gotten his
" Wine by lawful means, and many a
" hearty Prayer*, whereas I was going to
" tell a pack of Lies in order to hunt af-
" ter vain Glory, and to fell the Truth
" for empty Praife".

CHAP XXII.

*Of other Means more effectual for obtaining
the Virtue of* Humility, *to wit, the conftant*
Exercife *and* Practice *thereof.*

WE have already fpoken of the firft
kind of Means ufually affigned
for the obtaining of *Virtue*, to wit, certain
Reafons and Confiderations, both Divine
and Human. But yet fo great is the pro-
penfity we all naturally have to this Vice
of Pride, and fo deeply rooted in our
Hearts, is that fond Ambition and Defire

* Bene Optando.

of Divinity (*eritis ficut Dii*) which we inherit from our firft Parents, that no considerations are fufficient, wholly to fubdue the ftrong Impulfe and paffionate Defire, which we have to be Honoured and Efteemed, It happens to us herein as to one, who is naturally Cowardly and Fearful; What Reafons foever you bring to perfuade fuch a Perfon, that there is no manner of caufe for Fear, all the Anfwer you can get is this, I am fenfible that all you fay is true, and I would fain get the better of my Fears, but I cannot. Juft fo may fome fay in the prefent Cafe, I am fatisfied that the Reafons you have brought againft the Love of Praife and Eftimation of the World, are good and true, and they convince me that all is Vanity and Wind, —— meer emptinefs and fond Impertinence · but tho' I know all this, I can by no means prevail with myfelf to be indifferent I would fain be fo, if I could, but ftill I know not how, thefe kind of things tranfport and difquiet me ftrangely. Well then, as no Reafons, no Confiderations are fufficient to free the Timorous Man from his Pannick, till he can be perfuaded to put to his Hand and draw near enough to feel and touch thofe things, which feemed to be Ghofts or Spirits, and till he can be brought to go fometimes in the Dark by himfelf, and alone, to the Places where he thought he

faw

faw them, that fo he may find by experience, there was nothing in his Fright, but the vain illufion and miftaken Apprehention of a diftempered Imagination; this, when nothing elfe will do, may cure his Fears· In like manner the beft Remedy for correcting our vicious Love of Praife and worldly Honour, when no other Reafons or Confiderations are fufficient; is to fly into Action, and betake ourfelves to the Exercife of *Humility*, the principal and moft efficacious Means, which we, for our parts, can ufe for the obtaining of this or any other Virtue, being a diligent Application to thofe Acts, wherein the practice of it doth confift.

St *Bafil* tells us, *That as Sciences and Arts are acquir'd by Practice, fo alfo are the Moral Virtues.* Would a Man be a good Mufitian, a good Orator, a good Philofopher, or a good Work-Man in any Kind, let him exercife himfelf therein, and he will grow expert. So alfo, for obtaining the habit of *Humility*, or any other Virtue, we muft enure ourfelves to the Acts thereof, and by this means we fhall acquire them If any Man tell me, that for the compofing and moderating our Paffions, regulating the Affections of the Mind, and obtaining the habits of Virtue; the Confiderations and Reafons, the Documents and Counfels of holy Scripture are of themfelves

fufficient

sufficient, he is much deceived; for, as the same Saint goes on, *This would be like the Man, who would learn to build a House, and yet never lay to his Hand, but only spend his time in hearing Lectures on the Subject, and learning the Rules of his Art*; in this Case he might gain some Knowledge in the Theory, but would never make a good Work-Man. As little will he attain to *Humility*, or any other Virtue, who doth not exercise himself therein And in Confirmation hereof, he brings that of the Apostle St *Paul*, *For not the Hearers of the Law are just before God, but the Doers of the Law shall be justified*, Rom. 11 13 It is not enough to hear many Precepts and Instructions, without putting the same in execution. For Practice conduces more to the Accomplishment of any Business, than all the Speculation in the World. And tho' it be most true, that all Virtue, and every thing, that is good, must come to us from the Hand of God, and that we cannot compass it by our own Strength, yet the same Lord, who is to give it, expects and requires of us, to help our selves by our own Endeavours.

St *Austin* upon those Words of Christ *If I then your Lord and Master have washed your Feet, ye also ought to wash one anothers feet*, Joh xxiii 14. observes, that " it was this *Practical Humility*, which " our

" our Lord intended to teach us, by this
" Example of wafhing his Difciples Feet
" This *(faith he)* O bleffed *Peter*, is what
" thou didft not know, when thou would
" eft not confent, that Chrift fhould wafh
" thy Feet " He promifed that thou
" fhouldeft know it afterward , that *after*
" *ward* is now come , and now thou fhalt
" underftand it " If we will indeed ob
tain the *Virtue* of *Humility*, we muft exer
cife our felves in the Outward Acts thereof
For I (faith Chrift) *have given you an Ex-*
ample, to the end that you may do as I have
done Since the Omnipotent and Sovereign
Lord of all things did fo humble himfelf,
fince the Son of God abafed, and employed himfelf in fo mean and lowly Exercifes,
as wafhing the Feet of his Difciples, fer-
ving his bleffed Mother, and the holy *Jo-*
feph, and being fubject and obedient to
their Commands , let us learn of him, and
not think much to exercife our felves alfo
in humble and mean Employments , and fo
fhall we come to obtain the *Virtue* of *Hu-*
mility.

To the fame effect St *Bernard* faith,
" The humbling of the outward Man is
" as fure a Way to obtain the Virtue of
" *Humility*, as Patience is the means for
" obtaining Peace of Mind, and reading
" or Study for the gaining of Knowledge "
If therefore you would obtain the *Virtue*,
do

do not fly from the *Exercise* of Humility.
If you will not, or pretend you cannot,
comply with such an Exercise, as little
Mind have you to obtain the *Virtue* of
Humility. St *Austin* proves the same very well, and withal gives the Reason, why this Practical Exercise of *Humiliation,* is so useful, important, and necessary, for the obtaining of true *Humility* of
Heart. " The inward and the outward
" Man are so interwoven and united toge-
" ther, and the one depends so much upon
" the other, that when the Body is hum-
" bled and abased, the Heart is at the
" same time stirred up to an Act of *Humi-
" lity*" —That humbling myself before my
Brother, and doing him Reverence, hath
somewhat in it, that Teaches, as well as
Exercises *Humility*: That poor and plain
Coat, that low and mean Office, hath I
know not what, that contributes something
more than ordinary to the breeding of *Humility* in the Heart; and if it be there already, it preserves and encreases it.

To the same Purpose also doth St *Dorotheus* Answer this Question,—How should
a Man by the use of plain and ordinary
Cloathing, which belongs to the Body,
come to obtain the *Virtue* of *Humility,*
which reside in the Souls? " It is certain,
saith he, " that the Body in many Cases
" gives a good or ill Turn to the Soul: As we
" see

" fee, the Soul hath one kind of Difpofi-
" tion, when the Body is well, and ano-
" ther when it is fick , one, when it is full
" fed, and another when it is very Hungry ,
" fo in like Manner, the Soul feels itfelf
" very differently affected, when a Man is
" feated upon a Throne, or upon a Horfe
" richly adorned, and when he fits upon
" the Ground, or is riding upon a mean
" contemptible Horfe ; one kind of Dif-
" pofition it hath, when he is fet out in
" fumptuous Cloaths, and another when
" he is clad with a poor Coat". St *Bafil*
alfo notes the fame, " As gallant and fhin-
" ing Attire, faith he, lifts up the Hearts
" of worldly Men, and ingenders in them
" certain Fumes of felf Eftimation and
" Pride ; fo doth a poor and mean Habit
" awaken in the Heart of Religious Men,
" and in the Servants of God, an Act of
" *Humility*, and breeds a low Efteem of ones
" felf , it difpofes Men alfo the better to
" endure Contempt from others.

The fame Saint adds further, " That as
" worldly Men defire rich and fine Ap-
" parel, that they may be the more re-
" garded and efteemed ; fo the good Ser-
" vants of God, and fuch as are truly Hum-
" ble are contented to be poor and meanly
" Clad, and in confequence thereof to be
" regarded the lefs more efpecially be-
" caufe they conceive themfelves much af-
" fifted

" fifted hereby, both in the Confervation
" and Improvement of true *Humility*". A-
mong all the exteriour Humiliations, that
of plain and mean Cloathing, is not the
leaft, and for this Reafon we find it to have
been much ufed by fuch as were truly
defirous of being Humble.

How great an Influence towards the Attainment of *Humility* of Heart, or any
other *Virtue*, the external Exercife and
Practice of the fame Virtue hath, may appear alfo from this further Confideration,
that hereby the Will is much more excited to Action than by bare Defires. For as
we find by Experience, that prefent Objects move us more than abfent, and that
we are more affected by *feeing* things, than
by *hearing* of them ; from whence came that
Saying, *What the Eye fees not, the Heart
does not rue* . So the outward Act ftirrs
the Will more ftrongly, becaufe the Object
is there prefent, than any internal Act can
do, where the Object lies only in the Imagination or Conceit, and is not vifible to
the Eye. Hence it is, that one great Affront endured with Meeknefs and Equani-
mity, fhall contribute more to implant the
Virtue of *Patience* in the Soul, than many
Affronts will do, when you have only the
Defire, without the Deed. In like manner the fpending of one Day in the exercife
of fome ordinary and mean Imployment,

or

or the wearing fometimes plain and coarfe Apparel, will produce far greater Degrees of *Humility*, than many days and years of meer defires and impotent Wifhes will do. Experience often fhews that for a Day or two a Man hath great reluctance to perform one of the ordinary Mortifications, which are ufed in Religious Exercifes, but when that is over, he finds no further difficulty therein at all. Neverthelefs before he had recourfe to Action, he had formed many purpofes and defires in his Mind, but thefe alone were not ftrong enough to overcome the Difficulty To this we may add, what is faid by *School Divines, That when the Internal Act is accompanied by the External, it is commonly more efficacious and intenfe* Conclude we therefore, that nothing helps more towards the obtaining of the *Virtue* of *Humility*, than the employing ourfelves fometimes exteriourly in Things, which by the World are accounted Abject and Mean

And whereas every Virtue is preferved and augmented by the fame Means by which it is obtained, therefore as Exteriour Acts are neceffary for the obtaining the *Virtue* of *Humility*, it will alfo be neceffary for the retaining and increafe thereof; whence it follows that this Exercife is very important for all, not only Beginners, but alfo the greateft Proficients, as we faid before, when we were treating of *Mortification* *

tion *.   For it is a good Rule that is given by one in thele Words, —— *To perform thofe Offices with the greateſt Alacrity and Devotion, wherein* Humility *and* Charity *are exerciſed moſt, is the fureſt way to Perfection.* And in another Place he advifes, *to be be-fore band with Temptations, and to prevent them by their Contraries as when any one is inclined to* Pride, *be ſhould exerciſe himſelf in ſuch things as may ſerve to* humble *him* And in another Place, *Be ready to accept of ſuch Offices and Imployments, as are moſt mortify-ing and repugnant to the Pride of the Heart, whenſoever the Divine Providence is pleaſed to throw ſuch a Croſs in the Way; or it happens to be enjoined by the Will of Superiors.* So that I conclude, theſe two Things, *Humili-ty* and *Humiliation* ſhould help each other, the interiour *Humilty*, which confifts in de-fpiſing ſelf, and a contentedneſs to be held by others in ſmall Account, produ-cing the External *Humiliation*, and expreſ-fing itſelf thereby, and the Exteriour Acts of *Humiliation* which a Man performs, de-claring and difplaying the internal *Humi-lity* which is in the Heart.   Chufe you then *the loweſt Room,* as Chriſt our Lord ad-vifed, difdain not to converfe with Per-fons who are poor and mean, decline not the moſt inferiour Services; condefcend, if

* Tract 1 c 17.

need

need be, even to wash your Brethren's Feet, as your Lord did before you; and you will then find, that this Exterior *Humiliation*, if it flow from the inward Temper and Disposition of the Mind, will give a large Increase to that very Fountain, from whence it springs.

CHAP. XXIII.

That we must studiously avoid all Words that may turn to our own Praise.

THE Saints of old and Teachers of the Spiritual Life, such as St *Basil,* St *Gregory,* St *Bernard,* and others, advise us to take great heed of speaking any Words that may redound to our own Glory or Praise, according to that which Holy *Tobit* counselled his Son; *Never suffer Pride to have Dominion over thy Heart, or over thy Words. (Chap.* IV. 14. according to the Vulg*)* St *Bernard* produces that of Saint *Paul* to the same Purpose: *But now I forbear, lest any Man should think of me above that which he seeth me to be, or that he heareth of me* ∗ The Apostle had been

* 2 Cor XII. 6.

speaking

speaking great things of himself, and it was fit at that time he should do so for the Benefit of his Hearers, and the greater glory of God.——He might also have said greater things than these, since he had been caught up into the Third Heaven, and there seen and heard more than Tongue could exprefs, or was lawful for Man to utter. *But I forbear,* faith he, *to speak thereof, lest any Man should think of me more than he sees me to be, or that he heareth of me.* Upon which,——St *Bernard* faith, " O how well said the Apostle, I for-" bear!——The Proud and Arrogant, the " Vain-glorious Man forbears not such " things: he lets no Opportunity slip, to " magnify himfelf; to himfelf he afcribes " all that he is, and affects to appear all " that he is not; that so he may be the " more efteemed. But the truly Humble " Man *forbears* to lay hold of fuch Occa-" fions, and to the End he may be fure, " no more shall be attributed to him than " that which is true, he often conceals even " part of the Truth" And elfewhere, de-fcending more particularly into this Sub-ject, he faith, " you muft not fay any " thing, that favours of Self-Commenda-" tion, or feems to court the Applaufe of " others, whereby you may appear to be " more learned, or a Man of extraordi-" nary Piety and Devotion". That is in general, all that may any way tend to,

I your

your own Praife, muft carefully be avoided, as no lefs dangerous than vain. Or fuppofing you might fpeak it with much Truth, yea though it might be matter of Edification to others; and you may think it conducive to a good End, and for the Profit of another; yet as it is to your own Praife, that is fufficient to keep you from fpeaking it. Walk therefore with great wari nefs in any Difcourfe that concerns yourfelf, left otherwife you lofe the Benefit of that Good, which perhaps you had done

Bonaventure faith, " Boaft not of your " Knowledge or State in the World." That is, you muft never fpeak Words, that may infinuate to others, that you have eminent Parts, or that formerly you were of fome Account in the World. It looks ill in a Man profeffing Religion, to value himfelf on the Nobility and Riches of his Friends, for all fuch Pedigrees, or great Eftates, are no better than a little Wind To one that afked, what Nobility was good for? ano ther anfwered very well, ——— *To be Defpifed.* ——— St *Bafil* faith well, *He that is born of the Spirit, and by the New Birth, that hath contracted a Spiritual and Divine Relation with God, and received a Power to become His Son, fets but fmall Value on that other Kindred, which is according to the Flefh, but rather forgets it.* How worthy foever a Man may ... Words of Praife found ill out of his own Mouth; fo the Proverb faith, *for Men to fearch their own Glory is not Glory,* Prov. xxv. 27. And again, *Chap.* xxvii. 2. *Let another Man praife thee, and not thine own Mouth: a Stranger and not thine own Lips.* —— But in the Mouth of a Pious Man, all Appearance of Boafting, is fo contrary to Character, and fo inconfiftent with what he profeffes; that he lofes himfelf, and finks into Contempt by means of that very thing, whereby he meant to be Honoured. St *Ambrofe,* upon thofe Words of the Pfalmift, *Behold, O Lord, my Humility, and deliver me* *; faith, " That altho' a " Man be fick and poor, and of mean " Condition, yet if he grow not Proud, " nor prefer himfelf before any other, his " *Humility* will make him to be efteemed, " and beloved." So that *Humility* fupplies all Defects. —— On the other hand, tho' a Man be Rich, and Noble, and Powerful; tho' he be very Learned, of excellent Abilities, and bright Parts, yet if he boaft thereof, and look big upon it, he blafts his own Character, and finks into Contempt, defervedly forfeiting that Efteem and Refpect from others, which he vainly arrogated to himfelf.

History tells us of the devout *Arfenius,* " That altho' he had been fo Famous in the

---

* Pf xxv 19 *fec.* vuig.

World,

" 'World, and so Eminent for Learning,
" (for he had been the Tutor or Preceptor
" to the Emperor *Theodosius*'s two Sons,
" *Arcadius*, and *Honorius*, both which came
" afterwards to be Emperors,) yet no
" Word was ever heard to fall from him,
" after his Retirement into a Religious Or-
" der, which might favour the least of his
" former Greatness, or give Men to under-
" stand that he had any Learning; but he
" conversed and lived amongst his Brethren
" with so great *Humility* and Simplicity of
" Manners, as if he had never known any
" thing more than others; often asking
" Questions concerning the most ordinary
" Improvements in the spiritual Life, and
" affirming that in this sublime Science he
" needed to be their Disciple" It is also
related of St *Jerom*, that altho' he was of
very noble Extraction, yet we find not in
all his Works, that he hath so much as in-
sinuated any such thing.

This made *Bonaventure* say, (and an excellent Reason it is against Boasting) " If
" there be any one good thing in you wor-
" thy of Praise, it will shine out, and dis-
" cover itself to others, so that they can-
" not but understand and know it. if by
" Silence you conceal it, you shall gain
" greater Honour, and be thought the
" more worthy of Praise; not only for the
' Virtue itself, but for your hiding it,
                                    " but,

" but, if you will needs become the Pub-
" lifher thereof, and blow the Trumpet
" yourfelf; inftead of the Praife you ex-
" pect, they will but make Sport of you,
" And now vilify and defpife whom before
" they were Edified by, and Efteemed."
Virtue, in this Refpect, is like Mufk, the
clofer it is kept, the ftronger fmell it
yeilds, but if you carry it open, it lofes
it's Scent.

C H A P. XXIV.

*That the Examination of our Confciences con-
cerning the* Virtue *of* Humility, *fhould be
Particular.*

THE moft effectual Method of fub-
duing any one of the Mortal Sins,
and acquiring it's oppofite Virtue, is to refolve the fame into it's feveral Parts, and
to defcend to *Particulars.* A general Application to many Things at once, rather
diffipates the Attention, than forwards our
Succefs, whereas the moft difficult Tafk,
if divided into Parts, and purfued by little
and little, may by Degrees be brought to
a happy Conclufion. For this Reafon it
is, that if you have laid down a Refolu-

tion

tion to Root up the *Pride* of your Heart, and obtain the *Virtue* of *Humility*, you muft not fet about it in a General Way. Both *Humility* and *Pride* contain many Particulars ; and if you take them in the grofs, and fay, *I will be Proud in nothing, but Humble in all Things* ; it is too much to undertake at once : But you are to divide them into their feveral Parts, and fo go on by little and little. Confider in what Branches of *Humility* you are chiefly wont to fail, what kinds of *Pride* you are moft fubject to, and begin there , and when you have gone thro' one particular Thing, take another in hand, and then, another ; thus by degrees you will pluck up the whole Vice of *Pride* out of your Soul, and plant the *Virtue* of *Humility* in the Place thereof. Purfuant to this Method, let us take a View of fome particular Inftances, whereby we may gradually advance towards *Humility*, and at the fame time be the better enabled to judge of our Progrefs in fo neceffary a Virtue.

The firft fhall be, not to fpeak a Word that may tend to our own Commendation and Praife. —— So natural to us is the *Love of Praife*, and fo rooted in our Heart, that without thinking or reflecting, the Tongue is ever ready to fay fomewhat, that may directly, or indirectly redound to our Praife *Out of the Abundance of the Heart the Mouth*
fpeaketh.

fpeaketh. As foon as any Occafion offers, whereby Honour may be gained, we inftantly come in for our Share of it, by faying, *I was by. I was partly the Caufe:* —— *If it had not been for me, it would never have been done I faw how it would go: I faw, from the Beginning, how it would be, and therefore did not care to meddle.* —— And a hundred fuch Things we fay, which all fpring from a *fecret Pride,* and are fcarce ever attended to, before they be fpoken. 'Tis wife Advice therefore, that our Examination on this Head, be very *fpecial* and *particular,* that by fuch previous Reflection, and ufing ourfelves to a *Good* Cuftom, that other *Bad* one, which is fo natural to us, may be rooted out.

The fecond Advice may be that of St *Bafil,* St *Jerom,* and others, namely, *That we be not fondly defirous to hear our own Praifes; for in this there is great Danger.* St *Ambrofe* faith, that, " When the Devil fees he " cannot beat us down by Dejection, he " blows us up by Prefumption and Pride: " when he cannot overthrow us by Af- " fronts, he endeavours to fupplant us by " Honour and Praife; fpreading the *Net* " *of Flattery* in our Way, that fo we may " be caught, and perifh in that Snare." Hence St *Jerom* faith, " We are haftening " to our Home: let us turn a Deaf-Ear " to thofe *Syren's* deadly Songs." Beware

I 4 of

of their Enchantments, for they bewitch and deprive us of our Reason. So pleasing is the Melody of human Praise, so grateful to the Ear, that no *Syren's* Song was ever more charming, or more destructive. Stop we therefore our Ears to the Voice of those Charmers, charm they never so sweetly. —— Wise then is the Advice of *Climacus*, that when Men praise us, we should call our *Sins* to Mind, for by so doing, we shall improve our *Humility*, and draw Confusion from the very Honours that are given us. This therefore may be the *second* Particular, upon which you may examine yourself; namely, that you *Rejoice not* in being well spoken of, and praised by others. To which may be added, that you Rejoice and take Delight in hearing Others commended and praised. This is a Particular of no small Importance. —— Whenever you feel the least Motion of Envy at the Praise of Others, or too much Complacence, or vain Delight in others speaking well of Yourself, be sure to set it down for a Fault.

The *Third* thing is; *Not to do any thing in order to our being seen, or esteemed by Men* And this is what Christ our Lord advises us, *Matth.* vi. 1. *Take heed that ye do not your Alms* (or *Righteousness*, as some Copies have it) *before Men, to be seen of them; otherwise ye have no reward of your Father*
which

which is in Heaven. This is an Examination of the greateſt Uſe and Conſequence, and may be divided into many Parts. *Firſt,* it may be enquired, how far the Action was influenced by any *human* Reſpects. *Secondly,* if done chiefly for the Love of God. And *thirdly,* how well done, and if performed as in the Preſence of God, and as by one who ſerves not Men, but God. And this Exerciſe is to be continued ſo long, 'till, the Works be performed in ſo perfect a Manner, that they may rather ſeem to be Acts of *Love* to God, than Acts of mere *Obedience.*

The *Fourth* Point is, *Never to be too forward to excuſe ourſelves.* —— To fly to Excuſes, when we are told of our Faults, is a certain Mark of *Pride.* St *Gregory,* upon theſe Words of *Job, If I covered my Tranſgreſſions as a Man* * (So the *Latin* Verſion). well conſiders theſe Words [*Quaſi homo*] *as a Man,* and ſaith, " It is natural for " Man to cover and excuſe his Sin, being " derived to us from our firſt Parents. As " ſoon as the firſt Man had ſinned, he ". went inſtantly to hide himſelf among the " Trees of Paradiſe, and when God reprov- " ed him, for his Diſobedience, he excu- " ſed Himſelf, by accuſing his Wife, —— ". *The Woman, whom thou gaveſt to be with* " *me, ſhe gave me of the Tree, and I did* ". *eat.* The Woman excuſed herſelf in like

* Chap xxxi 33

I 5

" Manner,

" Manner, by throwing the Blame and
" Guilt upon the Serpent; *The Serpent be-*
" *guiled me, and I did eat.* God examined
" them about their Sin, to the end, that
" they knowing, and confessing it, might
" obtain Pardon for it: But, the Serpent,
" who tempted them to the Crime, and
" had no Title to a Pardon, He did not
" examine. Howbeit, our first Parents,
" instead of humbling themselves, and ac-
" knowledging their Sin, in order to the
" obtaining of Pardon, enhaunce and ag-
" gravate it by their Excuses: yea, in
" some Measure they stick not to cast the
" Blame upon God. *The Woman, whom*
" *thou gavest me,* &c. As if he had said;
" If thou hadst not given me Her for a
" Companion, no Part of this had hap-
" pened And as if the Woman had said,
" The Serpent, which thou didst Create,
" and suffer to enter into Paradise, de-
" ceived me if thou hadst not suffered
" it to enter there, I had not sinned."
" Thus, as the same Saint goes on, having
" heard that bold Lie from the Devil's
" Mouth, that they should be *as God,*
" seeing they could not become like him
" in respect of his Divinity, to inflame
" their Guilt, they endeavoured to make
" him such an one as themselves, in re-
" spect of their Sin; and so by Defend-
" ing, made it far more Criminal, than

" by

" by Committing it. Hence it comes to
" pafs, that as Men, and the Children of fuch
" Parents, we are all fubject to this In-
" firmity, and evil Cuftom, that when-
" ever we are reproved for any Fault,
" we inftantly feek an Excufe, and are
" for hiding ourfelves under our *Boughs*
" and *Fig-Leaves*; and fo flying from the
" Face of our Maker, to the Shades and
" Retreat of fome vain Excufe, to hide
" and conceal the Faults we have
" done."

Nor are we content to excufe Ourfelves,
but muft needs be cafting the Fault upon
Others. Such as are always ready at an
Excufe, are aptly compared to the Hedge-
Hog, which whenever fhe perceives herfelf in
danger of being taken, fhrinks in her Head
and Feet with extream Speed, and remains
like a Bowl, circled on every fide as it
were with Thorns fo that a Man cannot
touch her without receiving a Wound;
and you fhall fooner fee your own Blood,
than come at her Body Thus it is with
them, that are given to Apologies and Ex-
cufes if you but touch them, and reprove
their Faults, they inftantly defend themfelves like the Hedge-Hog. —— Yea,
fometime they'll prick and gaul you for
your Admonition, and tell you, you had
need of Reproof yourfelf. At other
Times they pretend there is a Rule, which

I 6   forbids

forbids finding of Faults. —— That others are as great Offenders; yet efcape Cenfure. Thus, I fay, touch the Hedge-Hog, and you'll wound your Fingers.

And all this grows from that exceffive Pride, which cannot bear to have our Failings known. It grieves us more to be charged with the *leaft* Fault, than to commit the *greateft*; and hence comes the mighty Pains, that fome take, to hide or excufe their Defects. Nay, there are fome fo unmortified in this kind, that even before you fay any thing, they prevent you, and begin to excufe and give Reafons for what they think you may diflike; *If I did this*, fay they, *it was for this Reafon*; *if I did that*, *it was for that*; *and the like*. But in the mean time, what is it that Stings you, and puts you upon defending yourfelf? 'Tis the Goad of Pride, which gauls you thus, and thus puts you upon the defenfive before you are attacked. It will therefore be well done of him, who finds in himfelf this vicious Difpofition, to examine himfelf particularly about it; 'till he come at length to conquer all Defire of covering his Faults and when he hath committed any, let him rather be glad, that he is blamed, and falls into Shame and Punifhment for them. Yea, tho' you have committed no Fault, and they reprehend you, as if you had, be not always forward to excufe.

The

The *fifth* Head of *Examination* is also of great use; namely, *To restrain and cut off all the Avenues, and first Thoughts of Pride.* Man is so Proud and Vain a Creature, that many idle and presumptuous Thoughts will be stealing in upon him; sometimes he will imagine himself to be in some high Office, and performing of some great Function. Another time fancy himself to be discoursing with great Applause and Apr probation, and that he acquits himself with great Success. Another time you conceive that you are Reading, or holding an argument, against such and such Points with great Acclamations of the Hearers. But all this grows from that Root of *Pride*, which lies implanted in the Heart. It will therefore be necessary to make a very particular Examination, in Relation to such vain and impertinent *Thoughts* as these After the same Manner it behoves us to put a Stop to, and instantly suppress all *impure* Thoughts, all rash Judgments, or any other Vice, to which we find ourselves inclined.

The *sixth* Point shall be, particularly to examine ourselves, whether we *esteem all Men as our Betters*, according to that Rule of *Humility*, which directeth us *in honour to prefer one another*, Rom xii. 10 Endeavouring, as well as desiring, to yield the Advantage to others, esteeming them all from our very Souls, as if they were our
Superiors,

Superiors ; and outwardly bearing them that Refpect and Reverence, which the Condition of every one of them fhall require, with Plainnefs, and religious Simplicity of Heart And howfoever there is a Difference to be obferved amongft Men, according to the Diftinction of their Perfons and Places, yet with refpect to the inward *Humility* of our Souls, every one of us muft hold Himfelf, for the leaft and loweft, and Others for his Superiors and Betters This therefore will be a very good and profitable Topic of Examination : provided it be not barely fpeculative, but active and fincere ; fo that in the Exercife and Practice thereof, we carry ourfelves towards all, with fuch *Humility* and *Refpect*, as if they really were our Superiours If you keep to this Rule of preferring others before yourfelf, you will at no time return a pettifh Anfwer, much lefs ufe fharp and angry Words · you will not rafhly pafs a Judgment ; nor take Offence, when treated in a Way you do not like And if in your Examen, you find fuch Symptoms as thefe upon you, mark 'em down for Faults and Imperfections.

The *feventh* Subject of this Self-Examination is, *whether you embrace all Opportunities that offer, towards the getting of* Humility. Are you troubled, when another fpeaks fome little Word to you, which
                                                        you

you like not to hear? or when they command any thing in too refolute and imperious a Manner; or when you think they make not fo much Account of you, as of others? Examine yourfelf how fuch things affect you, and what ufe you make of thefe, or any other Occafions, which fometimes prefent themfelves, tending to the leffening of your Honour or Credit. This is one of the moft profitable Examinations, we can ufe, towards obtaining the *Virtue* of *Humility* For befides, that we fhall thus prepare ourfelves for all thofe things which duly occur, and whereof we may ftand in need, we fhall by this Means advance towards Perfection, and go on to improve in this Virtue by thofe three Degrees, which we have affigned. *Firft,* you will perceive whether you bear all thefe things *with Patience.* *Secondly,* whether you bear them with fo much *Readinefs* and *Facility,* that they give you no Trouble or Regret And *thirdly,* whether you accept them *with Joy,* and take Pleafure in the Contempt of yourfelf, for in this (if duly regulated) the Perfection of *Humility* doth confift.

The *eighth* Point, upon which a Man may particularly Examine himfelf, either on this Subject, or others like it, is *to reflect what Acts be exerts, or what Exercife be ufes,* as well Interior as Exterior, whether it be of *Humility,* or any *other* Virtue, concerning

concerning which he Examines himfelf; meditating upon it fo many times in a Morning, and fo many times in an Evening, beginning with fewer Acts, and fo rifing up to more, 'till at length he get the Habit of the Virtue he ftudies to acquire. And now the Enemies being divided after this Manner, and we taking every one of them fingly, and by himfelf, they will the more eafily be overcome, and the Victory, which is defired, be the more fpeedily obtained.

CHAP.

CHAP. XXV.

How it may be consistent with Humility, *to admit of Honour and worldly Respect.*

THERE is a Question wont to be propounded concerning *Humility*, the Solution whereof doth much import us, that so we may know how to behave therein. We ordinarily say, and it is the general Doctrine of the Saints, that we must willingly submit to be Abased, Disesteemed, and Despised, and be contented that Men should not Honour or Esteem us in the least. But then it may be asked, What good we can do our Neighbours, if they Disesteem and Despise us, for in order to do them any good, it is necessary we should have some Credit with them, and that they have a good Opinion of us; therefore it may seem not an evil, but a good Thing that we should desire to be Valued and Esteemed of Men. St *Basil*, St *Gregory*, and St. *Bernard*, answer this Difficulty very well, and say, *That although it be true, that we ought to fly from worldly Honour and Esteem, by reason of the great danger which attends it, and that, with*
respect

respect to our selves, we must be content to be Disesteemed and Despised; yet for so good an end, as the Service of God, and greater good of our Neighbour, the Honour and Esteem of the World may Lawfully and Piously be desired. St *Bernard* saith also, *That upon our own Account, we may rather wish, that Men should think and esteem of us, as we think and esteem of our selves.* But he saith withal, *that whatever Contempt our Faults may deserve, it is not fit many times that others should be privy thereto, lest they should receive hurt thereby, thro the hindrance of their own Spiritual Improvement.*

Now it will be necessary to understand this Point very well, that we may walk therein with due caution; because such a Truth as this, instead of doing good, does many times much hurt to such as know not how to make a right use of it. The Saints therefore are careful to set forth this Doctrine in the plainest manner, that we may take no occasion of errour from thence St. *Gregory* saith, " Sometimes, even " Holy Men are glad that they are valued " and esteemed, but this happens when they, " find it a necessary Means for doing Good, " and helping their Neighbours Souls, " Now this is not to rejoyce at their own " Credit or Esteem, but at the Benefit and " Good that is down to their Neighbour", which is a very different case.—It is one thing for a Man to love worldly Honour

for

for its own fake, and his own fatisfaction,
and Content, that fo he may be counted
Great, and a Man of Confequence, (which
is a bad Principle and evil Defign;) and
another thing, when this is liked for fome
End that is truly good, fuppofing the Benefit of a Neighbour, and the Intereft of
Souls, which is a great and real Good: on
this view we may lawfully defire the Efteem
of the world, that fo their good Opinion of
us may tend to the greater Glory of God,
and Edification of others. For in this cafe
a Man will not rejoyce fo properly in his
own Honour, as in the Spiritual good of his
Brethren, and the greater glory of Almighty
God. And as he who for his Health defires
to take a Medicine, which he naturally abhors, may well fay, that he likes the Purge,
becaufe he loves his Health; fo he who upon occafion admits, and likes human Honour and Efteem, which otherwife he defpifes, (only becaufe in that cafe it is a neceffary, or at leaft a probable Means for ad-
vancing the Service of God, and the Good
of Souls) may affirm with Truth, that he
defires and likes nothing in it, but the Glory of Almighty God.

But, how may we know, whether a Man
delights in Honour and Eftimation, for the
fole glory of God, and the good of his
Neighbour, or elfe for his own fake, and
the mere Love of Praife? This indeed is a

nice

nice and subtile Point, wherein we are too apt to deceive our selves. St *Gregory* answereth thus: " Our Rejoycing in Honour " should be so disinterested, so intirely for " the sake of God, that when upon a change " of Circumstances, it happen in the least to " interfere with His Glory, and the good " of Souls, we should not only not rejoyce " therein, but be troubled at, and fly from " it". By this mark therefore shall you know, whether you take pleasure in Honour and Applause for your own sake, or the sake of God, and the good of Souls; If, when any occasion of *Humiliation* and Contempt is offered, you imbrace it as heartily, and in as good earnest, as you did before, the Compliment of Praise and Respect. It is also a good sign; when such a Sermon, or some other Undertaking hath succeeded well, and you are Valued and Esteemed for it, you can separate all selfish regards, and rejoyce not for your own Honour and Fame, but purely for the Glory of God, and the good of Souls which grows thereby. But if on the other hand, when an occasion of *Humility* is offered, you reject it; This is a sign that you are glad of a thing, which promotes your own Honour and Esteem, but do not unfeignedly rejoyce in the Glory of God, and the Interest of Souls.

So that we may truly say, the Honour and Esteem of Men is an not evil, but a good, if so be we use it rightly; in that case it may lawfully and virtuously be desired. Yea, even a Man's praising himself, may be holy and good, if it be done as it ought. For so we see, St *Paul* writing to them of *Corinth*, began to praise, and recount great things of himself, particularly the high Favours, which our Lord had imparted to him, not only saying; *That he had laboured more abundantly than the rest of the Apostles, but came to Visions and Revelations of the Lord*, and acquainted them with that glorious Rapture, whereby he had been *caught up to the third Heaven*. But all this he did, because it was convenient, yea necessary, for the glory of God, and the good of them, to whom he Wrote, that so being induced to hold, and value him for a *true* Apostle of Christ, they might the readier embrace his Doctrine, and be Edified thereby. He was conscious (as he himself Prefaces this Account) that it was *not expedient for him to Glory*, and therefore we may be assured, he spoke these Things of himself, with a Heart which did not only despise Honour, but even love Dishonour, for the sake of Christ our Lord, and when his own Honour was not necessary for the good of others, he knew very well how to empty and abase himself, saying, *That he was the least of the Apostles, not worthy to be called an Apostle, because he had persecuted the Church of God*, 1 Cor. xv. 9

In

In another place ſtiling himſelf *Blaſphemer,*
one born out of due time, and the *chief of Sin-*
ners, and when occaſions of Diſhonour and
Contempt for the ſake of Chriſt, were pre-
ſented to him, therein was his Glory and
his Joy. Such Hearts as theſe may well
be truſted with receiving Honour, and with
ſaying ſometimes ſuch things, as may tend in
ſome meaſure to their own Glory ; Becauſe
they will never do ſo, but when it may con
tribute to the greater glory of God, yea
and even then they do it, without aſſuming
any part of the Glory to Themſelves,
they do it, as if they did it not, It is not
their own Honour they Love or Deſire,
but the Honour of Almighty God, and
the good of Souls.

Hence it is that the ſame Apoſtle adds,
moſt gladly therefore wi'l I rather glory in
my Infirmities, that the Power of Chriſt may
reſt upon me. Therefore I take pleaſure in In-
firmities, in Reproaches, in Neceſſities, in Per-
ſecutions, in Diſtreſſes for Chriſt's ſake · For
when I am weak, then am I ſtrong.

But this is a Perfection in *Humility,* which
few can arrive at, it being a matter of
the greateſt difficulty to receive Honour,
and not to grow Proud of it, nor to take
any vain contentment, or complacence
therein Therefore the Saints, through
fear of the great dangers, which lie hid in
worldly Honour, in Dignity and high Places,

ces, fled as far as they could from it; chu-
sing rather to busie themselves in mean and
contemptible Employments, as the likeliest
way for profiting in *Humility*, as well as the
most secure. One said very well, *I am no*
Religious Man, If I take not Dishonour with
the same, both inward and outward joy, where-
with I receive Honour. If I joy in that Ho-
nour which others bestow, when I Preach, or
perform any Office of Charity, for Their *good ;*
(tho' I expose my Soul to some hazard, through
the danger of Vanity) how much more ought
my Soul to rejoyce in her own good, when so
effectually secured from Vanity, by the suffering
of Scorn and Re proach ?

It is the Dictate of Nature, and therefore
a self evident Truth, that we are more
obliged to joy in our own Good and Profit,
than in that of others, because *Charity, well*
ordered, begins at home. If then you joy in
any Act of your own, and the Honour it
meets with, when your Neighbour hath received a Benefit thereby ; why should you
not be equally glad of your own good,
when having done what was in you, and
yet despised for your Pains, you have the
opportunity of mortifying the swellings of
Pride, and performing an Act of sincere
Humility, which is far better, and more safe
for you? If you may be glad when you have
a great Talent committed to you, wherewith to do great Things for the good of
others,

others, why fhould you not be glad of promoting your own? If you rejoice when you
have Health and Strength, to labour for
the good of others, why fhould you not be
glad, when God is pleafed to bring Contempt upon you, for the Profit of your
own felf, and your greater furtherance in
Patience and *Humility?* By this fhall you
pleafe God more, than if you were a celebrated Preacher, or a wife and able Statef-
man, fince his Will is fo.

Hence it may appear how much they are
deceived, who have fet their Eyes upon
Honour, and the Opinion of the World,
under pretence, that it is a necefary Qualifi-
cation for doing good to others. Under Co
lour of this, they affect high Places, and
honourable Employments, giving a loofe to
their Ambition, and courting all that looks
Great. But this deceit is commonly punifhed by another very great one, that the
very thing, whereby a Man pretends to
gain Authority, is the moft certain Means
to fruftrate his Expectations, and defeat
not only the good he propofed, but the
Honour and Advancement he expected to
gain. Whereas the fureft Means for attaining either of thofe Ends, is that very way,
by which he feared to lofe them.

For if we confider the Thing in Queftion, by the Light of Reafon and Human Pru
dence you cannot ufe a more efficacious means
to

to gain Authority, and good Opinion amongft
your Neighbours, and confequently of doing good to their Souls, than by exercifing
your felf in fuch Things as feem mean and
bafe, (fuch as Catechizing Children in the
low and familiar way of fhort Queftions
and Anfwers, teaching, or feeing them
Taught, the firft Principles of Religion and
Manners, daily vifiting the Sick, the Poor,
the Ignorant, and humbly and kindly inftructing, comforting, and quickening them,
as occafion is offered.) And to do thefe
things fo much the more, by how much
the greater your Parts are. The World
hath fo high a conceit of Honour and
Preferment, and all thofe Things, which
contribute to that end, that it cannot but
look with Admiration on the Man, who defpifes thofe Advantages ; efpecially if he be
one of eminent and diftinguifh'd Merit, who
might worthily fill the higheft and moft
honourable Employments : to fee fuch a Perfon chufe to pafs his Hours in Things, that
are fo far beneath his Abilities, purely for
the fake of doing good, muft at length
raife a great Opinion and Efteem of the
Sanctity of fuch Perfons, and recomend the
Doctrine which they teach, as if it came
immediately from Heaven.

This is that kind of Authority, whereof
all have need, who labour for the good of
Souls ; to wit, that they bear the Character

of

of Humble, Holy Men, and faithful Preachers, and this, in a word, is the Authority, as well as End, that we fhould all purfue. As for other kinds of Refpect, Reputation and Punctilios, which carry a fmack and favour of the World in them, they do great hurt, and rather hinder our Neighbours Edification; as well as obftruct our own proficiency in the way of True *Humility*, and the Love of God.

Upon thofe words of our Lord, *I feek not mine own glory; there is one that feeketh and judgeth*, Joh. viii. 50. A Doctor faith very well; " Seeing our Heavenly Father *feeks*
" our Honour and Glory, we have no need
" to be follicitous about it ourfelves. Take
" you but care to humble yourfelves, be
" but fuch as ye ought to be, and for
" any Eftimation and Authority, which you
" may think you ftand in need of, for the
" good of Souls, leave that to God; by
" the very means you fhall ufe to humble
" and abafe yourfelves, even thereby will
" God raife you moft, and endow you
" with a Reputation in the World, far fu-
" periour to that which you would ever be
" able to raife to yourfelves, by thofe other
" means, and mere human Devices "

Some Men may think it behoves them to revere themfelves for the fake of the Religion they profefs, their holy Function, or the Station they are in. But this is too often a falfe Pretence, and only a Mafk to difguife an unmortify'd Pride, and the Defect of *Humility.* "I did this or that, *fuch a one will fay,* for the Honour of Reli-" gion, Credit of my Church, Profeffion, " Place, *&c*". I befeech you, let thefe Refpects alone ; what you are fo much concern'd for, will doubtlefs gain far greater Reverence and Refpect, if Men obferve you to be *Patient, Quiet* and *Humble.*—— The lefs you fhew of regard to the Efteem of the World, the greater will the World have for you, and confequently for the Station you hold.

CHAP. XXVI.

Of the Third *Degree of* Humility.

WE are now come to the *Third* Degree of *Humility,* and it is this ; when a Man poffeffing great Virtues, and great Gifts of God, and being in high Honour and Reputation for the fame, does not grow Proud in the leaft, nor attribute any thing to himfelf, but afcribes all to God, as the only Fountain thereof, from whom every good and perfect Gift proceeds. " This *Third*

" degree

" degree of *Humility* (faith *Bonaventure*)
" belongs to great and Perfect Men ; by
" how much the higher fuch are, fo much
" the lower do they humble themfelves.——
That a Man, who is imperfect and faulty,
fhould know he is fuch, and Efteem himfelf
accordingly, is no great matter. It is indeed a commendable, but no wonderful
thing ; any more than it is for a Plough-
man's Son, to be confcious that he is not
the Son of a King : or for a poor or fick
Man, to be willing that others fhould take
him for what he is: But for a Rich Man to
be content to be accounted Poor ; for a
Great Man to fubmit to be made little,
and placed on the fame Level with mean
Perfons, this is a condefcention juftly deferves to be admired. So for one who is
highly advanced in Virtue, and poffeffes
many extraordinary Gifts of God, and
is truely great in His divine Prefence,
to count himfelf Mean and inconfiderable ;
This indeed is great *Humility*, and worthy
of admiration. So St. *Bernard*, " A rare
" Virtue it is, that a Man fhould do great
" things, and yet not think himfelf great,
" that he fhould be admirable in the Eyes
" of others, and contemptible in his own.
" I Efteem this more, *faith he*, than all his
" other Virtues".

This kind of *Humility* was found after a
moft perfect manner, in the ever *Bleffed*
Virgin,

Virgin, who, tho' she knew she was chosen to be the Mother of God, did nevertheless with the profoundest *Humility* acknowledge herself to be his Servant. —— *Behold the handmaid of the Lord.* —— " God (saith the " same St *Bernard*) had chosen her to so " great an Honour, so high a dignity, as to " be His Mother, yet she calls herself His " Servant". —— When saluted by the Mouth of *Elizabeth*, as the most *blessed amongst Women*, she ascribed no Glory to herself, for all these transcendent Privileges, but said, *My Soul doth magnifie the Lord, and my Spirit hath rejoyced in God my Saviour, for he hath regarded the lowliness of his Handmaiden.* This is the very *Humility* of *Heaven* ; this is that kind, which the very Saints possess in Glory.

This (saith St *Gregory*) is the Moral of what St. *John* saw, in the *Apocalypse* ; the Four and Twenty Elders, *casting off their Crowns before the Throne*, signifies, the not attributing their Victories to Themselves, but their ascribing all to God, who gave them Strength and Power, to overcome. —— *Thou art worthy, O Lord, to receive Glory and Honour and Power* ; therefore we take the Crowns from off our Heads, and cast them at thy Feet ; *for thou hast created all things, and for thy Pleasure they are, and were created.* —— If we have done any thing that is good, it is of thy Gift, and all the Praise is due to Thee. This

then

then is the *Third* degree of *Humility*, when a Man afcribes not to himfelf thofe Gifts and Graces, which he hath received of God; but refers all to Him, as the Author and Giver of them all.

But fome Men may fay, if *Humility* confift in this, then all are humble; for who knows not, that all Good comes from God, and that of ourfelves we are nothing but Mifery and Sin? Who is he, that will not fay, If God fhould withdraw his Hand from me, I muft be the moft miferable Man in the World, according to that of the Prophet *Hofea*; *O Ifrael, thou haft deftroy'd thy felf, but in me is thine help,* cap. xiii. 9. All we have, and all we are, flows to us from the Bounty and Goodnefs of God. And this is found Doctrine.—It may feem then that we all have this *Humility*; for this is a Truth, we all believe, and whereof the holy Scripture is full. St *James* tells us, *Every good gift, and every perfect gift, is from above, and cometh down from the Father of Lights.* And St *Paul* faith, *We are not fufficient of ourfelves to think* [much lefs then to begin, to do, or to finifh,] *any thing as of ourfelves: but our fufficiency is of God,* 2 Cor. iii. 5. And what comparifon could more aptly exemplify this to us, than that, which Chrift our Lord himfelf makes ufe of in the Gofpel, *I am the Vine, ye are the Branches. He that abideth in me, and I in him, the fame bringeth* *forth much fruit, for without me ye can do no-thing.* John xv. 5. What is more fruitful than the Branch, while united to the Vine? What more unprofitable, and ufeless, than when it is divided from it? *What is the Vine Tree* (faith God to the * Prophet) *more than any Tree? fhall Wood be taken thereof to do any work? or will Men take a pin of it to hang any Veffel thereon? Behold it is caft into the Fire for fewel; the Fire devoureth both the ends of it, and the midft of it is burnt; is it meet for any work?* Juft fo are we, if we be not united to the true Vine, which is Chrift our Lord. *If a Man abide not in me, he is caft forth as a Branch, and is withered, and Men gather them, and caft them into the Fire, and they are burned,* John xv. 6. If we be any thing, it is by the Grace of God: fo St *Paul* teftifies of himfelf, and well may we fay the fame, *By the Grace of God I am what I am,* 1 Cor. xv. 10. All Men are fully fatisfied of the Truth of this, that we are to afcribe no good to ourfelves, but all to God, to whom alone the Honour and Glory of all is due; wherefore fince it is fo clear a Point of Faith, why fhould it be fet down for the moft *perfect* Degree of *Humility?*

It feems at firft fight a Degree of no difficult Attainment;— if we look fuperficially

* Ezek xv.

upon

upon it, it appears an eafy thing ; but in reality is very hard. *Caffian* faith, " That " to fuch as are but Beginners, it feems " to be but an eafie thing, for a Man to at- " tribute nothing to himfelf, but to refer " and afcribe all to God ; howbeit, upon " trial, it will be found very hard". For firce we alfo contribute fomewhat on our part, towards good Works, and are as St *Paul* fpeaks, *Fellow-workers,* and concur jointly *with God,* we grow infenfibly, and without perceiving it, to confide in our-felves ; and a fecret Prefumption and Pride fteals upon us unawares, tempting us to think, that this or that was done by our Diligence and Care ; till by degrees we grow vain enough to afcribe all the Works we do, to ourfelves, as if the whole merit were our own.

To evince the Perfection of this kind of *Humility,* it might fuffice that the Saints fet this down, for the *higheft* De-gree of that Virtue, and call it the *Hu-mility* of eminent and great Proficients To receive extraordinary Gifts from God and to do extraordinary things, yet ftill to give God the Glory of all, and attribute no part of the Praife to ourfelves, is a Point of great Perfection. Honour is the Shade and Reflection of every fhining Virtue, and follows it wherever it moves , but to be praifed for a Saint, and yet receive no more Impreffion of Pride in the Heart, than if

the

the Man had done nothing, is a Task too
hard for human Nature, and few there be
who attain to it. 'Tis God-like to do good
merely for the fake of Good: It therefore
requires a more than ordinary Virtue to perfect us in this *third* Degree of *Humility.*

St *Chryfoftome,* who was a fkillful Judge
in fuch matters, faith, " That to live in the
" midft of Honour, and not be affected
" therewith, is like converfing with Beauti-
" ful Women, without the leaft glance of
" a wanton Eye." It is doubtlefs both a
difficult, and a dangerous thing; and a Man
had need of much Grace, and ftrong Refo-
lutions to fecure his Virtue. For a Man to
climb high, and not be giddy, he had
need have a good Head; very few have
Brains proof againft turning, when they are
raifed to an uncommon height. 'Tis plain
Lucifer and his Angels wanted this firmnefs
of Mind; the very Height of their Station
made them giddy and proud; and this caft
them down into the bottomlefs Pit. For
this, it is thought, was the Sin of the fallen
Angels, that God having created them fo
beautiful, and enriched them with fo many
both natural, and fupernatural Gifts, they
retained not their Union with him, nor gave
him the Glory of all; but yielding to the
dictates of Self-love, they fell away from
their firft Eftate, and wou'd needs fubfift of
themfelves: not that they conceived they

V

had thefe things of themfelves, (for they knew well, that all came from God, that they depended upon him, and that they were his Creatures) but (as the Prophet *Ezekiel* faid of the King of *Tyre*, *Thine Heart was lifted up becaufe of thy Beauty, thou haft corrupted thy Wifdom by reafon of thy brightnefs*, ch. xxviii. 17.) They grew proud of their Beauty, and gloried in thofe Gifts, which they had received of God, as if they pof-feffed them of themfelves : They gave not Him the Honour and Glory thereof : With their Underftanding, they could not but know the Praife of all was due to God, yet with their Will they robbed him of it, and ufurped it to themfelves.

You fee then, this degree of *Humility*, is not fo eafie, as at firft it feems to be ; fee-ing it proved too hard for Angels to main-tain that Height, wherein God had placed them ; and if Angels fell, how much more reafon have we to fear, and *take heed leaft we fall*, whenever we are raifed on high. Such miferable Creatures are we Men, that as the *Pfalmift* fpeaks, *We vanifh like the fmoak.* For as fmoak, the higher it rifes, the more it fcatters and diffolves into Air : So Man, by Nature, is fo wretched, and yet fo Proud a Thing, that the more he is Ho-noured, and exalted to a high Eftate, the more vain and intoxicated he grows.

How

How well did Chrift our Lord admonifh us of this ! The Holy Gofpel relates, that having fent his Seventy Difciples to Preach, they returned to Him full of Joy ; and being, as it were, fomewhat elated with the Succefs of their Miffion, they faid thus to Him, *Lord, even the Devils are fubject unto us through thy Name.* But the Saviour of the World, by the Anfwer he made, feems to correct the Vanity, which he faw fpringing up in their Hearts ; *I beheld Satan as Lightning fall from Heaven,* Luke x. 18. as much as to fay, take heed of vain complacence in yourfelves ; know that *Lucifer* fell from Heaven, becaufe in that high State, wherein he was created, he was vainly pleafed with himfelf, and with thofe Gifts and Graces which he had received ; not afcribing all to the Honour and Glory of Almighty God, as he ought, but affuming a part to himfelf. That the like happen not to you, take heed that ye grow not high-minded, by reafon of the great and wonderful things, which you do in my Name, nor take any vain Self-Content therein Then he concludes with this moft excellent Advice. —— *Notwithftanding, in this rejoice not, that the Spirits are fubject unto you ; but rather rejoice, becaufe your Names are written in Heaven,* ver 20. See that you wax not Proud, how great things foever are done by you, for the good of

others,

others, and becaufe many Souls are gained by your means. Beware that you take no Pleafure in the Applaufe and Opinion of Men, and in the great Refpects they pay you. Be fure you affume nothing to your felves, nor fuffer the love of Honour and Vain-glory to cleave at all to your Hearts; for this is that, which caft *Lucifer* down to Hell, that, which of an Angel made him a Devil. *You may fee* (faith St *Auguftin*) *how deteftable a thing* Pride *is, fince it makes* Angels Devils; *and on the other hand, how Excellent a thing* Humility *is, fince it makes* Men *to become* Angels.

CHAP. XXVII.

Wherein the Third Degree *of* Humility *confifteth.*

WE have not yet fufficiently declared wherein the *Third Degree* of *Humility* confifts; it may be therefore worth while to treat fomewhat more largely hereon, that fo we may the better reduce it to practice, this being the main thing we are to aim at. The Saints affirm, That the Third Degree of *Humility* confifts in know‑
ing

ing how to diſtinguiſh between the pure
Gold of thoſe Graces and Benefits, which
come to us from God, and that Droſs or
Miſery, which we abound with in ourſelves,
and then to give every one his due ; to
God, that which is His ; to ourſelves, that
which is ours; and this chiefly with regard to
Practice ; for *Humility* doth not conſiſt in
knowing *ſpeculatively*, that, of ourſelves,
we are good for nothing, and can effect
nothing ; that all good things come to us
from God, and that it is *He that worketh in
us both to Will and to Do, of his good pleaſure,*
as the Apoſtle ſpeaks, *Phil.* ii. 13. (For
to know this *ſpeculatively* is a very eaſie thing ;
becauſe it is a Dictate of Faith, which all
Chriſtians know and believe ;) but to know
it *Practically*, and be ſo grounded and ſettled in it, as if we ſaw it with our Eyes,
and touch'd it with our Hands. *This* (as
teſtifies St *Ambroſe*) *is a ſingular Grace and
Gift of God.* To prove which he brings that
Paſſage of St. *Paul, We have received not
the Spirit of the World, but the Spirit which
is of God, that we might know the things that
are freely given to us of God,* 1 Cor. ii 12.
For a Man to know, and even feel the
Graces which he hath received from God,
and yet with ſuch Purity and Self-abſtra-
ctedneſs, as to eſteem them wholly anothers, diſclaiming all Propriety in them, and
acknowledging them to have been imparted,
and

and given to be enjoyed by the meer Liberality and Mercy of Almighty God, is a moft particular Favour and Gift of His. The wife *Solomon* calls this, *found Wifdom* *. To inftance in a particular Virtue :—the Gift of *Continence* is a thing, which we are not able to acquire by our own Strength ; nor by any Induftry or Endeavour of our own. Now to underftand this, and know it *practically*, that it is the fole Gift of God, and that we muft have it from his Hand, is a great *Point* of *Wifdom* †, for fo the wife Man, *When I perceiv'd that I could not otherwife obtain to be Continent, except God gave it me (and that was a point of Wifdom to know whofe Gift it was,)* &c. To conclude, *to receive the Spirit which is of God*, to afcribe all we have, and all we are, to him, and diveft ourfelves of *the Spirit of the World*, which St *Paul* fpeaks of, is that *found Wifdom* mentioned by the Wifeman, wherein this *Third* Degree of *Humility* confifts, *What have we, that we have not received ?* †† it was none of ours, for of ourfelves we have no good thing ; and *if we did receive it,* that

---

* Sound Wifdom in the Original is expreffed by a Word that properly fignifies *Subftance, real Effence,* which can mean no lefs than GOD himfelf And the truely Humble Man refolves all into God, confeffes him to be All in All ; GOD to be the Subftance; Himfelf, Nothing   * Prov iii 21, and viii 14.
† Wif viii 21. †† 1 Cor iv. 7.

is, if it be from another, and not from ourfelves, *why do we glory, as if we did not receive it*; — as if it were properly our own?

This was the proper *Humility* of the
Saints; they were enriched with the Gifts,
and Graces of Almighty God; they were
raifed by his Holy Spirit to the very top of
Perfection, and thereby to Honour and
Efteem even in this World; neverthelefs
they appeared *Vile and Bafe in their own
Eyes*, and their Souls remained immovably
fixed in the knowledge of their own Mean-
nefs and Mifery, as if they had poffeffed
no fuch Graces at all. Their Hearts did
not admit the leaft Vanity, or flighteft Impreffion of that Honour and Efteem, which
the World gave them; they knew well,
how to diftinguifh between what was their
own, and what was anothers; and therefore
lookt upon all thofe Gifts, and Graces, that
Honour and Eftimation, as things extrin-
fecal to themfelves; as received from the
Hand of God; and to him they afcribed,
to him they returned all the Glory and
Praife thereof. Though the whole World
exalted them, they would not exalt Themfelves, nor fuffer the leaft breath of that
Popular Air to ftick to their Hearts, but
referred all thofe Praifes to God, to whom
they belonged, and in whofe Glory they
placed all their own Glory and Joy.

With

With much reason then is it affirmed, that this is the *Humility* of Great and Perfect Men. *First*, Because it necessarily presupposes great Virtue, and great Gifts of God; for this only can make us great in His sight. *Secondly*, It is a Mark of great and wonderful Perfection, for a Man to be truly great in the sight of God, and to have made an eminent Progress in Virtue, and for this Reason to be highly Valued and Esteemed, both before God and Man, and yet in the midst of all this, to appear little and base in his own Eyes. This is indeed an uncommon Degree of Virtue. This is what St *Chrysostom* and St *Bernard* do so much admire in the *Apostles*, and others, who being so great Saints, and so richly filled with all Divine Graces, and, by the Power of God, working such extraordinary Wonders and Miracles, so as even to raise the Dead to Life again; and for these things, and the incomparable Sanctity of their Lives, to be so highly esteemed and reverenced by the whole World, yet nevertheless to remain so deeply fixed in the Sense of their own Unworthiness, as if they had nothing in them; as if it had been some other, and not they, who did those great things; and as if all that Honour, Esteem, and Praise belong'd not to them, but to other Persons. " It is not much, " faith St *Bernard*, that a Man in Pover-

" ty should Humble himself; the very
" State he is in, forces him to know, and
" think meanly of himself : but for a Man
" to be generally Honoured and Esteemed
" as an Excellent Man, and a Saint, yet
" remain so well grounded in the Sense
" of his own Vileness, and of his nothing,
" as if no part of those other things, were
" in him, this is indeed a Rare and Excel-
" lent Virtue, this is a Point of most high
" Perfection".

 " Such Men (adds the same Saint) let
" their light shine, according to the Com-
" mand of our Lord, not for the glorify-
" ing of themselves, but of their Father,
" who is in Heaven". These are those
true imitators of St *Paul*, and of the First
Preachers of the Gospel, who preached
not themselves, but the Lord Jesus Christ.
These are those Good and Faithful Servants,
who seek not their own Advantage, nor
ascribe any thing to themselves, but all,
and that most faithfully, to God : to him
they give the Glory of all, and therefore
shall be sure to hear from the Mouth of
their Lord, those joyful Words of his, *Well
done thou good and faithful Servant; thou
hast been faithful over few things, I will make
thee Ruler over many things; enter thou into
the Joy of thy Lord,* Mat. xxv. 23.

C H A P.

CHAP. XXVIII.

The foregoing Argument is further deduced.

WE have said, that the *Third Degree* of *Humility* confifts in this; when a Man hath great Virtues and fingular Gifts of God, and withall, is in great Honour and Reputation with the World, yet grows not Proud thereof, but attributes all to God, as the Fountain Head, and giveth him the Glory of all; containing himfelf all the while within the Verge of his own Unworthinefs and Vilenefs, as if he nothing did, or nothing had. Yet we infer not hence, that we do no work, or that we have no part in thofe good Works we do; for this were an Errour of affected, rather than real, Ignorance

It is certain, our Will is free to co operate with God in all the good Works we do; for Man has a power to confent there to, or not: Therefore operates concurrently with God, when he does well; and it is in his Choice, whether he will act or no And this indeed is it, which makes *this Degree* of *Humility* fo hard to be attained: for

on

on the one hand, we are to use all our Diligence, and employ all the Means we can, to obtain Virtue, and to resist Temptations; and so to labour, that all things may succeed well, as if our own Endeavours alone were able to effect it : On the other hand, when all that is done, we are to distrust ourselves as much, and hold ourselves as unprofitable, as if we had done nothing at all; placing our whole confidence in God, according to that Precept of our Lord's, * *When you shall have done all those things, which are commanded you,* (where note, he saith, *all,* not some *things* only) *say, we are unprofitable Servants* : And to say this aright, you will have need of no small share of Virtue. *Cassian* tells us, " That he who knows, and " can truly say, that he is an unprofitable " Servant, who is convinced, all his own " endeavours and diligence are not able " to accomplish any one thing, but that all " flows from the gracious Gift of Almighty " God; this Man will not grow Proud, " when he succeeds in any thing; as knowing he obtained it, not by his own labour, " but by the Free Grace and Goodness of " God, which alone could give a Blessing " and Success to his Endeavours". This is what our Lord saith, *Without me ye can do nothing.* This is also the same with that

---

* Luke xvii. 10.

of St. *Paul,* * *What haſt thou, which thou didſt not receive?*

St *Auguſtin* brings a very good compariſon to illuſtrate this Truth ; " Without
" the Grace of God (ſaith he) we are no
" more than a Body without a Soul. As
" a Body, which is dead, cannot move or
" ſtir itſelf, ſo we, without the Grace of
" God, cannot perform any Act of the
" ſpiritual Life, or do the leaſt thing
" that ſhall be pleaſing in his ſight. So
" that as that Body were a mad kind
" of thing, which ſhould aſcribe the Acts
" of living and moving to itſelf, and
" and not to the Soul, which dwells
" therein, and gives it Life ; ſo that Soul is
" moſt miſerably blind, which doth attri-
" bute the good Works it doth, to itſelf,
" and not to God, who infuſed into it the
" Spirit of Life, which is His Grace, to
" enable it to perform them". And in
another Place he ſaith, " That as our Cor-
" poreal Eyes, be they never ſo ſharp-
" ſighted, except they be aſſiſted by a pro-
" per Medium of Light, can diſcern no-
" thing ; ſo a Man, how Juſt ſoever he
" may be, cannot continue to live well,
" unleſs he be enabled by the Light of
" God's Grace. If the Lord keep not the
" City, ſaith the Prophet *David,* the watch-
" man waketh but in vain". Oh ! ſaith

* a Cor iv. 7.

the

the fame Saint, " That Men would at
" length know themfelves, and confefs,
" that they have nothing in themfelves,
" whereof to Glory, but only in Almighty
" God !" ——— O that God would fend us
fome Beam of Light from Heaven, whereby we might apprehend, and underftand
our own Darknefs; and that there is no
Good, nor Strength in any Created Being,
but fo far only as our Lord vouchfafes to
beftow it, and is ftill pleafed to continue
it!

Herein then doth this *Third Degree* of *Humility* confift.—But alas, what words of ours
can fufficiently exprefs the Profundity and
great Perfection which is therein ! Notwithftanding all that we have faid, or can fay,
fometimes after one manner, and fometimes
after another ; not only the Practice thereof is hard, but even the Speculation alfo.
This is that Self-Annihilation, which is fo
often by our fpiritual Writers recommended,
as the moft genuine Act of the fpiritual
Life, and moft confummate Degree of
Humility. This is that perfect Abnegation
of ourfelves, that entire Reliance upon
God, which is fo highly commended in Holy
Scripture. This is that bleffed *Poverty in
Spirit*, that Firft and peculiar Leffon of our
Mafter Chrift, which we are to learn of
Him, which we fhould ever be talking of,
ever hearing, and ever learning. And Oh
that

that we could get this Leſſon by Heart, and ever retain it there! That we might under-ſtand Experimentally, and in very Deed, as a Man who ſees things with his Eyes, and touches and feels them with his Hand, that of ourſelves we neither Have any thing but Miſery, nor can Do any thing but commit Sin; and that all the Good we effect or work, we neither do it, nor have it of our ſelves, but of God; that He alone is the Author and the Finiſher of all; —— *He worketh all our Works in us.* —— That the Honour therefore and the Glory of all, is due to Him alone.

After all that hath been ſaid, if you yet underſtand not fully the Perfection of *this Degree* of *Humility*, do not wonder at it; for this is a very high Point of Divinity, and not eaſily underſtood; yea never to be underſtood, except it be felt. A certain Doctor ſaid very well, " As it hap-
" pens in Arts and Sciences, that any body
" may attain to the Knowledge of ſuch
" things as are common and plain, but
" ſuch as are Curious and Choice, are to
" be attained by thoſe only, who are Men of
" Parts, and Eminent in that Science or
" Art". Juſt ſo it is in the preſent caſe, the ordinary and uſual things belonging to any *Virtue*, are underſtood by all the World, but ſuch as are extraordinary, and choice, and nice, and high, can only be compre-
h_nded

hended by such as are Eminent Practitioners, and fully possessed of that *Virtue.* And this is what *Laurentius Justinianus* saith, " That no Man knoweth well what *Humili-* " *ty* is, but he who hath received the Gift " thereof from God".

Hence it is that the Saints, who were indued with a profound *Humility,* thought, and said such things of themselves, that we, who come so far short of them, cannot fully apprehend their meaning ; their Speeches seem mere Hyperboles and exaggerations, when they say, they were *the greatest of Sinners,* and the like. — But of this I shall have occasion to speak more particularly In the mean time, I have only to observe, that if wecannot say, or think such things as they did, no nor even understand their meaning, it is because we have not yet arrived to so great *Humility* as theirs was, and so we understand not the eminent and more sublime Precepts of this excellent Virtue —*Study then to be humble ;* the more you improve in this Science, and the more you profit therein, the more you will understand, how such things as those, may be Thought of with Sincerity, and spoken with Truth.

CHAP.

CHAP. XXIX.

The Third *Degree of* Humility] *is further explained, and whence it comes, that the truely* Humble *Man thinks himself* the least of all.

THAT we may yet better underſtand this *Third Degree* of *Humility*, and ground ourſelves well therein, it will be neceſſary for us to go back, and take a nearer review of this Divine Virtue. According to what we ſaid before (*Chap.* 6,) our very Being, and all the natural Operations which we have, are derived from God.——Once we were not, and then had no Power either to Move, to See, to Hear, or Taſte; to Underſtand, or Will. But God who gave us our Being, gave us alſo theſe Faculties and Powers; ſo that to Him are we to aſcribe, not our Being only, but theſe Natural Powers, and to Him alone In the ſame manner, but with much greater reaſon, muſt we ſay of our Supernatural Being, and the Works of Grace, which are ſo much Nobler, and more Excellent than thoſe; we have them not of ourſelves, but

of

of God. Yea, our spiritual Being is so entirely the Gift of his Grace and Favour, that it
takes its very Name from thence, because,
of his *Free Grace* and meer Goodness He
added it to our Natural Being. *For by
Nature we were the Children of Wrath, even
as others; but God, who is rich in Mercy,
for his great Love, wherewith he loved us,
even when we were dead in sins, hath quick-
ned us together with Christ; for by Grace are
ye saved through Faith, and that not of ourselves, it is the Gift of God*. He it was that
brought us out of Darkness into his marvellous
Light †. Of Enemies, made us Friends;
of Slaves, Sons; of Aliens and Strangers,
having no hope, and without God in the World,
hath he made us accepted in the Beloved ‖.

And the Cause of this unspeakable Favour was not any respect either to our Merits past, or Services to come; but only
his own Free Bounty and Mercy, through
the Merits of Jesus Christ our only Lord
and Saviour; So St *Paul* saith; *Being justi-
fi'd freely by His Grace, through the Redemp-
tion that is in Jesus Christ* ‖ ‖. Now then,
as we were not able to emerge out of
that Nothing, wherein we first were, into
this Natural Being, which we now have;
nor were able to perform any one Act of

---

* Ephes. ii 3 &c.   † 1 Pet ii 9
‖ Ephes. i 6.   ‖‖ Rom. iii. 24.

L

the

the Sensitive Life, to See or Hear, or Feel ; but all was the gracious Gift of God ; to whom therefore we must a-scribe it all, without taking any part of the Glory to ourselves ; so neither could we ever have come out of that Darkness of Sin, wherein we were, and in which we were conceived and Born, had not God, of his infinite Goodness and Mercy, drawn us out from thence ; nor could we now perform the least Work of the Spiritual Life, did He not give us his Grace to that End For as it is not the bare Metal or intrinsick worth of our Money, which gives it a le gal Value and Currency, but the Royal Stamp and Inscription, which it bears, so the *Virtue* and Worth of our Good Works grows not from that part thereof, which they have from us, but from what they re-ceive from the *Grace* of our Lord ; and therefore we must not ascribe any Glory at all to ourselves, but all to God, from whom both our Natural and Supernatural Powers are derived ; carrying ever that of St *Paul*, both in our Mouths, and in our Hearts, *By the Grace of God I am what I am* *.

To this we may add, that as God not only drew us out of our Primitive No thing, and gave us that Being, we now

* 1 Cor xv 10

have

have ; but continues ſtill to ſuſtain, uphold, and conſerve us with the Hand of
his Power, that we may not fall back into
that former Abyſs of Nothing, from whence
He took us before: In the ſame manner it
is that we ſtand indebted to him for our
Supernatural Being; his Favour not only
brought us out of the Darkneſs of Sin,
wherein we were, into the marvellous
Light of his Grace; but he is ever ſupporting and holding us up with his Hand,
that we may not relapſe into it again : Yea,
were not his preventing Grace inceſſantly
vigilant over us, ſhould he but for one
moment take off his Guardian Hand, and
give the Devil free Liberty to Tempt us,
we ſhould not only return to our former
Sins, but fall into far greater.. This it
was, made *David* ſay, *I have ſet God al-*
ways before me, for he is on my right-hand,
*therefore I ſhall not fall**. And again, *The*
Lord upholdeth all ſuch as fall, and lifteth up all
thoſe that are down†. As if he ſhould ſay ;
" It is thy work, O Lord, to raiſe me
" from Sin; thine to keep me from re-
" turning to Sin again. If I roſe up, it
" was becauſe thou gaveſt me thine Hand;
" and if I now ſtand, it is becauſe thou
" keepeſt me from falling".

* Pſ l xi   † Pſal cxlv.

L 2   But

But if, as we said before, it be sufficient-ly Humbling to reflect, that of ourselves we are nothing, we were nothing, and should be nothing, did not God perpetually preserve us in Being; so much more mortifying is it, and should make us abhor ourselves, as worse than Nothing, that we are miserable Sinners : that of ourselves we ever were, and ever shall be Sinners, if God uphold us not with his holy Hand.

To confirm this, *Albertus Magnus* saith, that " Whosoever is a Lover of *Humility* must plant the Root thereof in his " Heart, that is, must so know his own " Weakness and Misery, as to understand " not only how vile and wretched he is " now, but how vile and wretched he " might have been ; yea, and would be " even now, if God with his Powerful " Hand, did not restrain him from Sin, " did he not remove the Occasions, and " assist and strengthen him in Temptati " ons". Into how many Sins had I fallen, O Lord, if thou through thy Infinite Mercy hadst not held me up ! How many occasions of Sinning hast thou prevented, which were sufficient to have cast me down, if thou, knowing my Weakness, hadst not hindred them ! How many times hast thou tied up the Devils Hands, to the end he might not tempt me at his
Will

Will! or if he tempted, that yet he might not overcome! How often, and how truly might I have said those words of the Psalmist; *If the Lord had not helped me, it had not failed, but my Soul had been put to silence; But when I said, my foot hath slipped, thy mercy, O Lord, held me up* *. How often might I say, —— *Thou hast thrust sore at me, that I might fall, but the Lord was my help* †. Thy powerful and gracious Hand came instantly to my Succour; *When I said, my foot hath slipped, thy mercy, O Lord, held me up* ‖. How often should we have been lost, eternally lost, if God of his infinite Mercy and Goodness had not preserved us? This Consideration therefore we should ever have in our Minds, what we are in our own Nature, what we were, and what we shall be again, if God withdraw his Hand and Custody from us.

Hence it was that the Saints Despised, and Humbled themselves so far, that they seemed not content to Esteem little of themselves, and to hold that they were wicked, and sinful Men ; but they professed themselves the meanest of all others ; yea, the most unworthy, and most sinful Men in the World. Thus St *Paul* affirms touching himself; *Christ Jesus came into the World*

---

* Psal xcv. † Psal cxvi, 13 ‖ Psal xciv. 18.

L 3

to save Sinners, of whom I am Chief*. And in order to obtain this *Humility*, he advises, that *in Lowliness of Mind each should esteem others better than themselves* †. And again, *Be kindly affectioned one to another, with Brotherly Love, in Honour preferring one another* ||. And the Apostle, as St *Augustin* observes, " deceives us not, when " he bids us hold ourselves for the least of " all, and would have us Esteem all " others as our Superiours, and Betters"; neither yet doth he command us hereby to use any Words of Flattery, or Compliment towards them. It was not with counterfeit *Humility*, or telling a Lie, that the Saints professed themselves the greatest of Sinners; but with Sincerity and Truth, because they thought so in their Hearts, and because they really thought so of themselves, they gave us also in Charge that we think, and say the same thing; not only *that every Man amongst us should think soberly, and not more highly of himself than he ought to think* |||| ; but to yield the Preference to all others, without Compliment or Fiction.

To this purpose St *Bernard* ponders very well that saying of our Blessed Saviour, *When thou art bidden to a Wedding, go*

---

* 1 Tim 1 15   † Phil 11. 3 || Rom. xii

10. |||| Rom xii 3

and fit down in the loweft room *. " He
" faid not, choofe a *middle* Place, or fit
" *amongft the loweft,* or in the laft place
" *but one* ; but will have you fit in the very
" *loweft* Place of all ; to be fo far from
" preferring yourfelves to others, as not fo
" much as prefume to compare or equal
" yourfelves with any ; but rather Efteem
" yourfelves to be the moft miferable
" Sinners in the whole World. It ex-
" pofeth you, *faith he,* to no danger
" fhould you Humble yourfelves too
" much, and take the very loweft room ;
" but to prefer yourfelves before others,
" cannot but do you a great deal of mif-
" chief. He then brings this comparifon.—
" When you go in at a low Gate, the
" ftooping too much with your Head can
" do you no hurt ; but if you ftoop
" never fo little lefs than the Gate re-
" quires, you may bruife your Head.
" So it is alfo with the Soul : To Hum-
" ble yourfelf too much, cannot be hurt-
" ful, but to fall fhort of *Humility,* though
" it be but a little, and to prefer or equal
" your felf to any one, is a dangerous
" thing. What knoweft thou, O Man,
" whether that One, whom thou takeft to
" be worfe than thyfelf (for fo perhaps it
" may feem to thee now, that thou haft

*Luke xiv 10

L 4

" begun

" begun to lead a good Life) yea, to
" be a wicked Man, and a great Sinner ;
" may not prove the better Man of the
" two ; that perhaps he is so already in
" the sight of God?" Who knows if
God will not change Hands, as *Jacob* did*
in the Case of *Joseph*'s Sons : that the Blessing also will be changed ; and *that* of the
Right hand fall to the other ; *that* of the
Left hand prove to be thine ? How knowest thou what God hath wrought in that
Heart since yesterday ; yea, within this
last Minute? *It is an easy thing in the sight
of the Lord on the sudden to make a poor Man
rich.* † In an Instant is God able to make
Apostles of Publicans and Persecutors, as
He did of St *Mathew* and St *Paul.* — Of
Sinners more stony, and hard than Ada-
mant, can God *raise up Children to Abraham.* How did that Pharisee deceive himself, who pass'd his Censure on *Mary Mag
dalen*, and judg'd her to be a wicked Wo
man ! For this our Lord reproved him,
and gave him to understand that she, whom
he held for a notorious Sinner, *was better
than he.* Hence *Aquinas* sets this down for
one of the Twelve Degrees of *Humility*,
*that a Man confess and think himself the
worst of Men.* Nor is it enough to say so
with the Tongue, but it must be felt with

---

* Gen. xlviii 14.   † Ecclus xi. 21.

t   the

the very Heart. Our Progrefs in *Humility* bears ever a Proportion to the Senfe we have of our Sins. "Think not, fays *Kem-*
" *pis*, you have profited at all, except in
" all Things you efteem yourfelf the mean-
" eft of all Men, and the chief of Sin-
" ners.

CHAP. XXX.

How Good and Holy Men, may with Truth Efteem themfelves lefs *than others,* yea, *and affirm themfelves to be the* Chief *of* Sinners

IT is not a matter of Curiofity or meer Speculation, but of great Ufe and Benefit to fhew how *Good* and *Holy* Men may with Truth Efteem themfelves *lefs than all*, and even affirm that they are the greateft of Sinners; for we have faid that this is a Point we muft labour to attain to. Some of the Saints have refufed to anfwer the Queftion, how this may be; and content themfelves with believing fo of themfelves, and having a Senfe of it in their Hearts. St *Dorotheus* relates, "That Holy *Zofimus*, as he was one Day fpeaking of *Humility*, and
" faying

" faying fo of himfelf ; a certain Philofopher,
" who was prefent, asked him, How he
" could call himfelf fo great a Sinner,
" when he knew he kept the Commands
" of God?" The Holy Man made only
this reply, " What I have faid is true, and
" what I fpeak, I think ; therefore ask
" me no more Queftions". Others give a
Solution to this Queftion ; but divers ways.
That of St. *Auftin* and *Aquinas* is, that a Man
who fixes his Eyes upon his own Defects;
and knows not the fecret Gifts, which his
Neighbour hath, or fhall perhaps receive
of God, may with Truth affirm of himfelf,
that he is one of the vileft, and greateft of
Sinners ; for fo he muft appear in his own
Sight, feeing he knows his own Defects,
but knows not thofe of any other. Befides,
he gives not himfelf leave to judge his
Brother . His Charity fees another Man's
Graces and Gifts; His Modefty fees not
his own. — O ! but fay you, I fee that he
commits many Sins, which I commit not.
But in the firft Place, how know you, as
we faid before, what God hath wrought in his
Heart fince that time ? In a moment, may
God have fecretly imparted his Gace, and
made him by far the more excellent Man.
This was the very Cafe of the *Pharifee*,
and the *Publican* in the Gofpel, who went
up to the Temple to pray. *I tell you* (faith
Chrift in the Conclufion of his Parable)

this

his Man (whom the Pharisee despised) went down to his House justified rather than the other.

This, I say, this alone might serve to check all vain Thoughts, and teach us not to presume of our own Merits. But indeed the truly *Humble* Man, as he considers in other Men, the Goodness and Virtue which they have, and in himself, looks only at his own Defects; he is so intent on the knowledge and redress of these, that he hath no leisure to observe the Faults of Others, no time to spare from attending to his own. Hence it is that he despises no one, but Himself; that he holds other Men for *Good*, in comparison of himself, and himself as the *chief of Sinners.* — But the principal Reason is this, by how much the more Holy any Man is, so much the more tender will his Conscience be; the clearer and more poignant his Sense of Sin. For divine Illumination encreasing, in the same Proportion as our Virtues encrease, he discovers more and more the Deformity and Guilt of Sin; and consequently more and still greater Cause of *Humility*; —— for all these things go together.

Besides this, the greater Light he receives from Heaven to know Himself, and see his Errors; —— the more knowledge will he have of the Goodness and Mercy of Almighty God; And the more He contemplates the Holiness and Perfections of God, the more profound Understanding will he come to have of his own Misery, of his own nothing ; thus *Abyſſus abyſſum invocat* *. *One Deep calleth another*, the Deep Senſe and knowledge of the Goodneſs and Majeſty of God, calls up and diſcovers that other profound Deep of our Miſery, and makes us able to diſcern the infinite little Moats of our Imperfections, with a thouſand Blemiſhes we never obſerved before. Wherefore if we ſet any Value on Ourſelves, it muſt certainly be, becauſe we have but ſmall knowledge of God, and but little acquaintance with ourſelves. 'Tis a Sign the Beams of the Sun of Righteouſneſs have not yet entred in at our Window ; ſo that we not only ſee not the Moats, which are our leſſer Defects and Imperfections, but are ſo ſhort-ſighted, or rather indeed ſo blind, that we ſcarce diſcern our greater Sins.

To this may be added, that God ſo loves *Humility* in us, and is ſo pleaſed to behold us lowly in our own Eyes ; that for this very End, he is wont many times in the Caſe of his moſt eminent Servants, to whom he imparts many high Graces and Favours, to diſguiſe his Gifts, and to com-

---

* Pſal. xlii. 9

municate

municate them in fo fecret and wonderful
a manner, that even the Man himfelf who
receives them, doth not always comprehend them, nor perceive that he is indued
with them; as St *Hierome* obferves; *All
the Beauty of the Tabernacle was covered with
the Skins of Beafts*; fo is God wont to conceal and cover over the Beauty of Men's
Virtues, and of his own Graces, with variety of Temptations, yea fometimes of
Errours and Imperfections, that they may
be the more fafely conferved. So alfo
burning Coals are kept alive under the
Afhes of their own making; they are hidden from the Eye, but retain their Heat
the longer.

Job was an *upright* and *perfect* Man; this
God himfelf teftified of him · And fo he
was, as to every Human Virtue, and every Divine Grace except one, and that was
Humility towards God. To teach him this,
was the End and Defign of Providence,
in all his Sufferings. —— But thefe failing
of their full and intended Effect, God was
pleafed, firft by the Reproof of *Elihu*, a
mere Youth, and then by himfelf out of
the Whirlwind, to teach him what he yet
wanted, the important Leffon of *Humility.*
God fhewed him *to Himfelf*, that fo the very
beft of Men may be convinced of their
real Imperfections and innate Mifery.
God fhewed Himfelf *to Him*, that he
might

might not prefume of the Virtues he had.
And when, by the fplendour of the Divine
Majefty he was brought to a Sight of
thofe Two Effential Points of *Humility*, he
crys out with the utmoft Vehemence, ——
*Lord! I abhor myfelf and Repent in Duft
and Afhes**. Thus *we have heard of the
Patience of Job,* and *thus have we feen the
End of the Lord*†. He exercifed his Patience, that he might at once *hide Pride
from him,* and teach him *Humility.*

Hence St *John Climacus* afferts, That as
the Devil lays our Virtues and good Works
before our Eyes, that we may grow Proud,
and be undone ; God on the contrary, defiring
our greater good, gives a particular Light
to His Servants, to fee their Imperfections,
but not to fee all the Graces which he gives
them. And this is the common Doctrine of
the Fathers. St *Bernard* faith, "To conferve
" *Humility* in his Servants, the Divine Good-
" nefs difpofes things in fuch fort, that the
" more a Man advances in Piety, the lefs he
" conceives himfelf to Profit , —— and even
" when he is arrived to the higheft De-
" gree of Virtue, Almighty God per-
" mits in him fome Remains of Imperfecti-
" on, even as to the very firft Degree ; to
" the end he may feem to himfelf, not to
" have fully attained fo much as to that".

* Jam v. 11. † Job xxxiii. 17.

After

After the fame manner doth St *Gregory* fpeak in many Places; and St *Paul* himfelf had the Meffenger of *Satan* fent to buffet him; that he might not be puffed up above Meafure.

To this purpofe fome make the following Comparifon, that as when the Sun appears the Stars are hid; fo when *Humility* is in the Soul, other Virtues are not feen. —An Humble Man conceives he hath no Virtue at all. St *Gregory* faith, *The Virtues of fuch are manifeft to all Men, only himfelf fees them not* *Mofes* when he came from fpeaking with God, had a great brightnefs on his Face; the Children of *Ifrael* faw it; but for his part, he faw it not. So the humble Man fees not his own Virtues; all he fees are his Faults and Imperfections; his Sins, as *David* fpeaks, *are ever before him* *. Yea, he believes, that the leaft part of his Failings and Miferies, is that which he knows, and that he is ignorant of much the greater. After all this, what wonder is it he fhould count himfelf of all Sinners to be the Chief?

Moft certain it is, that as there are many ways, whereby God is wont to Conduct his Elect, fo he leads many by this way; namely, of concealing his Gifts from them, that fo themfelves may not conceive that

---

* Pfal 1.

they

they have them; yet he manifefts them to others, that they may efteem his Servants, and hold fuch in Reputation. —— Yea, he fhews thefe his Gifts to themfelves, when they have Strength of Mind fufficient to bear them, or when it is for his own greater Glory. As St *Paul* might therefore fafely fay, — *We have received not the Spirit of the World, but the Spirit which is of God, that we might know the things that are freely given to us of God*; So the holy Virgin *Mary* did very well both know, and acknowledge the great Graces and Gifts, which fhe had received from Almighty God; as fhe faith in her Canticle, *My Soul doth magnifie the Lord, becaufe he that is mighty hath magnified me.* And this, as we obferv'd before, is not only not contrary to *Humility* and Perfection, but is accompanied with an *Humility* fo very much elevated, and high, that for this Reafon, the Saints are wont to ftyle it, *the* Humility *of great and perfect Men.*

There is an Error of no fmall danger, whereof we are advertifed by the Saints, and it is this, when fome think they have more Grace than indeed they have. In this unhappy miftake was that Perfon, to whom God in the *Apocalypfe* * commanded it to be faid, *Thou fareft that I am rich, and increaf-*

---

* Chap iii. 17.

ed

ed with Goods, and have need of nothing, but knowest not that thou art wretched and miserable, and poor, and blind, and naked In the fame Errour, was that Pharifee who gave God thanks, that he was not like other Men, fondly believing that he had what indeed he had not; and therefore *trufted in himfelf that he was righteous and defpifed others* And this kind of Pride fteals in upon us fometimes fo fecretly, and with fuch Difguife, that infenfibly, and before we are aware, we grow full of ourfelves, and fwell with Self-Efteem. The beft Remedy for this is, ever to keep our Eyes open to the Virtues of others, and fhut to our own; this will keep us in a conftant holy kind of Fear, whereby we ourfelves fhall be more fafe, and the Gifts of God be better preferved.

But forafmuch as our Lord is not tied to this or that Method, He conducts his Servant, by feveral ways. Sometimes concealing his Graces, fometimes as St *Paul* faith, *Shewing to his Servants the things which they freely have received from God.* And herein lies the great difficulty of refolving that Queftion, which I propofed, namely, " How holy and fpiritual Men, " who fee and well know the fublime " and extraordinary Gifts, which they have " received from God, can yet with truth " efteem themfelves to be the very *meaneft*

" *of*

" *of Men,* and the *greateſt of all Sinners ?*"
I confeſs, when our Lord conducts a Man
by that other way of concealing his Gifts
from him, ſo that he ſees nothing of Virtue ; yea, nothing but Faults and Imperfections in himſelf, the Caſe has no ſuch
difficulty in it.   But where God is pleaſed
to manifeſt to a Man's own Mind the
Graces he beſtows, it may well admit of
a Diſpute how it can poſſibly be.   Nevertheleſs that the thing is not impoſſible,
your own Experience will convince you,
if ſo be you imitate the *Humility* of a certain Holy Man, who being often queſtion'd
by his Friend, how he could reconcile it
with Truth, to ſay he thought himſelf
one of the *greateſt Sinners,* made this reply,
" It is my firm Belief, that if God had
" imparted to the moſt wicked Man alive
" the Mercies and Favours he has indul
" ged to me, he would have prov'd a
" better Chriſtian, and more grateful to
" his Benefactor than I have been ——
" Beſide this, I do verily Believe, and
" am perſwaded that if God ſhould with-
" draw his Hand from me, and let go his
" hold, I ſhould immediately fall into
" more enormous Crimes than other Men,
" and of courſe be more wicked than
" they. —— And this, ſaid he, is my Rea-
" ſon why I call and think myſelf the
greateſt

" greateft Sinner of all Sinners, and moft
" ungrateful of all Men.

This was indeed an Anfwer truely excellent, containing an Inftruction no lefs
admirable, than the *Humility* was profound. —— This is the Knowledge, and
this the Confideration, which has conftrained Holy Men to deprefs themfelves to the
loweft Degree of Abjection, to *lay their
Body as the ground, and as the Street to them
that went over* *. In a word, to count
themfelves the greateft of all Sinners ——
They had in them that Root of true *Humility*; to wit, a deep Senfe and Confcioufnefs of their own Weaknefs and Mifery. —— They perfectly underftood, what
they had, and what they were in themfelves. —— Convinced of this, they well
knew, nothing but the Reftraining Hand
of God kept them from falling into Sins
of the deepeft Die. And as for the Gifts
and Graces they had received from God,
They look'd not on them as their own, but
as the Goods and Property of another,——
as a Talent entrufted to their Care, and only
Lent —— Yea, fo far was this Confideration from leffening the Senfe of their own
Vilenefs and Self-Dejection, that it proved
no fmall inducement to humble themfelves
ftill the more, for the much flighter Im-

* Pf. li. 23

provements

provements they made in Virtues, than might well be expected from such Advantages as these. —— Thus which way foever we turn our Eyes, whether inward, upon what we have of ourfelves, or whether upward, upon what we have received of God ; we fhall find occafion more than enough to be humbled, and to efteem ourfelves the vileft of Men, and *lefs than the least of his Mercies.*

Upon this Occafion St *Gregory* ponders thofe Words of *David* to *Saul,* after he might have killed him in the Cave, — *After whom is the King of* Ifrael *come out? after whom doft thou purfue, after a dead dog, after a flea ? David* " was already " Anointed King, and underftood from " the Prophet *Samuel,* who Anointed him, " that God would take the Kingdom from " *Saul,* and give it him ; neverthelefs " he humbled and leffened himfelf be " fore him, though he knew that God " had preferred him, and that in the fight " of God he was a better Man than *Saul* " By this are we taught to Efteem our " felves lefs than others ; efpecially when " we know not in what Degree of Favour " they ftand with Almighty God.

CHAP.

CHAP. XXXI.

That this Third Degree *of Humility is the most effectuall means to overcome all kinds of Temptations, and to acquire Perfection in every Virtue.*

*C*Assian tells us, it was the general Opinion of the Ancient Fathers, and held as a firſt Principle in the ſpiritual Life, That no Man will ever attain to Purity of Heart and the Perfection of Virtue, except he firſt underſtand and know, that all his own Endeavours, all his Induſtry, and Pains will be wholly inſufficient for that purpoſe ; except he unfeignedly acknowledge, that it cannot poſſibly be obtained, without the eſpecial Grace and Aſſiſtance of God, who is the prime Author and Giver of every good and perfect Gift He ſaith moreover, That this knowledge muſt not be barely ſpeculative, becauſe we have Heard it or Read it, or becauſe it is a Doctrine of Faith, but we muſt know it practically, and by experience, and be ſo convinced, ſo reſolved and ſettled in this Truth,

Truth, as if we saw it with our Eyes, and touched it with our Hands.

And in Truth herein confists principally that *Third Degree* of *Humility*, whereof we now treat. Which kind also it is, that the holy Scripture fpeaks of, when it Promifes fo great, and fo many Bleffings, to fuch as are *Humble*. With good Reafon therefore the Saints affign it for the laft and moft *perfect* Degree of *Humility*, calling it the Foundation of every Virtue, and the Preparation or Difpofition for receiving all kind of Graces and Gifts from God. And as we have before, out of *Caffian*, applied this Rule to the particular Virtue of *Chaftity*, we fhall here add an Example to confirm the fame. *Palladius* relates, That Abbot *Moyfes* having been a Man of great corporal Strength, and withal of a moft vicious Mind, was afterwards converted, and became a great Penitent. At the firft, he was grievoufly tempted, efpecially to Impurity By Advice of his fpiritual Director, he imployed his utmoft endeavours to Conquer it Six Years he paffed in Prayer, fpent the greateft Part of many whole Nights in Devotion, remaining ftill upon his Feet , ufed much and hard Labours, eat nothing but dry Bread, and that in fmall quantity , went carrying Water to the old Monks in their Cells, and ufed many other great Mortifications, and

and Aufterities. Yet all was vain : he was not freed from his Temptations ; but rather feem'd the more enflamed ; was often in danger to fall away, and to forfake his Purity. Being in this trouble, the Holy Abbot *Ifidore* came to him, and told him on the part of God, " That from that time " forward his Temptation fhould ceafe " Accordingly it did, and never affaulted him more. " 'Till then, as the Holy Man, ob- " obferv'd to him, God had not thought fit " to give him a Compleat Victory, left " he fhould have grown Vain and Proud ; " as prefuming he had Conquered by his " own Strength, that therefore God had " fo long permitted it for his greater good." *Moyfes* had not it feems yet learned to diftruft himfelf: that he might learn this, and not grow Proud by confiding in himfelf, God left him for fo many Years to contend alone, and by his own Strength, with that unruly Paffion, not granting to all his Labours and Exercifes, the Compleat Victory over a Temptation, which many others by lefs Diligence had obtained.

The fame Author relates the like Cafe to have happened to one *Pachovius*, who even at the Age of Seventy was very much molefted by Temptations to Impurity. He adds, that the other affirmed it to him with an Oath, that after he was fifty Years Old, the Combat had been fo continual, and withal

fo

so very Fierce, that there had not passed either one Day or Night in all that time, wherein he had not been assaulted by that Sin. He did very extraordinary things to free himself from the Temptation : but they did not answer the End. And lamenting one Day, and even half fearing, that our Lord had forsaken him, he heard a Voice which interiourly said thus to him *Know that the Cause why God hath permitted these sharp Assaults to be made against thee, is to make thee know and feel thy own Poverty and Misery, and the little, or rather the nothing, which thou hast of thyself, see therefore that thou humble thyself hereafter, and confide not in thyself at all ; but in all things have recourse for help to me.* He said, he was so comforted and strengthned by this Intimation from Heaven, that he never felt that Temptation again. In fine it is the will of our Lord, that we place all our confidence in him; that we ever distrust our own Strength; not relying at all on our own Skill, or any human Means.

Neither is this the Doctrine only of St *Augustin, Cassian,* and those ancient Fathers, " to ascribe all our Virtues to the Bounty " and Free Grace of God," but of the Author of the Book of Wisdom *, where the Wiseman speaking of *Wisdom,* and the

* Ch viii 21

way

Way to obtain her, exprefly fets down both the Theory and Practice of this point in thefe Words; *When I perceived that I could not otherwise obtain her, except God gave her to me (and that was a Point of Wifdom alfo to know whofe Gift fhe was) I prayed unto the Lord, and befought him,* &c. Solomon, or whoever the Author was, knowing that our Appetites and Paffions are not to be contained within thofe Bounds of Moderation, in which true Wifdom con-fifts; and that fuch Wifdom is only to be obtained by the efpecial Gift of God, he had Recourfe to God, and begged this Gift of him with his whole Heart. So that the only Means, whereby a Man may become virtuous, and be able to continue fo; to reftrain and govern his Paffions, con-quer all Temptations, and attain to the Perfection of every Virtue, is to feek to God for his Grace; to hold all that is good in us as of his fole Gift; and nothing properly our own, but what is refufe and bad. This the Pfalmift underftood well when he faid, *Except the Lord build the Houfe, their Labour is but loft that build it. Except the Lord keep the City, the Watch-man waketh but in vain.* * It is He muft give us all good Things; it is He muft

* Pfal cxxvi. 1, 2

M preferve

preferve them to us ; elfe all our Labour will be loft, and in vain.

C H A P. XXXII.

That Humility *is not contrary to* Magnanimity, *but rather the Foundation and Caufe thereof.*

AQUINAS, treating of the Virtue of *Magnanimity*, propounds this Queftion, *Forafmuch as both Saints and Scriptures are agreed, that on one Hand* Humility, *on the other, that* Magnanimity *is very neceffary, efpecially for thofe who are advanced to Stations of Dignity and Honour* ; *how can thefe two Virtues (feeming fo contrary the one to the other) fubfift together, and meet in one and the fame Subject* ? Magnanimity is a greatnefs of Mind prompting to enterprife Great and Arduous Things, which in themfelves have a View and Tendency to Honour ; whereas Humility declines both the one and the other. To attempt great Things, feem not to fuit the Nature of this Virtue, becaufe one of the Degrees of Humility is *To confefs our unworthinefs, and hold our felve*

selves unprofitable Servants ; and for a Man
to attempt that which he is not fit for,
seems to be Presumption and Pride ; whereas the truly humble Man must be far from
even desiring Honour and Esteem.

To this Question *Aquinas* answers very
well, *That although in Appearance, and by
the exterior Sound of the Words, these two
Virtues may seem opposite to each other, yet
in Effect and Truth, no one Virtue can be
contrary to another* ; that as to these two, of
Humility *and* Magnanimity, *if we will but
attentively cast our Eyes upon the Truth and
Nature of the Thing, we shall find them so
far from being contrary, that they have a
most strict Affinity, and mutually depend upon
each other.* This he illustrates well in the
following manner : *As to the first,* saith he,
*which is to undertake and attempt great
Things (and is proper to the* Magnanimous
Person*) this is not only not contrary to the
Humble* Man, *but rather very consistent with
his Character* ; *he alone being capable of
going about such Things in the Manner he
ought, and performing them with Honour.
Whereas, if relying on our own Ability only,
and our own Strength, we undertake great
Things, it savours plainly of Presumption and
Pride* ; *for what great, yea what small
Thing is our own simple Strength equal to,
seeing the Apostle witnesseth,* we are not sufficient *so much as to think any Thing as

of ourfelves, but all our Sufficiency is of God *. The very Foundation then of this Virtue of *Magnanimity* is to be laid in the Diftruft of ourfelves, and of all human Endeavours, and placing our whole Confidence in God ; and what is this but the very Effence and Spirit of *Humility?*

St. *Bernard* upon that Place of the *Canticles* ; *Who is this that cometh up from the Wildernefs leaning upon her Beloved* †, declares how all our Virtue, all our Strength, and all our good Works, are to rely and reft upon our *Beloved* Redeemer. And to prove this, he brings for Example, that of St. *Paul* to the *Corinthians* : *By the Grace of God, I am what I am, and his Grace which was beftowed upon me, was not in vain : but I laboured more abundantly than they all* ‖. The Apoftle had been recounting his Labours, and the Sufferings, Afflictions and Perils he had undergone in the Preaching of the Gofpel, and for the Service of the Church, till at length he came to fay, he had laboured more than all the reft of the Apoftles. St *Bernard*, addreffing himfelf to the Apoftle, "O "holy *Paul*, faith he, take Heed what "you fay. Howbeit, that you may "with Safety fay this, and not lofe the "Reward of your Labour by faying it,

---

* 2 Cor. iii. 5. † Chap. viii. 5. ‖ 1 Cor. xv. 10.

"rely

" rely upon your Beloved : " But, as he goes on, the bleſſed Apoſtle ſhews that he relied upon his Beloved, when he adds immediately, *Yet not I, but the Grace of God which was with me.* And writing to the *Philippians,* * he ſaith, *I can do all Things* ; but then inſtantly he leans upon his Beloved, by ſaying, *through Chriſt which ſtrengtheneth me.* In God we ſhall have. Power to endure all Things ; by His Grace we ſhall be enabled to do them ; on Him alone we ought to reſt.

He alone muſt be the Foundation of our Magnanimity. And this is what the Prophet *Eſay* intimates to us, when he ſaith, † *They that wait upon the Lord ſhall* || *change their Strength.* They ſhall exchange the Strength of Men, which is meer Weakneſs, for the Strength of God, which is Omnipotence ; they ſhall change their Arm of Fleſh and Blood, for the Arm of our Lord : So ſhall they have Strength for all Things, for they ſhall be able to do all Things in God. Well therefore did *Leo* ſay, *Nothing is hard to the Humble, nothing is harſh to the Meek.* The truly Humble, is the truly Magnanimous and Couragious Man ; Bold to enterpriſe, and Hardy to execute the greateſt Things : Nothing

---

* Chap. iv 13. † Chap. xl. 31. || According to the Hebrew.

will

will be too hard to him, becaufe he confides not in himfelf, but in God; and
looking up to Him, contemns all Dangers:
*Through God we fhall do valiantly: for He
it is that fhall tread down our Enemies.* *
In him the Humble Man can do all Things.
And this is what we have all fo much
Need of, namely, an invincible Fortitude
of Mind, a generous Spirit, and great Confidence in God, not a faint Heart, which
damps the Courage, and takes away all
Appetite to our Duty Wherefore in ourfelves, we muft be Humble, as knowing
that of ourfelves we are nothing, that we
can do nothing, and are good for nothing;
but in God, and in His Power and Grace,
we are made not only able, but refolute,
and of undaunted Courage, in the enterprizing of great Things.

St. *Bafil* explains this very well upon
thofe Words of the Prophet, *Here am I,
fend me* †.   God was refolved to fend one
to preach to His People; and forafmuch
as He is pleafed to work Things in us,
with our good Will and Confent, He
asked (and asked it fo, as that *Efay* might
hear him;) *Whom fhall I fend, and who
will go for us?* To this the Prophet anfwers, *Here am I, fend me.* He faid not,
as St. *Bafil* well obferves, Lord, I will go,

---

* Pfalm lx. 12.   † Ifaiah vi. 8.

and

and effect the Bufinefs ; for he was humble, and confcious of his own Weaknefs :
He knew too well the Prefumption it
would be to promife for himfelf, that he
would perform fo great a Work ; but he
faid, *Here am I,* ready and willing to receive what thou fhalt be pleafed to give
in Command : *Send me* ; for upon thy
Warrant I will go. As if he had faid, If
Thou, Lord, fhalt fend me, I may well
go, for going in thy Name, I fhall be
able to perform the Work. Then God
faid to him, *Go.* " See here, faith Saint
" *Bafil,* how the Prophet *Efay* took his
" Degree, as it were, for a Preacher and
" Apoftle of God ; becaufe he was well
" verfed, and could anfwer well in the
" Doctrine of *Humility* : He placed no
" Hopes of Succefs in himfelf, but ac-
" knowledged his own Infufficiency and
" Weaknefs ; he repofed all his Confi-
" dence in God, believing he could do all
" Things through him, and that if God
" fent him, he might fafely go. For this
" Reafon, God gave him the Charge, bid
" him go, and made him his Preacher,
" Embaffador, and Apoftle. " The like
Reliance upon God is our Strength and
our Magnanimity, for the enterprizing
and undertaking great Things. Be not
therefore difcouraged, or difmayed, when
you look upon your own Infufficiency and

Weak-

Weakneſs. *Say not I am a Child* (faith God to the Prophet *Jeremiah* *) *for thou ſhalt go to all that I ſhall ſend thee, and whatſoever I command thee, thou ſhalt ſpeak. Be not afraid of their Faces, for I am with thee.* So that this Part of *Humility* is ſo far from being contrary to Magnanimity, that 'tis rather the Foundation and Root thereof.

The ſecond Point, which belongs to the *Magnanimous* Perſon, is, To deſire to do great Things, and Things that in themſelves may be worthy of Honour. But neither is this contrary to *Humility, becauſe*, as *Aquinas* faith, *although the Magnanimous Perſon deſires to do ſuch Things, yet he deſires it not for human Honour, nor makes* this *his End.* He will take Care indeed to deſerve it, but not *therefore* to deſerve it, that he may gain Eſteem. He hath a Heart, that deſpiſes both Honour and Diſhonour; he holds nothing to be Great, but Virtue; and for the Love of this, he is moved to do great Things, and ſits ſuperiour to all the Honours, which Men can give. For Virtue is a Thing ſo excellent, that it cannot be ſufficiently rewarded by Men, and therefore expects its Honour and Reward from Almighty God. Wherefore the Magnanimous Perſon values not the Honour of the World; it is a Thing

Chap. i. 7, 8.

of

of no Price at all with him; his Ambition takes a higher Flight. He is moved only by the Love of God and Virtue, to do Things that are great, and despises all Considerations besides. Now that a Man may have a Heart so great, so generous, such a Despiser of the Praise and Dispraise of Men, such as the *Magnanimous* Person is wont to have, it is necessary that he have also a great Degree of *Humility.* Without this how can a Man arrive to so great Perfection, as to be able to say with St. *Paul, I know both how to be abased, and I know how to abound · every where, and in all Things, I am instructed both to be full, and to be hungry, both to abound, and to suffer need**. And again, *By Honour, and Dishonour, by evil Report, and good Report, as Deceivers and yet true ; as unknown, and yet well known, as dying, and behold we live?* † How is it possible, without a deep and firm Foundation of *Humility* and *Wisdom* from above, to keep a steady Course against such stiff, and such contrary Winds, as those of Honour and Dishonour, of Praise and Contempt, of Favours and Persecutions, that they shall cause no Change in us, nor make us stumble, or shrink from our Duty? To continue unwearied in well-doing, and abound in all good Works, while you abound in

---

* Phil. iv. 12. † 2 Cor. vi. 8, 9.

M 5   Plenty

Plenty and Eafe, feems to be a Thing neither difficult or ftrange : To fuffer Poverty with Patience, and to be Humble in the midft of Difhonours and Affronts; this alfo perhaps you may be able to do . But to be Humble in Honours, Chairs, Pulpits, and the higher Rank of Miniftries, [*Hic labor, hoc opus eft*] This is a Difficulty, that few are equal to . This is a Temper of Mind, that requires both a Greatnefs of Soul, and a profound *Humility*. Alas! thofe Angels, once of Heaven, knew not how to do this ; they were intoxicated with their High Station, grew proud and fell. *Boetius* juftly obferves, that *Though both Eftates are to be feared, yet Profperity more than Adverfity.* * It is much harder for a Man to keep himfelf humble in Honour and the Efteem of the World, in high Employments and great Places, than in Difhonour and Contempt, and in the Difcharge of fuch Offices as are mean and poor ; for thefe Things draw *Humility* after them, but thofe others, Vanity and Pride. [*Scientia inflat*] Knowledge, and all other high Things, do naturally *puff us up*, and make us giddy: hence therefore the Saints are wont to fay, That it is the *Humility* of great and per-

---

* Cum omnis fortuna timenda fit, magis tamen timenda eft profpera quam adverfa.

fect

fect Men, to know how to be Lowly, and yet Great ; to be *Magnanimous*, and yet *Humble*.

This Degree therefore we must, thro' Grace, endeavour to arrive to; such of us especially as are called to any Eminence in the Church or State, we are called to this very End, that we should not be shut up in Corners, or be hidden under a Bushel, but set up on high, like a City upon a Hill, or like a Candle upon a Candlestick; to shine, and to give Light to the World. And to answer this high Purpose, it will be necessary for us, to lay a very low and sound Foundation. We see then, that *Humility* is not contrary to, but the very Root and Support of *Magnanimity:* The deeper the Root descends, the taller and firmer will that sublime Virtue grow. And as to ourselves, altho' a profound Knowledge of our own Misery, our Baseness, and our Nothing, may make us contented, and even willing, to endure Shame and Reproach, when we deserve it, and even to rejoice in Contempt, when we deserve it not ; yet the *highest* Pitch of Virtue, is, to bear either Extreams with a noble, dispassionate, and holy Indifference : This is true *Magnanimity*, this is a sincere and genuine *Humility*.

C H A P.

CHAP. XXXIII.

Of the great Benefits and Advantages which are contain'd in this Third Degree *of* Humility.

ALL *Things come of thee, and of thine own have we given thee,* said King *David,* * when he had prepared much Gold and Silver, and many rich Materials for the Building of the Temple, and was offering them up to God   This is what we muſt do, and ſay, in all our good Works, *Thine, O Lord, are all our good Works, and of thine own do we return thee.* St. *Auguſtin* therefore had Reaſon to ſay, " He " that goes about to recount the Services " he hath done thee, O Lord, what doth " he tell thee of, but of the Benefits " and Gifts, which he hath received from " thy Hands. † "   This is one gracious Effect of thy infinite Mercy and Goodneſs to us, ſo to qualify thy Benefits and Gifts to us, that they may become our Virtues:

---

* 1 Chron. xxix. 14.   † Conf. L. 9. 13.

When

When therefore thou payeft us for our Services, thou rewardeft thine own Benefits; and for one Grace of thine well ufed, thou giveft us another, even *Grace for Grace* Our Lord is pleafed to deal with us like another *Jofeph*; he gives us not only Corn, but repays back the Price and Money which it coft : He gives both *Grace and Glory.* * All is God's Gift, and all muft be afcribed, all returned to Him.

The firft great Help and Benefit which is to be reaped by this *Third Degree* of *Humility*, is, That it is the moft genuine and trueft Gratitude and Thankfgiving, for the Favours and Mercies we have received at the Hand of God. It is well known how highly the giving of Thanks is recommended in Holy Scripture ; fince we fee that whenever God vouchfafed any remarkable Benefit to His People, He inftantly ordained, that fome Commemorations, or Feafts of Thankfgiving fhould be inftituted in Remembrance of it ; becaufe Gratitude doth fo greatly contribute to our receiving of new Gifts and Graces from our Heavenly Benefactor. Now this is moft effectually performed by this *Third Degree* of *Humility*, which con-

---

* Gratiam & Gloriam dabit Dominus. Pf. lxxxiii 12. Vulg

fifts,

fifts, as hath been often faid, in a Man's attributing nothing to himfelf, but all to God; and giving Him the fole Glory of all. And in this very Thing confifts true Gratitude, and the moft acceptable Thankf-giving; not in faying with the Tongue only, *Lord I thank thee for thy Benefits.* Howbeit we are not to omit praifing God, and giving him Thanks with the Tongue. But if you do it with the Tongue *only,* that will not be *giving,* but *faying* of Thanks; and Words without Deeds is the very Reverfe of Gratitude. That it may not therefore be *mere* Thanks, the Heart muft accompany the Mouth, and both confpire to acknowledge, that all the Good we have is from God; retaining to ourfelves no Part of that Honour, which we fee to be none of our own, but divett-ing ourfelves, and giving the Whole to God, to whom it belongs.

And this is what our Lord intended to fignify to us in the Gofpel, when having cured Ten Lepers, and One only returning to give Him Thanks, He faid, *There are not found that returned to give Glory to God, fave this Stranger.* * And when God ad-monifhed the People of *Ifrael,* that they muft be grateful, and not forget the Bene-fits they had received, He gave them the

* Luke xvii. 18.

Com-

Command, *Beware that thou forget not the Lord thy God, in not keeping his Commandments and his Judgments, &c. left when thou haft eaten and art full, and haft built goodly Houfes, and dwelt therein ; and when thy Herds and thy Flocks multiply, and thy Silver and thy Gold is multiplied, and all that thou haft is multiplied : Then thine Heart be lifted up, and thou forget the Lord thy God (which brought thee forth out of the Land of Ægypt, &c.) and thou fay in thine Heart, My Power, and the Might of my Hand hath gotten me this Wealth* .* For a Man to afcribe the Gift of God to himfelf, is the gicateft Ingratitude, into which he can fall. Take Heed then you have not fuch a Thought as this. *But,* as he goes on, *Thou fhalt remember the Lord thy God ; for He it is that giveth thee Power to get Wealth.* And this not for any Defert of yours, but *that he may eftablifh his Covenant, which he fware unto thy Fathers.* This is the Gratitude, this the Praife, wherewith our Lord God will be honoured, for the Benefits and Favours, which He confers upon us. So *Pfal.* l. 23. *Whofo offereth me Thanks and Praife, he honoureth me.* This is the Sum of St. *Paul's* Doxology : *Now unto the King Eternal, Immortal, Invifible, the only Wife God, be Honour and Glory, for ever*

---

* Deut. viii. 11, &c.

and

*and ever, Amen.** To wit, that God *only* fhould have the Glory of all.

Another Benefit, which a truly Humble Man derives from this *Third Degree* of *Humility*, is this, That although he may have many Gifts of God, and be univer-fally efteemed for the fame, yet doth not he value himfelf the more in the leaft, but remains fo confirm'd in the Knowledge of his own unworthinefs, as if none of thofe Things, which they afcribe to him, were to be found in him. Yea in the very Act of receiving the Gifts of God, he is rather the more humbled and confounded there-by: For he knows very well, how to di-ftinguifh between what is anothers, and what is his own, and to afcribe to each their due. Hence he looks not on the Gifts and Benefits he has received of God, as his own Property, but as the Goods of anothers, and a mere Loan. He has ever an Eye to his Frailty and Wretchednefs; and confiders what he fhould be, did God withdraw his Hand, and not continually uphold and preferve him. Yea the more Favours and Graces he receives from God, the more ftill is he humbled, the greater is his Confufion. " For as it happens " with Trees, faid St. *Dorotheus*, fuch as " are loaden with Fruit, their Boughs bend

---

* 1 Tim. i. 17.

" down fo low, as almoft to break with
" their great Weight ; whereas the Boughs
" which bear no Fruit, remain ftrait, and
" lift up themfelves on high ; and as Ears
" of Corn, when they are very full, hang
" their Heads fo low, as if they would
" bear down the Stalk whereon they grow ;
" but when they ftand bolt upright, it is
" a fhrewd Sign that they have no Grain
" in them ; fo it happeneth, faith he, in
" the Way of the Spirit, they who are
" empty and without Fruit, look Big and
" Lofty, and hold themfelves for Gallant
" Men ; but they on the other Side, who
" bear much Fruit, and are full of the
" Graces and Gifts of God, are the more
" humbled thereby, and more abafed in
" in their own Eyes. " The greater the
Gifts and Benefits the true Servants of
God receive, the greater Occafion they
take to mortify their Pride, and to walk
with the more Warinefs and Fear ; which
St *Gregory* illuftrates by another very per-
tinent Similitude.

" As a Man, faith he, who hath bor-
" rowed a great Sum of Money, is glad
" he hath borrowed it for the prefent Sup-
" ply of his Need ; but this Joy is foon
" damp'd, by reflecting on the Obligation
" he is under to pay it again, and the
" Uncertainty, whether he fhall be able to
" comply, when his Bond is due ; fo the
" Man,

" Man, who is truly humble, the more
" Gifts he receives from the Hand of
" God, the more deeply indebted he ac-
" knowledges himself to be, and the more
" obliged to serve him ; and he is still
" jealous of himself, that his Services are
" not equal to such Graces, nor his Thanks
" to such extraordinary Favours : He con-
" ceives and believes, that to whomsoever
" God would have shewed that Goodness,
" which he had indulged to him, that
" Man would have made better Use of it,
" been more grateful, and a better Man. "
And indeed one of the Considerations,
which makes the true Servants of God to
be very much humbled and confounded at
the receiving of extraordinary Favours, is
this ; They know that God will not only
call them to account for their *Sins commit-*
ted, but also for his *Favours received*; and
they know, that to whom God hath given
much, from him shall *much* be required.
Hence Holy *Macarius* faith, " That the
" humble Man looks upon the Gifts and
" Favours of God, as a Steward or a
" Treasurer ought to do, who hath his
" Master's Effects in his Hands ; such a
" one will rather live in Fear and Care,
" than in Vanity and Pride, left somewhat
" should by his Fault be lost, when he is
" called to give an Account. "

Another

Another Benefit arifing from this *Third Degree* of *Humility*, is this, That the Man, who has attained thereto, *defpifes no other Man*, whatfoever Defects and Sins he may perhaps fee him fall into ; neither will he thereby grow vain of his own Worth, or efteem himfelf one jot the more for that ; but rather take Occafion to humble himfelf the more, by feeing his Brother fall ; confidering that the other, and himfelf, are both made in the fame Mold ; and that when the other falls, he alfo falls together with him ; forafmuch as that other is in himfelf. For, as St. *Auguftin* faith, " There is no Sin which is committed by any one Man, which another " would not, or might not commit, if the " Hand of God's Mercy withheld him " not. " And fo an ancient Hermit, when he heard that any Man had fallen, was wont to weep bitterly, and fay ; " To " Day for him, and to morrow for me : " As he fell, I might as well have fallen, " fince I am a weak Man as he is. I muft " efteem it a moft particular Bleffing of " our Lord, that I fell not too. " And thus do all the Saints advife, " That as " when we fee one Man Blind, another " Deaf, another Lame, another Maimed, " or Sick, we muft efteem all thofe Mife- " ries of theirs to be Benefits of ours, and " give Thanks to God, for not having " made

" made us Blind, or Deaf, or Lame, or " Maimed, as he made any of them; " So also, we muſt make account, that the Sins of other Men, are as ſo many Benefits to us, for that there is none of us but might have fallen into the ſame, if our Lord, of His Infinite Mercy, had not interpoſed to prevent it. It is by this means the Servants of God preſerved themſelves in *Humility.* St. *Gregory* ſaith well; *True Juſtice makes us have Compaſſion of our Neighbours when they fall ; falſe Juſtice maketh us diſdain and ſcorn them.* But ſuch Deſpiſers have Reaſon to be afraid of that Warning of St. *Paul, Gal.* vi. 1. *Conſidering thyſelf, leſt thou alſo be tempted ;* and to pray God, they may not be tempted in that very Thing, which they condemn in others ; and that they may not find to their Coſt, how great that Miſery is, which is generally the Puniſhment of this Sin. *In three Things,* ſaid one of the antient Fathers, *have I judged others, and myſelf fell into them all* And this is permitted by the Divine Will, to the End we may know by Experience , that ourſelves alſo are but Men ; and to learn, neither to *judge,* nor *deſpiſe* others.

C H A P.

CHAP. XXXIV.

Of the great Graces and Favours which God vouchsafes to the Humble, and the Cause why he so exalts them.

ALL *good Things together came to me with her,* * said the Wise Man concerning Divine Wisdom. We may as fitly apply them to *Humility,* and say, That all good Things come to us therewith , seeing it is also said, *Where Humility is, there also is Wisdom.* † The Pious *David* intimates to us the same, in these Words, *The Testimony of the Lord is sure, making wise the Simple* Psal. xix. 7. We are also taught this Truth in divers other Places, both of the Old and New Testament ; where great Blessings and Graces are promised to the *Humble,* by Almighty God ; sometimes by the Name of the *Lowly* ; sometimes, of *Little ones,* and other times, of the *Poor in Spirit* ; for by these, and such other Names, are they, who are truly *Humble,*

* Wisd. vii. 11. † Prov. xi. 2, See Vulg.

called.

called. So God by the Prophet, * *But to this Man will I look, even to him that is Poor, and of a Contrite Spirit, and Trembleth at my Word.* Upon Thefe doth God caft a gracious Eye, to fhew them Favour, and even fill them with Benedictions. So also the Apoftles St. *Peter* †, and St. *James* §, in their canonical Epiftles, *God refifteth the Proud, but giveth Grace unto the Humble.* We are likewife taught the fame by the Bleffed Virgin in her Canticle ; *He hath put down the Mighty from their Seats, and hath exalted them of low Degree ; He hath filled the Hungry with good Things, and the Rich He hath fent empty away* ‖. And this is that, which the Royal Prophet had faid before : *Thou wilt fave the afflicted* [or *Humble*] *People, but wilt bring down the high Looks of the Proud* **. That alfo which Chrift our Lord faid in the Gofpel ††, *Whofoever exalteth himfelf, fhall be abafed, and he that humbleth himfelf, fhall be exalted.* As the Waters flow to the Valleys, fo the Rain of God's Grace defcends upon the Humble : And as Valleys are moft fertile, and wont to abound with Fruit, by Reafon of the Plenty of Water wherewith they abound ; (and to *ftand fo*

---

* Ifaiah lxvi. 2 † 1 Pet. v. 5. § Chap. iv 6
‖ Luke 1 5-, 53. ** Pfalm xviii. 27. †| Luke xiv. 11

thick

thick with Corn *) fo they who are lowly
in their own Eyes, bring forth much Fruit,
through the many Gifts and Graces, which
they receive from God. Yea, St. *Augustin*
affirms, *That* Humility *draws down the moſt
High God to itſelf.* " *God is High,* faith
" he, *above all Nations, and his Glory above*
" *the Heavens* ; yet if you humble yourſelf,
" *He humbleth himſelf* likewiſe, and will
" deſcend to you : If you lift up yourſelf
" and grow proud, he will fly from you. "
And why doth he ſo favour the *Humble,*
ſo abhor the *Proud ?* The Reaſon is plain :
The *Humble* are Loyal Subjects, acknowledging his Sovereignty, and ſubmitting
to his Will ; the *Proud* are Rebels to his
Laws, and deſpiſe his Authority ; therefore, *Though the Lord be High, yet hath he
Reſpect unto the Lowly* ; that is, to preſerve
and watch over them for their Good. *But,*
as it is added, *the Proud he knoweth afar
off* †. As when we ſee a Man *far off,* we
know him not ; or, as when we will *not
know* the Man we do not like, ſo doth
God deal with the Proud; he *knows them
not,* ſo as to ſhew them any Countenance or
Favour. And dreadful is the Puniſhment
contain'd in thoſe Words, *I know you not,*
being the very Term of that great Doom,
by which the Wicked at the laſt Day ſhall

* Pſalm lxv. 14. † Pſalm cxxxvii , 6.

be

be turned into Hell *. *Bonaventure* faith, " When Wax is foft, it readily takes the " Impreffion of the Seal; fo doth *Humi-* " *lity* difpofe the Soul to receive Virtue " and Grace from God. " When *Jofeph* invited his Brethren to eat with him, *the leaft* and *youngeft* of them all had the *largeft* Mefs.

Let us now confider, why God raifes the *Humble* fo high, and is pleafed to do them fo great Favour. It is becaufe all his Goods do thus come back again to him-felf. For the *humble* Man carries nothing away ; he attributes nothing to himfelf; but intirely afcribes and reftores all to God, and gives him the Honour and Glory of all ; *For the Power of the Lord is great, and he is honoured of the Lowly.* Ecclus iii. 20. " Such as thefe (we may fuppofe " God to fay) may very well be trufted " with our Goods We may well put our " Riches and Bleffings into their Hands, " for they are faithful, and will not de- " fraud, or run away with them. " God proceeds with them, as in a Cafe entirely his own ; becaufe all the Honour and Glory is ftill his, and wholly referved for his Ufe. And as a great Lord or King difplays his own Greatnefs, by raifing a Man fometimes out of the very Duft, who

* Luke xiii. 27.

be-

before was nothing: So is the Bounty and Greatness of the King of Heaven and Earth the more visibly shewn, by pouring his Favours on the Humble and Meek. To this Effect spake the Apostle, *We have this Treasure* [of the Graces and Gifts of God] *in Earthen Vessels, that the Excellency of the Power may be of God, and not of us.* * For Clay hath no such Value or Excellence in itself. For this Cause therefore doth God exalt the *Humble*, and shew them so many Favours: And for this doth He *send the Rich* and the Proud *empty away*; because the proud Man confides so much in himself, and in his own Ability and Skill, and ascribes so much to himself, taking a vain self-Complacence in the good Success of his Business, as if all had been atchieved by his own Industry and Pains. This is a kind of sacrilegious Robbery, and steals away from God that Honour and Glory, which is wholly due to His Divine Majesty. No sooner have we made some little Progress in the Exercises of Devotion, or sprinkled our Prayers with a few Tears, but we conceive ourselves to be Holy and Spiritual Men, and great Proficients in Prayer. Another Time we are vain enough to be drawing Comparisons between ourselves and others,

---

* 2 Cor. iv. 7.

pre-

preferring ourſelves before them, as Perſons who have profited leſs, and are leſs
devout than we. For this Reaſon our
Lord is conſtrained, either to withhold his
Favour, or elſe to take that from us, which
he had given; leſt what ſhould have
been for our Wealth, prove unto us an Occaſion of falling, and our Health be turned
into Sickneſs, our Medicine into Poy-
ſon; that is, leſt his Benefits and Gifts
ſhould prove the Means of our Damnation,
thro' our ill Uſe thereof; as in the Caſe
of a ſick Man who hath a weak Stomach,
though the Food be good, yet the Phy-
ſician allows but a ſmall Quantity of it,
becauſe he hath not Strength to digeſt it,
and more would corrupt, and turn to ill
Humours. The miraculous Oyl of the
Prophet *Eliſha* never ceaſed running, till
ſuch Time as Veſſels were wanting to receive it; but then, the Holy Scripture
ſaith, *The Oyl ſtayed*, 2 Kings, iv. 6. Now
ſuch is the Oyl of the Mercy of God;
in itſelf it is not limited; for the Graces
and Mercies of God have on his Part no
Limits or Bounds at all : God hath not
ſhortened or cloſed his Hand, nor is his
Nature changed; for *He is the Lord, and
changeth not,* * nor can he change, but ever
remains the ſame, and is ever more ready

* Mal. iii. 5.

to give, than we to receive, or even ask. The Fault is wholly on our Side, who want Veſſels, to receive the Oyl of the Graces and Mercies of God. We are too full of ourſelves, and put too much Truſt in our own Strength. *Humility,* and the Knowledge of our own Weakneſs, empties the Heart of all carnal Sufficiency, * takes a Man off from himſelf, and makes him diſtruſt all human Helps, and aſcribe nothing to himſelf, but all to God : To ſuch Men as theſe, God diſpenſes his Favours with full Hands. — *Be humble towards God, and expect his Hand.* †

* Dat Dominus ibi benedictionem ſuam ubi vacua invenerit Et quanto perfectius infimis quis renuntiat, & magis ſibi ipſi per contemptum ſui moritur, tanto gratia celerius venit, copioſius intrat, & altius liberum or elevat Kemp. L 4. cap 15.
† Ecclus. xiii. 9 See Vulg

CHAP.

CHAP. XXXV.

How much it imports us to have Recourse to Humility, to supply what is wanting in us of Virtue and Perfection; left God take us in Hand, to humble us, by Correction.

THE mellifluous St. *Bernard* faith, " A very Fool and Madman is " he, who trufts to any thing but *Hu-* " *mility*; for, alas, in many Things we " offend all, and can have no Right to " any Thing from God, but Punifhment." *If Man*, faith *Job*, *will contend with him, he cannot anfwer him one of a Thoufand.* Chap. ix. 3. To a Thoufand Things laid to his Charge, he will not be able to give one good and fufficient Anfwer. What then remains, but only to betake ourfelves to *Humility*; and thereby fupply our Want of other Graces ?

And becaufe this is a Remedy of fuch Importance, the fame Saint repeats and inculcates it many Times, both in thefe, and other like Words ; " Let that which " is wanting, as to Purity of Confcience, " be

" be supplied by a Sense, and humble Con-
" fession of such Want : Let what you
" fall short of in Fervour and Perfection,
" be made up by a hearty Confusion for
" such a Defect. " Another Holy Man
(as St. *Dorotheus* tells us) used often to
recommend the same Thing, with great
Earnestness to his Friends. " Let us
" Humble ourselves a while, *said he*, that
" we may save our Souls, if, thro' Weak-
" ness, we cannot labour so much as others,
" let us at least endeavour to be as *Hum-*
" *ble* · By this Means, I trust, we shall
" hereafter be admitted into the Society
' of those, who have laboured much. "
Supposing, for Instance, you have committed many Sins, and find yourself dis-
abled to go through all the Discipline of
Repentance and Mortification, for Want
of Health and Strength ; walk on quietly
in the plain and low Way of *Humility*, and
there you will find a most effectual Means
to promote your Salvation. Again, If
you find yourself indisposed for *Devotion*,
and less able to attend the Exercise of
Prayer, enter at least into an humble Sense
of your Infirmity ; and that shall be as
prevalent, as the most fervent Supplication.
If you conceive that you have no Talent
for Things of great Importance, have recourse to *Humility* ; and that will make
up for all Deficiencies.

Let

Let us then but confider, how fmall a Matter our Lord asks of us, and with how little he is content. He requires that we fhould know, and acknowledge our own Bafenefs, and humble ourfelves accordingly. Should God ask of us extraordinary Faftings, great and many good Works, great and high Contemplations ; fome Men might excufe themfelves, and fay, that they have no Strength for the one, nor Talent, or Ability for the other. But for the not Humbling ourfelves, we have no Reafon or Excufe to alledge. You cannot fay, you have not Health to be Humble, or that you have no Talent or Ability for That. *There is nothing more eafy* (faith St. *Bernard*) *than for a Man to Humble himfelf, if he have but a Mind to do it.* This we can all do, if we will; and we have Matter enough for it, if we but look into our Hearts. *Thy Cafting down is in the midft of thee*, faid the Prophet *Micah*, Chap. vi. 14. All the Furniture of *Humility* thou haft at Home. Hither let us therefore retire, and fupply by Humility, what is wanting to us of Perfection ; fo fhall we be able to move the Bowels of God to Mercy and Pardon. Are we poor? 'Tis but fit we fhould be Humble too ; and this will be as acceptable to God, as to be rich in good Works : But to be poor and *proud* is as prepofterous in itfelf, itself, as it is offensive to him. Of three Things, which the Wise Man notes, to be much abhorred of Almighty God, this is the First, *A Poor Man that is Proud.* Ecclus xxv. 2. And it is no less odious even amongst Men.

Above all, let us Humble *ourselves,* left *God should Humble us* ; for thus he is very ordinarily wont to do. *He that exalteth him-self shall be abased.* Luke xiv. 11. If then you will not have God to humble you, take Care to humble yourself. This is a Point of great Moment, and most worthy of Consideration; so we learn from the great St. *Gregory.* " It is the usual Procedure of God, saith " he, towards good Men, that although " he endue their Minds for the most Part " with great and eminent Virtues, yet, in " some Respects, he permits them to be " imperfect ; that so, notwithstanding " many shining Excellencies , which ap- " pear to others, their own Eyes being " intent on their Failings, and frequently " lapsing into them, they may not be " exalted above Measure for Things of " greater Moment ; that finding them- " selves unequal to lesser Duties, they " may not presume on the Merit of " their most perfect Actions. —— Would " you know, saith he, how much God " loves Humility, and how greatly he ab- " hors Pride and Presumption ? He ab-

N 4
" hors

" hors it fo much, that he fuffers us firft
" to fall into many little Faults, in order
" to convince us, that feeing we are not
" able to keep ourfelves from *little* Sins
" and Temptations, we are certainly much
" lefs able, of ourfelves, to avoid thofe
" that are *greater.* " By fuch Difcipline
as this he likewife prevents our being
proud, when we fall into great and ftrong
Temptations ; neither ftubbornly refifting
his Will, nor relying on our own Strength,
but walking on with Humility and Fear,
and commending ourfelves wholly to God's
Favour and Grace.

St. *Auguftin*, upon thefe Words, *And
without him was not any Thing made that
was made.* John 1. 3. and St. *Jerom* upon
that of the Prophet *Joel*, *I will reftore to
you the Years that the Locuft hath eaten, the
Canker-Worm, and the Caterpiller, and the
Palmer Worm.* (Chap. ii. 25.) Say, that
it was to humble Man, and to tame his
Pride, God created thefe little Animals,
and vile Infects, which are fo troublefome
to us; that, to chaftize and fubdue the
proud Heart of *Pharaoh* and his People,
he could as eafily have fent Bears, Lions,
and Serpents upon them; but he thought
fit to correct them rather by the bafeft
Sort of Creatures, by Lice, Flies, and
Frogs, that fo the Contemptiblenefs of the
Scourge might humble them the more.

This

This is often the Cafe with us : God permits our Fall into *little* Faults, and fome
leſſer Kinds of Temptations, which are
like Gnats, and feem not to have any Body or Bulk in them, that fo we may be
led to underſtand our own Weakneſs and
Mifery. For if we confider attentively,
what it is that fometimes difquiets us, we
ſhall find they are certain Things of little
Confequence, and mere Trifles, which being well fifted, and looked into, have no
Subſtance in them at all. — " What did
" they mean, by faying fo and fo? Or, they
" faid it in fuch a manner, or in fuch a
" tone, as look'd like a defign'd Affront; "
and the like. But what matters all this,
more than the Buz of a Fly, which paſſes
through the Air ? However, Man is vain
enough to build fuch a Caſtle of imaginary
Trouble in this Air, as ſhall deſtroy all the
Peace and Quiet of his Mind. —— What
would then become of us, ſhould God let
loofe fome Lion, or Tyger againſt us ; if
we are put into fuch Diforder by a Gnat
or Fly ? How ſhall we bear up under a
great and grievous Temptation, when fo
eafily maſter'd by a fmall one ? Howbeit,
This Advantage are we to make of thefe
fmall Trials, that we convert them into
Opportunities of improving our *Humility*,
and confounding our *Pride* ; " For if, as
" St. *Bernard* faith, this Benefit be drawn

N 5   " from

" from thence, it is a great Mercy and
" Favour of God, that such Means as
" these, though seemingly very inconsi-
" derable, should never be wanting to us,
" in order to make, and keep us Hum-
" ble. "

But if these slight Things will not answer that End, then know, that God will
proceed to more severe Methods, as he is
wont to do. For so highly doth he abhor Presumption and Pride, and so greatly love *Humility*, that as the Saints affirm,
through a just and most secret Judgment,
he often suffers a Man to fall into the most
enormous Sin, that he may be reclaimed
from Pride, and duly humbled thereby.
Thus, say they, he sometimes punishes secret Pride with open Lust. To which
Purpose they bring that of St. *Paul*, concerning those Philosophers, whom for their
Pride, *God gave up to uncleanness, through
the Lusts of their own Hearts, to dishonour
their own Bodies between themselves.* Rom. i.
24. *Professing themselves to be wise, they*
not only *became Fools*, but fell into the
most filthy Sins, not fit to be named; God
so permitting it for their Arrogance and
Pride, to the end they might be humbled,
and confounded with Shame, when they
found themselves turned into Beasts, and
given up *to vile Affections*, more brutal than
the very Beasts that perish. *Who would*
not

not fear thee, O King of Nations ? said the Prophet. * Who will not tremble at this judicial falling from one Sin into another ? a Punishment so great, there is none greater on this Side Hell ! for were it not for Sin, there could be no such Thing as Hell. *Who knoweth the Power of thy Anger ? or who is able to relate it,* † through the great Fear, which ought to be had thereof ?

The Fathers observe, that God is wont to use two Kinds of Mercy towards us, a greater and a less : The lesser Mercy is, when he succours us in our less considerable Distresses, which are the Temporal, and such as only concern the Body : The great Mercy is, when he supports us under, or removes, our greater Miseries, which are the Spiritual, and such as concern the Soul. Thus when *David* saw the Greatness of his Misery, in being abandoned and forsaken of God, for the Adultery and Murther, which he had committed, he cried out with great Vehemence, and most earnestly implored the *great* Mercy of God; *Have Mercy upon me, O God, after thy* great *Goodness.* Psal. li. 1. So on the other Hand, they say, that there is also a great, and a less *Anger* of God : The lesser is, when he punishes Men here with Temporal Los

---

* Jeremiah x. 17.   † So the vulgar Latin.

of

of Goods, of Honour, Health, and the like, which only relate to the Body ; but the *great Anger* is, when the Punifhment goes fo far, as to reach to the interiour Part of us, even to the Soul; according to that of the Prophet, *The Sword reacheth unto the Soul.* Jer. iv. 10.   And this is that which God faith by the Prophet *Zachary.   I am angry with my* * *great Anger, with the Heathen that are at Eafe.* Chap. i. 15.   Now when God forfakes a Man, and judicially permits him to fall into heinous Crimes, for a Punifhment of his other Sins, this is the *Great Anger* of God ; thefe are Wounds, which are given by Divine Indignation; they are Stripes, not of a Father, but of a juft and righteous Judge.   Of which Wounds, that of the Prophet is to be underftood ; *I have wounded thee with the Wound of an Enemy, with the Chaftifement of a cruel one.* Jer. xxx. 14.   fo alfo the Wife Man ; *The Mouth of ftrange Women is a deep Pit · He that is* abhorred *of the Lord fhall fall therein.* Prov. xxii. 14.

Finally, Pride is a Thing fo wicked, and fo much hated by Almighty God, that the Saints fay, The greateft Good that can befall the proud Man, is to be fharply punifhed by the Divine Juftice, that fo he may come to be cured of his *Pride.*   Par-

* So the Vulgat. *Irâ magnâ.*

ticularly

ticularly St. *Auguſtin* ; " I may venture to
" affirm, ſaith he, that it is profitable and
" good for *Proud Men*, to be permitted to
" fall into ſome viſible and notorious Sin,
" that ſo, having been too well pleaſed
" with themſelves, and already fallen, tho'
" they perceived it not, they may begin
" to know their own Frailty, learn to be
" Humble and diſtruſt themſelves, for the
" Time to come, and be convinced of that
" Saying of the Wiſe Man, *Pride goeth*
" *before Deſtruction, and an haughty Spirit*
" *before a Fall.* Prov. xvii. 18. " St. *Baſil*
teaches the ſame Thing ; ſo doth *Gregory*
alſo, who taking Occaſion from the Sin of
David, to ask, why God permits the Elect,
and ſuch as be the Heirs of Salvation, on
whom he hath heaped many Graces and
Gifts, ſhould fall ſometimes into carnal and
filthy Sins ; he anſwers, that the Reaſon
of it is, becauſe ſometimes, they who have
received great Graces, are apt to fall into
Pride, and have it ſo rooted, and even
wrought into the very inmoſt Folds of the
Heart, that they themſelves perceive it not ;
but are ſo pleaſed with, and ſo confident of
themſelves, as to think that God and they
are all one. As it happened to St. *Peter*
the Apoſtle, who little thought, that thoſe
Words of his flowed from Pride, when he
ſaid, *Though all Men ſhall be Offended be-*
cauſe of Thee, yet will I never be Offended.
Matth.

Matth. xxvi. 33. He rather conceived it to be a holy Courage in him, and the Effect of that extraordinary Love, which he had for his Master.

To cure such Pride as this, which lies so close, and is so disguised, that the Man who hath it, is already fallen, tho' himself perceive it not, our Lord permits such Persons to fall sometimes into the most flagrant and shameful Crimes; to the end they may know themselves better, and look more strictly into the State of their Souls: This, if any Thing, will discover to them their Pride, which while they continued insensible of, they looked for no Remedy, and so must have come to perish; but now, by means of such gross Falls, they are brought to know their Weakness and their Danger; and being deeply humbled in the Sight of God, they repent both of the one, and the other; and so obtain a Remedy for both their Maladies at once, as we see St. *Peter* did; who by that apparent and shameful Fall of his, came to know the Pride, which had lain so secretly within, and to repent of both. Happy then was the Fall, which prov'd the Cure of his Pride. The same, we may presume, happened also to *David*, from what he saith, *It is good for me, that thou hast * humbled*

* So the Vulg. *humiliasti me*

me, that so I may learn thy Statutes. A wise Phyfician, when he finds the Diftemper lurking wholly within, and the peccant Humour fo rebellious and malignant, that he cannot make Nature digeft and overcome it, endeavours to draw it to fome extream Part of the Body, that fo it may be the better cured ; juft fo, for the Cure of certain haughty and rebellious Spirits, our Lord permits them to fall into fome grievous and fcandalous Sins, that they may know themfelves, and learn to be *humble :* That by means of that Abafement, which outwardly befalls them, the malignant and peftilent Humour of Pride may alfo be cured, which lay fo clofe within. This is that *Work which God worketh in* Ifrael, *which whofoever comes to hear, both his Ears fhall tingle* : Thefe, I fay, (to wit, this punifhing of one Sin with another) are thofe great and fore Judgments of God, the very hearing whereof, fhould make us tremble.

Neverthelefs, our Lord, who is full of Benignity and Mercy, doth not employ this fo rigorous Punifhment, nor this fo fevere and defperate a Cure, till all fair and gentle Means have failed. He firft adminifters Lenitives, fome gentle Correction *to* humble us ; fome flight Sicknefs, fome Contradiction, fome Reflection, and Lofs of Honour, when our Credit fuffers, suffers, and our Reputation is blemished. But when these Temporal Applications will not prevail to humble us, he passes on to Spiritual: And first he begins with Things of less moment; then proceeds to greater, permitting fierce and grievous Temptations to befall us, such as may bring us within a Hair's Breadth of some horrid Crime, and even make us to doubt, whether we consented to the Sin or no. This is done, that a Man may see and find by sad Experience, that he is not able of himself to master the least Frailty or Temptation; that he may feelingly understand his own Misery, and the absolute Need he hath of Help from Heaven, so as to humble himself in the profoundest manner, and never to trust to his own Strength. If all this will not do, then comes that other so violent and costly Cure, of suffering a Man to fall into some mortal Sin, and to be quite overcome by the Temptation. Then, I say, is applied this Cautery, which is made even of the very Fire of Hell; 'tis a kind of desperate Cure, by which, after a Man hath almost destroy'd himself, he may be brought to a due Examination and Knowledge of what he is; and at length be prevailed on to humble himself by this means, since he would not be wrought upon by any other.

By this Time I hope we fee, how very much it concerns us to be humble, and not to confide or trûft in ourfelves : But let every one fearch out his Spirits, examine faithfully how the Account ftands between God and his Heart, and confider what Improvement he has made of thofe Occafions, which God daily fends him, for the healing of his Pride, in the Quality of a Tender-hearted Phyfician, and of a kind indulgent Father; that fo there may be no Need of thofe other Medicines, which are fo violent.— *Correct me, O Lord, but with Judgment, not in thine Anger, left thou bring me to nothing :* Chaftife me, but with the Chaftifement of a Father · Cure my Pride with Afflictions, with Difeafes, Difhonours, and Affronts, with as many Humiliations as thou art pleafed to fend; but fuffer me not, O Lord, fuffer me not, by Way of Punifhment for my Pride, to fall into deliberate and wilful Sin. Let Satan have Power to touch me in point of Honour, or in my Health ; let him make another *Job* of me ; but permit him not to touch my Soul, nor fmite down my Life, my *Spiritual* Life, to the Ground : So Thou, O Lord, forfake me not, nor ever permit me to fall away from Thee, whatever Tribulation may come upon me, it fhall never do me Hurt ; but rather turn to my Profit, and procure me that

greateft

greateſt Good, the Virtue of *Humility*, which is ſo very acceptable to thee. Grant this, O Lord, for JESUS CHRIST his Sake, our only Saviour and Redeemer. *Amen.*

CHAP. XXXVI.

How Children *may be trained up to the Virtue of* Humility.

HERE I ſhall take Leave of my Author.--- His *laſt* Chapter concludes with certain Examples of uncommon Humility ; but moſt of them ſavour ſo much of *Superſtition*, and ſo little of the true Spirit of *Chriſtianity*, that I flatter myſelf the *Proteſtant* Reader will not think himſelf wronged, if I omit this, as I have done three or four other Chapters, which are of the ſame Leven ; and in the Room thereof ſubſtitute one, on the Subject of Implanting this excellent Virtue of Humility in the Minds of Children. And this I humbly offer, not as a Perfect Rule, or even as a Tried Preſcription, but as a Caſe of ſuch Importance, as highly deſerves to be Conſidered and Tried, by all that are

con-

concerned ; and is the Refult of fome Thoughts I had, while that Subject requir-red my Confideration.

Divine Truth hath affured us, That all are born in Sin, and bring with them into the World a Depravity of Nature, derived from our Firft Parents. All then who have the Care and Management of *Children*, fhould obferve carefully the Symptoms and Tokens of fuch *innate* Corruption, as foon as ever they begin to appear ; and be pre-pared, by proper Methods, to weed them out ; or at leaft to check their further Growth. To do this effectually, it will be neceffary they fhould, like able Phyfi-cians, be well skilled in the Nature, De-grees, and Symptoms of the Vice, they are to cure ; and provide themfelves with fuch proper Helps, as may furnifh them with a competent Information herein.

A watchful Eye will difcover very ear-ly in Children the Motions of *Pride, Envy, Covetoufnefs*, &c. And there is one *gene-ral* Remedy, which, with prudent Appli-cation, will prove an Antidote to all thefe ; and it is this, Contrary to the *ufual* Cuf-tom, to inure Children to fubmit their *Defires*, and to go without their *Longings*, from the very firft. Their *Will*, wherein the Depravity doth principally lie, is care-fully to be watched, and difcreetly re-ftrained from every Irregularity and Per-

verfenefs.

verfenefs. This will more plainly appear, if we come to Particulars; but, for the prefent, I fhall confine myfelf only to the Vice of Pride.

As to *Pride*; avoid every Thing that may ftir up, and encourage this Vice: Suffer no flattering and fawning Speeches to be ufed to the Child; efpecially for thofe Things, which are merely the Gifts of God and Nature, as *Beauty*, *Wit*, &c. much lefs for the Advantages of *Drefs* and *fine Cloaths*.

A foolifh Affectation of winning the Heart of Children, and expreffing our Delight in them, is the common Caufe of all fuch fulfome Flattery; which though defign'd only to *pleafe* them, is, in Effect, a moft fatal Incentive to *Vanity* and *Pride*; and fpreads a dangerous *Snare for their Feet*, (Prov. xxix. 5.) For perceiving they are looked on with Delight, that every Thing they Say, or Do, tho' never fo trifling, is obferved and admired; they from hence accuftom themfelves to an Opinion, that they are poffeffed of more than ordinary Excellence; and that they have a Right to be praifed and admired by all; fo that all fuch as pay not this Court and Homage to them, become diftafteful and unwelcome Company.

" This

" This imprudent Treatment of Chil-
" dren, all Applaufe and no Contradiction,
" is apt likewife to fill them with chime-
" rical Hopes, which makes Way for in-
" finite Difappointments, for the whole
" Courfe of their Life that is to come.
" Care therefore is to be taken of Chil-
" dren, without letting them fee, that we
" think much of them . make 'emfee that
" it is purely out of Kindnefs, and the
" Need they are in, of being redreffed
" and helped, that you are mindful of
" their Conduct, and not out of any Ad-
" miration of their Parts. " [*Cambray*]

Another *ill Effect* of this indifcreet A-
dulation is very obfervable in Children of
forward Parts : That very Pregnancy of
Wit, which gains 'em fo much Praife and
Compliment, is thereby often ftifled, or
check'd. For Flattery is of an intoxicating Quality ; few *Men* are Proof againft
it, much lefs can the weaker Heads of
Children bear it Their *Fancies* may be
lively enough to excite Admiration, but
their *Judgments* are too feeble to fupport
it Applaufe, on *proper Occafions*, is doubtlefs neceffary, but *improperly*, or too libe-
rally beftow'd, is like Excefs of every
Kind, very dangerous and deftructive :
'Tis as Mildew to Corn, or too much Oil
to the Lamp. Hence we often fee a very
fprightly Infancy degenerate into a ftupid
or

or fantaftical Manhood; and all the Hopes of riper Years blafted, by the peftilential Breath of Flattery.

The moft unhappy Confequence of all, is, the evil Effect it has upon the *Will,* rendring it refiactory to all Laws and due Reftraints, and making the Mind averfe to Obedience, and the Difcipline of *Virtue.* As *Pride* is the Firft and moft immediate Offspring of *Self-Love*; fo is it juftly ftyled *The Mother of all other Vices*; infomuch, that without a diligent and watchful Care, to weed it out betimes, or at leaft to ftop its Growth, 'twill over-run our new Plantation, and deftroy every *good Seed* you fow therein. But how will it poifon the Ground, and render it incapable of any good Principles, if, as too much the Fafhion is, you cocker and encourage it! And many, I fear moft, Parents take more Pains to cherifh, and even inftil *Pride* into their Children, than to correct and fuppref's it.

The Pride of the Eye is the firft Kind of Pride, that appears in Children; and the chief Fewel and Incentives to it, are gaudy Cloaths, and rich Dreffes, fine Trinkets, and fhowifh Play-Things. Outward Ornaments ought rather to be forborn a while; at leaft till their Reafon be grown capable of judging of the *Ufe* or *Abufe* of fuch Things, of the Vanity of fetting a

Value

Value on them, and the great Weakness of valuing themselves for them. Take the first Occasion that offers, to instruct the Child that it is not the *Gaiety of Dress*, &c. but *a wise and modest Carriage*, which recommends most, in the Sight of God and Man: Instance some known Examples of Children, who are aukward and disagreeable, though *finely dressed*; of others *plainly clad*, but well esteemed and beloved for their Neatness, and ingenuous Behaviour. Acquaint the Child with the Original and first Occasion of Cloathing, which was *Sin*; and therefore what little Reason we have, to be *proud* thereof; but rather, on the contrary, have Cause to be much humbled and ashamed, as having lost that Innocency, which was a much greater Ornament, than any the most glorious Apparel can be. That the chief Ends of Cloathing being to cover our Nakedness, to fence the Body from Cold, and for Distinction of Persons and Sex, our Apparel ought, in the first Place, to be *modest* (such as may answer the End of covering our Shame) next, *decent*, and suitable to our Condition and Quality.

After such Lectures, 'twill not be amiss, for Experiment sake, to change your Hand, and on a *suitable Occasion*, that so the Child may apprehend the Reason of the Change; (and here, by the Way, let this be a

standing

ſtanding Rule to the Managers of Children, not only to govern them conſtantly
by the Dictates of Reaſon, but now and
then to make the Child apprehend, according to its Capacity, that what is to
be done, is *reaſonable*, and fitting; ſo as to
exerciſe the Child's Judgment, and inure
it betimes both to approve of the Gover-
nor's Conduct, and to conform its own to
the Rules of *Reaſon* and *Prudence*) · On
a *ſuitable Occaſion* therefore, ſuch as any
conſiderable Solemnities, as *Chriſtmas*,
Birth-Days, *Viſits* to Perſons of Honour,
&c. let their Dreſs be *ſumptuous* and *fine* :
apprizing them, as before, of the Reaſon
of the Change.   Then obſerve narrowly,
whether it produce any *Change* in the
Mind ; that is, if it exalt 'em ; or if any
Symptoms of *Pride* appear in their Behaviour.   If ſo, take this Occaſion to convince the Child, that Rich Apparel is indeed a great *Temptation to Pride*, and that
therefore it has been ſo long withholden
from it, till the Mind was grown ſtrong
enough to bear the Trial.   That *Humility*
does not conſiſt in *plain* or *ſordid Cloaths*,
nor *Pride* in going *Fine*, but in the Temper, wherewith the Mind is affected by the
one or the other, Virtue or Vice being
ſeated in the *Soul*, and not in *Outward
Things* · He that is aſhamed to wear ordinary *Cloathing*, being as Proud as he that

is puffed up with *Rich* Apparel. That therefore the true Virtue of *Humility* lies in an even, unaffected Frame of Mind, under either Condition; regarding the *Use* and *Reason*, and not the *Shew* and *Appearance* of what we wear. —— Here relate the Story of *Esther*; particularly that Instance of her *Humility*, which she expressed in her " hating the Glory of the Unrighteous, " and abhorring the Sign of her high " Estate, which was upon her Head, on " the Days wherein she was obliged to " shew herself; and that she wore it not, " when in private by herself. " *Esther in the Apoc. Chap.* xiv. 16.

But alas! the contrary to this is too much practifed towards Children; as it is described, and severely reproved, by St. *John Chrysostom*, in his *Golden Book of Education.* " No sooner, says he, is the Child " born, but the Father beftirs himself, that " he may magnificently set him out, and " adorn him with Jewels and rich Appa- " rel; by this means effeminating his Son " from the very Cradle, soft'ning the Vi- " gour of his Sex, and engrafting into " that tender Age a superfluous Love of " Riches, and such Things, as are wholly " unneceffary and vain. Some may, per- " haps, *(as he goes on)* deride these Dis- " courfes, as small and inconfiderable Mat- " ters; but I tell you, they are not small

O

" Mat-

" Matters, but of the greatest and most
" important Consequence. —— A Maid,
" who, in her Mother's Chamber, hath
" learned to Long after the various Tires
" and Ornaments of Women, will prove
" to her Husband both a troublesome, and
" an expensive Wife. "

To propose therefore, as is too commonly done, *Fine Cloaths* to Children, as *Rewards* of any Duty, is a very pernicious Method of Encouragement : For when you promise your Son a fine Cravat, or new Suit, upon Performance of some of his little Tasks, what do you, by proposing these as *Rewards*, but allow them to be the *good Things*, he should aim at; and thereby authorize his longing for them, and accustom him to place his *Happiness* in Them ? Whereas such a Proceeding serves but to increase, and to strengthen those wrong Inclinations, and Propensity to Vanity and Pride, which it is our great Business to subdue and master : It foments and cherishes in him *that*, which is the Spring, whence all the Evil flows, for though it may seem to train him to Obedience and Acts of Duty, it does it on such base Motives, and mean Views, as, in Effect, is sacrificing the Child's Virtue to Selfishness and Pride, and quite inverting (as Mr. *Lock* observes) the Order and Design of Education.

The

The next Kind of *Pride* is that *of the Tongue*. This is generally inftilled into Children by that indifcreet *Flattery*, we have already remarked, as too much ufed towards Children, and is the natural Effect of it : For what Wonder is it to hear thofe Perfons fetting forth their own Praife, whofe Ears have been fo long accuftomed to hear it from others? And though, when grown up, their better Senfe may fuggeft the Unbecomingnefs of Vain Glory and Self-Commendation ; yet what Arts will they not ufe, to publifh their own Merit ! forcing fuch Difcourfes, as may help to raife a Reputation with others, and to gain Efteem : too often making free with *Truth*, in Favour of *Vanity* ; adding or diminifhing, as may be ferviceable to this End ; laying open the Failings or Indifcretions of others, as a Shade to fet off their own Advantage over them : and upon any Oppofition, breaking out into paffionate Apologies, or outragious Revilings , not being able to bear any Thing that is provoking, or feems to derogate from that Efteem and Deference, they have been fo often *taught*, to look upon as their *Due*.

A *Third* Kind is the *Pride of the Heart.* Here, indeed, is the Seat or Root of Pride; what we have already mentioned, being but the Branches, or outward Expreffions

of

of it. But whereas it is by thefe *apparent* Symptoms only, we can come to the Knowledge of this Vice in *Children*, and confequently know how to apply the proper Remedies ; in order to attain the greater Skill herein, let us look firft into *Ourfelves*, and confider the Motions and Operations of *Pride, in our Own Hearts*. And here a due Attention will inform us, that altho' *Pride* in all Mankind proceed from the very *fame Caufe*, namely, the Prevalence and Afcendency of the *Animal* Life above the *Spiritual* ; or, in other Words, from an Excefs of *Self-Love*, and a Defect of Love towards *God*; yet it varies its Symptoms or Appearances, according to the Soil it grows in ; I mean, according to the Perfon's Genius, Education, or Circumftance of Life : So that we may obferve in general, that in different Perfons, there are *Two Sorts* of Pride, widely different from each other : One a *Mean* and *Bafe*, the other a *Nobler* and more *Ingenuous Pride*. The Firft, the Effect of a confcious *Unworthinefs* , the other, a Senfe of *real Merit*, of Parts and Accomplifhments truly laudable. While the One is ambitious of difplaying its own *Excellencies*, in the Purfuit of Glory, Fame, and Applaufe; the other is making ufe of mean Shifts and Artifices, to conceal and difguife its *Defects*. While the one deceives *itfelf*, by

affuming

affuming an Honour, which is only due to God, for the Gifts He has beftowed; the other is bufied in deceiving *Others*, by a counterfeit Shew and Pretence of Gifts, it never had.

To trace a little further this fecret working of *Pride*; you'll obferve in Perfons of diftinguifhing Abilities, it generally exerts itfelf in thofe Inftances, wherein they moft excel. The *Couragious* piques himfelf in Feats of Arms and Military Exploits; the *Wife*, in Policy and Counfel; the *Learned*, in Knowledge of Arts and Sciences, *&c.* and *thefe* Ends they purfue fo intently, as generally to neglect and defpife all the leffer Accomplifhments of *Drefs, Equipage*, and *Fafhion*, as trifling and inconfiderable. Whereas the Man, who knows himfelf not poffeffed of any fuch Noble Qualities, applies himfelf wholly to improve the Gifts of *Fortune, Beauty*, and other *afcititious* Advantages, that fo he may, by fuch *Fig-Leaves* as thefe, hide the Nakednefs of his Mind, and by *falfe* Colours beguile the Eyes of the Beholders into Praife and Admiration. To this Confcioufnefs of the Want of *real* Worth, is owing the *pert Coxcomb* and *fantaftical Coquet*, the *demure Prude* and *precife Hypocrite*, the *vain Fop* and *painted Jezebel*; and, in general, all Sort of Affectation. But the Fallacy is fo

O 3 eafily

eafily detected, that it commonly meets with Contempt and Shame;

—— *Movet Cornicula rifum*
Furtivis nudata Coloribus. ——

These two Extreams, and very differing Kinds of *Pride*, though not *equally* destructive of that Honour and Applause from Men, which *Pride* ever proposes to itself; yet are *equally* contrary to *Humility*, and to that Honour and Gratitude, which is due to God, for every Gift we possess, or expect; and must therefore equally fall short of his Grace Here, and Glory Hereafter. To obviate therefore both these Extreams, and prevent their taking Root in the Child, the foregoing Directions, concerning the *Pride of the Eye*, and the *Pride of the Tongue*, or whatever other Symptoms shall appear, are diligently to be obferved; together with all such other Methods, as the particular Temper, Capacity, Age, or Circumstance may fuggeft to the prudent Parent or Instructor. And, for their Encouragement, they may be affured, that if they fucceed in removing, or preventing this Radical and Fundamental Corruption, the *Pride of the Heart*, all the other Vices will of Course, give Way (being more properly *Scions* or *Branches* of Pride, than of a Species distinct from it.) The tender

der Soil will likewise be duly prepared, for the Seeds of Virtue and Religion. By this Method will effectually be accomplished that wise Design, which the *Persian* Policy aimed at, in the Institution of their Youth; the Discipline they made Use of (as *Xenophon* informs us) being calculated to prevent, rather than to punish, every Crime and Disorder. While other Nations framed particular Laws against Overt-Acts, with severe Penalties annexed for Correction of Offenders; but at the same Time permitted their Youth to be trained up in so loose and licentious a Manner, as necessarily led them into the Breach of those very Laws; the *Persian* Institutes were levelled at the Cause, and struck at the Root of every criminal Action: by an early and virtuous Education, forming every Subject from the Beginning, to *love* Justice, rather than to *fear* it; to hate Evil for its own Sake; to dread the Crime more than the Punishment; in a Word, to live by Reason, and be a Law to themselves.

We may also say, such *early Care of Youth* is indeed making (what the Wise Men among the *Jews* called, the *Septum Legis*) a Hedge or Fence about the Law, to keep Men from breaking through; or what the Forerunner of Christ most appositely calls, *laying the Ax to the Root of the Tree. Pride* is this *Root*; a Root, that we bring with

O 4

us

us into the World ; a Root of Bitterneſs, whence all other Vices ſpring, or have a near Affinity with : And if this be plucked up, it 's, in Effect, deſtroying all the reſt at once ; or, at leaſt, making the Cure of them very practicable and eaſy.

Thus have I adventured to propoſe a Method, how *Humility* may be *firſt* planted in the Heart. Our Author, in the foregoing Chapters, has indeed given many Rules, for acquiring and improving that Virtue ; but *this* Rule, which relates to *Children*, though of the greateſt Importance, he has wholly omitted, and paſſed over in Silence. I hope, therefore, what has here been offered, will ſerve for a Hint, at leaſt, to all that are concerned, and have a ſincere Deſire to promote Virtue and true Piety in the World, how and where the firſt Step is to be taken, and the firſt Stone laid. The beſt Ground is *Humility,* * the beſt Seaſon is *Youth*.

As to this Treatiſe, it is not to be expected it ſhould have any good Effect, except where ſome *early* Impreſſions of *Humility* have been firſt made : Where that has been neglected, and a contrary Spirit prevailed, it is as vain to hope this Book ſhould do ſuch Perſons any Good, as it is impoſſible to gain any *other Virtue*, without

---

* See Chap. iiī.

begin-

beginning firft with *Humility*. Our Lord began his Sermon with it, and fo muft we our Courfe of Virtue. The *earlier* we fet out, the more fuccefsful, as well as fpeedier, will our Progrefs be. His Words intimate to us a *Certainty* of Succefs, as well as affure us of a Bleffing : *Bleffed are the Poor in Spirit, for theirs is the Kingdom of* HEAVEN. No lefs than a Kingdom, a Heavenly Kingdom is here promifed; yea not only promifed, but immediately beftowed on the *Humble Man* —— Heaven IS His ——The Virtue and the Reward go together : No fooner does *Humility* begin the Race, but it wins the Crown.

Before I conclude, let me intreat all Parents, and thofe, who have the Education of Children entrufted to their Care, to confider, that by thus initiating them in the Practice of *Humility*, they not only prepare and fit them the moft effectually for the Exercife and Habit of every *other* Virtue; but are taking the fureft Method, that can be taken in this World, for fecuring fuch Children from all the Calamities, Cares, and Afflictions, to which the Life of Man is expofed. —— For what are they all owing to, but to *Pride* ? —— Either as Corrections from God, or the froward Impatience of our own rebellious Paffions; ever refifting, and being ever refifted by the Hand of him, who is a profeffed Ene-

my

my to this Vice, and has declared, *though Hand join in Hand, the Proud shall not go unpunished.* But remove the Cause, by the timely Cure of *Pride*, in the Hearts of your Children, and you effectually prevent all those fatal Effects. —— If *Job* was *defective* in ought (as who is not?) it was in *Humility*. —— This brought on him those grievous Sufferings : But no sooner was he convinced of his Error, and turned the secret, and before unobserved, Risings of *Pride*, into a lowly *Self-Abhorrence*, but God *turned* also *his Hand*,* and gave him *Double* for all he had suffered ; *blessing his latter End more than his Beginning ;* as if he would teach us, that even in his *best* Servants he will not let *Pride* go unpunished ; and that the obtaining of this One Virtue of *Humility*, shall even *double* to us all his other Gifts and Graces.

The following *Prayer* we may suppose was added by the *Protestant* Editor of this Treatise, it not being found in the *Latin* or *English Popish* Editions, but deserves well to be continued. And whoever desires a more full and particular Form on the same Subject, may have Recourse to *Gother's Complaint of a Sinner.*

* Isaiah i. 25.

I hope

I hope the Reader will excuse the Addition of two or three *Poems* : They may be of Use to *Children*, to imbue their tender Minds and Memories with Impressions in Favour of *Humility* ; and let the Dignity of the Subject attone for the Meanness of the Poetry.

A Verse may find him, who a Sermon flies,
And turn Delight into a Sacrifice.

A
PRAYER
AGAINST
PRIDE.

Nothing, O bleſſed Lord, is more diſpleaſing to Thee than Pride; nothing more hateful than Self-conceit. Did I conſider this as I ought, there need no other Motive to perſuade me, that I ſhould not only diſlike, but abhor it, as a mortal and damnable Thing; ſince thou, O Lord, doſt ſo deteſt it, that the Angels, whom thou createdſt with ſo many Perfections, and adornedſt with ſuch Beauties and Gifts, giving them the Poſſeſſion of thy inmoſt Heaven, yet for this Sin only didſt thou for ever baniſh them from thence into the infernal Pit, there to ſuffer the condign

Puniſh-

Punifhment of their heinous Offence. And from that Time until this prefent, and from this Time for ever to come, the *Proud* thou always haft, and ever wilt abhor. Thefe are they, on whom thou delighteft to fhew the Power of thy mighty Arm; humbling them, cafting them down, and making them equal with the Earth, that they may underftand themfelves to be but Men, and not dare to lift up their Heads againft thee. That thou abhorreft Pride in Bodily Strength, thou haft declared in *Goliath*, giving him over into the Hands of a Young and Beardlefs Stripling, for fuch was *David*. That thou detefteft it in Self-Conceit and Vain-Glory, thou fhewedft in abafing *Haman*, making him ferve for Page, to Herald and proclaim the Virtues of *Mordecai*, whom he fought to deftroy. That it is abominable to thee in thofe, who have a vain Opinion of their own Beauty, we are taught by the Fate of *Abfalom*, whom thou fufferedft to be hanged by that Hair, of which he was fo proud. That it is deteftable to thee in the Greateft of Men, who glory in their great Riches and Dominions, we have a terrifying Inftance in *Nebuchadnezzar*, whom thou draveft out to live and feed among brute Beafts. That it is odious to thee in them, who are opinionated of their own Wifdom, was manifefted in *Achitophel*, whom thou fufferedft

to

to become his own Executioner, by an ignominious Death, becaufe his Counfel was not followed. Thou hateft it in Words, thou hateft it in Virtue and Goodnefs itfelf, knowing it to be the Moth and Canker thereof; for this thou haft taught us in the prefumptuous *Pharifee,* fending him away defpifed and rejected, becaufe he vaunted before thee of his own Worth, and fet forth his own Praife. Wifely therefore did thy Servant *Tobit* * advife, —— *Suffer not* Pride *to reign in thy Underftanding, nor in thy Words, for all Deftruction took its Rife from thence.* The Confideration of thefe Things, O Lord, and of thefe Examples, plainly evincing that Pride is fo abominable to thee, and fo feverely punifhed, wherever thou findeft it, were more than fufficient, if I had the leaft Underftanding, to breed an Abhorrence of it in my Heart, and lay a conftant Reftraint, not only on my Deeds and Words, but alfo on the moft inward Thoughts of my Heart. For though I were Valiant, yet fhould I not be like *Goliath :* Had I Power and Command, yet would it be lefs than *Holofernes :* though a Favourite, yet could I not match *Haman :* Did I furpafs Others,

---

* See the Vulgat. Superbiam nunquam in tuo fenfu, aut in tuo verbo dominari permittas; in ipfa enim initium fumpfit omnis perditio. Chap. iv. 14.

yet how far should I fall short of *Absalom*, in Beauty; in Majesty and Power, of *Nebuchadnezzar*; in Wisdom, of *Achitophel*; in Holiness and all other Excellency, of the Angels, before their Fall? Yet all these, in the several Kinds of Pride, whereby their Hearts were lifted up, were by thee brought down to the lowest Degree of Shame and Confusion, of Misery and Calamity, in Proportion to their Pride and Vanity. But if to this I add the Consideration of mine own Frame, and the Condition of those Things in themselves, for the Sake of which I am lifted up in my own Conceit, either I must forsake all Pride, or else entirely quit all Claim to the Understanding of a Man : For my Being is but Earth, a Clod of Earth, so frail, so vile and beggarly, that I can neither cloath myself without stripping other Animals; nor maintain my own Life, without taking away their Lives from Birds, or Beasts, or Fishes. I can neither breathe without Air, nor see without Light, nor hear without Sound, nor live at all, without the Help of thy meanest Creatures. And besides all this, I am so encompassed with Necessities, so invironed with Wants, of Hunger, Thirst, and Sleep, so soon tired with Labour, so beset with Dangers, so overwhelmed with Miseries, that if I rightly take the Estimate of my Case, I must judge myself, of all thy other Works, the moſt wretched and contemptible. —— And what alas ! if I truly weigh them, are thoſe Things, which make me ſwell, but lighter and leſs worth than this wretched Life itſelf? Every Injury of Weather diſtempers my Health ; the lighteſt Sickneſs abates my Strength ; the leaſt Pain overthrows my Content ; but a few Hours Want of Suſtenance enfeebles me, a few Days Want kills me ; Riches ſlip away like Water from between my Fingers, and if not rightly uſed, they but add here to our Sorrows, and increaſe our Torments hereafter. Honour vaniſheth like Smoak ; Nobility is Baſeneſs, except it be ſet in Virtue. The Applauſe of the World paſſeth like a Dream, both in them that give, and them that take it. Favour of Princes laſteth no longer than themſelves, and they periſh, when they leaſt think it. Friendſhip is Flattery and private Intereſt. Love is unſound in Subſtance, and fickle in Duration. Wiſdom is Folly, and Learning a wearineſs of the Fleſh. And if the Account be ſtated aright, our Knowledge amounts to no more, than what we reduce to Practice. So that on all Hands, if I rightly conſider, there is no Ground in Man, or what belongs to Man, but for *Humility* ; no Colour but for Lowlineſs. *Pride was not made for Man,* nor his Enjoyments

joyments given to miniſter to his Pride; but all Things rather, in their ſeveral Kinds, cry out, that I have in me infinite Matter of Confuſion and Shame; nothing at all to glory in, or prize myſelf for, except it be my Folly; which, as I am, is more truly the Cauſe of puffing me up, than any real Merit I have to pretend. This is it, and only this, which makes me lofty, preſumptuous, ſelf-conceited, vain. Lord, heal me of this Frenzy, and reſtore me again to a right Underſtanding, that with ſuch *Humility* of Spirit as I ought, I may henceforth ſerve thee, eſteeming myſelf of all Others, the *leaſt*, —— towards Thee, *nothing, Amen.*

Praiſe

Praiſe *of* HUMILITY.

HUMILITY ! *The* Firſt, *the* Faireſt
          Gem,
That can adorn the Chriſtian Diadem !
Tho' of external Splendour not poſſeſt,
It gives their Worth and Luſtre to the reſt.
Humility ! 'tis *every Virtue's Soul :*
Gives each it's Form, and animates the Whole.
Take this away, the brighteſt Virtues are
But blazing Meteors, but a falling Star.
The moſt exalted Graces without This,
Loſing their Names, degenerate to Vice.
Thro' Want of This, an Hoſt of Angels fell,
Devils commenc'd, and chang'd their Heaven
          for Hell.
The Loſs of This loſt Adam *Paradiſe,*
Depriv'd at once of Innocence and Bliſs.

Would you then, Fair One, *in true Beau-*
          ty ſhine ;
Would you in Dreſs *be exquiſitely fine ;*
Humility's the beſt Coſmetic to the Face;
Cures each Defect, and heightens every Grace.

Humi-

Humility's *a plain, but rich Attire,*
Attracts the Chaſte, *and curbs the* looſe
          Deſire.
Be cloath'd * *with this, no* Royal Garment
          may
In Grandeur vie, or nobler State diſplay.

     Then truſt no more your Toilet, truſt not
          Dreſs ;
Nor ſeek for Beauty from ſuch Aids as theſe.
By This *your faithful* Glaſs, *by this you may*
Adjuſt your Mien, your Face, your whole Array.
This every other Mirrour far outdoes,
Improves *Good Features*; mends *the Faults*
          it ſhows.
Directs the Conduct, *regulates each* Senſe,
And by a ſweet harmonious Influence,
To every Part will Symmetry *reſtore,*
And make you truly Beautiful *all o'er.*

     *   1 Pet. v. 5.

Character *of* Humility.

Taken from Bishop *KENN's* Poems,
with Alterations.

HAIL *Son of God ! hail Virgin's Son,
     let me*
Thy Humble *Mother's Virtue learn of* Thee.
This Faireft Beauty of the Human Mind,
In which blefs'd Mary *all her Sex outfhin'd,*
Invited Thee to fix thy Choice on Her,
And to thy Heaven's *Blifs, a* Virgin Heart
     prefer.
The Humble *ftill engage thy chiefeft Cares ;*
They Firft, *of Heaven are made Adoptive Heirs ;*
They Firft, *in Rank of Blefsings take their*
     Place,
Firft *gain the Prize of Innocence and Grace.*
The Mighty God, who haughty Minds repels,
Familiar with the Humble *Spirit dwells ;*
Defcends with Pleafure to this lowly *Sphere,*
And brings his Heaven down, to fix it here.
The Lowly *more to* Grace, *than* Gifts *afpires,*
To Honour God, *more than* himfelf *defires ;*

Is

Is better pleas'd with one self-humblingThought,
Than if his Hand a Miracle had wrought.
Flies all Observance ; loves the loweſt Seat ;
To worldly Pomp prefers ſome hid Retreat.
His Mien ; *of Affectation void, or Art :*
Modeſt and few his Words, *the Language of*
         his Heart.
Leſs than the leaſt of Mercies, ſtill he cries ;
Chearful his Will, *with Heaven'sWill complies.*
In him no Honours *vain Emotions raiſe,*
Him no Contempt *dejects, no* Croſs *diſmays.*
Yet, of the Two, Contempt *he'd rather chuſe,*
The ſafeſt State ; th' unlikelieſt to abuſe.
But dares not ſeek Contempt, or fondly ſtrive
From others Sins *his Virtues to derive.*
Good Name's *a Bleſſing, which from Vir-*
         tue flows :
The precious Odour no Wiſe Saint *foregoes.*
Saintſhip he keeps in hon'rable Repute :
Fair Fame *is Virtue's fair and genuineFruit.*
The Tree, which bears it, by theFruit we trace,
And leſs revere the Perſon, than the Grace.
All he receives from God, he reconveys ;
He's but the Conduit of his Maker's *Praiſe.*
Of his own Frailty has a lively Senſe ;
That of himſelf he can no Good commence :
Is nothing, nothing Has, *can nothing* Do,
Which may ſuſtain the Teſt of God's Review.
Conſcious that Virtues, which ſuch Weakneſs
         ſhare,
To Heaven's Rewards can no Proportion bear.

                                    But

But if he meet with Causeless *Hate and*
  Scorn,
His humble Mind they sink not, but adorn :
He knows they're Med'cines *from Paternal*
  Love,
To heal Defects, and Virtues to improve.
If doubtful Cases Conscience *discompose,*
To his Soul's Guide the mourning Patient goes;
Conceals no Part of Frailty, or of Blame ;
Gives God the Glory, *takes himself the* Shame.
Of Counsel *glad he lends attentive Ear ;*
Respects Superiors with a Filial Fear.
To just Reproof *with grateful Heed inclines :*
Can value Virtue, which his own outshines.
On others Grace ; on his own Guilt *reflects ;*
And less computes his Virtues than Defects.
Searches no Neighbour's Faults, to veil his
  own ;
Is always to his conscious Self best known.
More Evil in himself, than others spies,
And worthless *seems in his own lowly Eyes.*
For slightest Wrongs he Pardon first entreats,
For an offensive Word, or angry Heats.
The Name of Coward *rather undergoes,*
Than rob the God of Vengeance, to avenge his
  Foes.
Yet with calm Courage *he the* World *outbraves,*
Nor any persecuted *Virtue Waives.*
When Duty *calls, he dares the* hardest *Things,*
And gains the Conquest by his Sufferings.

Frequent

Frequent *Self-Scrutinies* the **Humble** *makes,*
Inceffant Prays, nor *his ftrict Watch forfakes.*
Ne'er acts befide his Providential Sphere ;
God ever Prefent careful to Revere.
Strives of himfelf like Thought with God to
     frame,
Nor grieves if Others think of him the fame.
The vile Materials which frail Man compofe,
His Lapfe, Curfe, Dangers, Death, and nu-
     merous Woes ,
His own Defaults and Sins he oft recalls,
Omiffions, vicious Habits, Slips and Falls ;
Neglects of Opportunities enjoy'd,
Cold wandring Pray'rs, and Talents mifem-
     ploy'd ;
Woful Experience, a perfidious Heart
From Perfeverance ever prone to ftart ;
Subtle Temptations, fierce Affaults of Hell,
Remains of Luft, which in laps'd Nature
     dwell,
The Spots in Saints, who greateft Height
     acquire,
With all that can Humility *infpire ;*
The Majefty of God, the Judgment Day,
Which with unerring penetrating Ray
Shall all Mankinds moft fecret Crimes dif-
     play.

Thefe are the Topicks, thefe the Leffons are,
By which the **Humble** *forms his Character.*

His

His Conduct steering by this Golden Rule,
(First and Peculiar to the Christian School;)
With persevering, tho' unequal Pace,
His Master's Steps he studies how to trace.

    But while from this Original Divine
His Care and Zeal was copying every Line,
A sudden Calm compos'd his weary'd Breast·
The Grace transcrib'd, another Form exprest,
And where he sought HUMILITY *to find,*
There smiling REST* *appear'd, and gladsome*
Peace of Mind.

* Matth. xi.

Self·

Self-Annihilation.

Man is as a Thing of Nought.

SEE in the Sunshine of a Summer's Day
   Ten thousand thousand little Atoms play;
But if a Cloud, or Shadow intervene,
Not one of all the busy Number's seen.
Thus, Lord, if Thou, my Sun, withdraw
     thy Ray,
O, Cloudy Passions intercept the Day;
Invisible, I vanish, if Alone:
A mere Non-Entity, when THOU art
     gone.

P   Self-

Self - Abnegation.

Not unto me.

I.

THY *Glory be my only View,*
  Thy *Honour my sincere Design :*
If *thy Hand act the Good I do,*
  'Tis *fit the Praise should all be* Thine.

II.

So poor, so frail an Instrument
  If Thou, my God, vouchsafe to use ;
'Tis *Praise enough, to be* employ'd :
  Reward *enough, if Thou* excuse.

III.

If thou excuse, yet work thy Will
  With so unfit *an Instrument ;*
It will at once thy Goodness shew,
  And prove thy Skill Omnipotent.

T H E

THE
Frontifpiece Explained.

*B*Lefs'd Lord ! who can without Emo-
tion fee
This Paradox of thy Humility ?
In every Face appears devout Surprize,
To fee their Mafter *in fuch* Servile Guife *!*
None but a Judas, *Slave to Love of* Gold,
Can Unconcern'd fuch Love of Man *behold.*
His fullen Paffions ficken at the Scene ;
Around his Brow a gloomy Cloud *is feen :*
His Pride *difdains fo mean a Sight as this,*
And adds Contempt *to his Vile* Avarice :
Scorn, Anger, Malice, Shame *of falfe Difgrace*
Darken each guilty Feature of his Face ;
Sit plotting Treachery in every Line ·
Refolve upon ; then juftify the horrible Defign.

Reverfe to this the Meek Redeemer *fee,*
Before a Mortal, *with a* Bended Knee :
With Towel girded , rifen from his Seat,
Equipp'd to wafh his own Difciple's Feet.

H

His Robe *laid by, which once outshone the*
          Light,
When Tabor's *Mount beheld the Mystic Sight,*
Laid by; yet still retentive of the Ray,
Now occupies the Seat, *where He discumbent*
          lay.

Peter *abash'd, repels his Master's Hand;*
Reluctant yields, and scarce obeys Command.
Unknowing of Himself, and of his GOD,
He yet the Form *of neither understood:*
Jesus *the Form of* Both *at once unfolds,*
Of Man, *as* Humble *and Abas'd; of* God,
     as Cleansing Souls.

If any Reader, unacquainted with Antiquity, be curious to know the Character of the Authors cited in this Treatise, and the Ages they lived in, he will find an Account of them in Dr *Cave's Lives of the Fathers*, his *Scriptorum Ecclesiasticorum Historia Literaria*, Lond 1688, and in Monsieur *Dupin's History of Ecclesiastical Writers*, in several Volumes, *English* Edition. The Volumes and Pages referred to, are respectively set against every Author's Name, together with the Year wherein he flourished.

	A.D	Cave's Lives	Cave's Hist	Dupin
St. IGNATIUS, Bishop of *Antioch* - - - -	101	V. I p 99	p. 26	V. I p 35
TERTULLIAN, a Presbyter of *Carthage* - - -	192	— p. 201	56	— p. 69
SERAPION, an *Ægyptian*, Bishop of *Thmuys* - - -	347		160	V II. p. 58
St BASIL, the Great, Bishop of *Cæsarea*, in *Cappadocia*	370	V II 215	192	— 122
St AMBROSE, Bishop of *Milan* - - - -	374	— 359	212	— 198
St. JEROM, Cotemporary with St. AMBROSE - - -		—	218	V III 73
St. AUGUSTIN, Bishop of *Hippo* - - - -	396		242	— 124
St JOHN CHRYSOSTOM, Bishop of *Constantinople* - -	398	— 447	252	— 6
THEODORET, a *Syrian*, Bishop of *Cyrus* - - -	423		314	V IV 55
JOHN CASSIAN, a Monk of *Marseilles* - - -	424		319	— 9

	A.D	Cave's Hist	Cave's Appen	Dupin.
John Climacus, so called, from the Title of a Book which he wrote - - - - - - - -	564	421	———	Vol. V. p 69
Gregory the Great, so called from his worthy Actions, the first Pope of that Name - - - - - -	590	430	———	——— p. 72
Dorotheus, Abbot in *Palestine* - - - - - -	———	444		
St Anselm, Archbishop of *Canterbury* - - - - -	1093	627	———	V. IX. 21, 91
St Bernard, Abbot of *Claravall*, called Dr. *Mellifluus*	1115	643	———	V. X p 42
Bonaventure, Bishop of *Albano*, and Cardinal - -	1255	728	———	Vol. XI 68
Thomas Aquinas, called the Angelical Doctor - -	1155	726	———	——— p. 69
Gerson, Chancellor of *Paris* - - - - - - -	1404	———	79	V XIII p 59
Laurentius Justinianus, a Noble *Venetian*, Bishop, and afterwards Patriarch of *Venice* - - - - -	1431		107	——— p 83
Thomas a Kempis - - - - - - - - - -	1450		132	p. 90, & 142
See a large Account in the Preface to a Translation of some of his Works, recommended by Dr. Hicks, and printed 1710				
Francis *de* Borgia, Duke of *Gandia*, and Grandee of *Spain*, enter'd into a Religious Order about - - -	1550			

THE

CONTENTS.

Chap. I. OF the Excellency of the Virtue of Humility, *and how great Need we have thereof.* Page 1

II. *That Humility is the Foundation of all the other Virtues.* 8

III. *Wherein is declared more particularly how Humility is the* Foundation of all the Virtues. 13

IV. *Of the particular Necessity which they have of this Virtue, who profess the* Cure of Souls. 21

V. *Of the First Degree of Humility, which consists in a* Man's *thinking meanly of himself.* 39

VI *Of the Knowledge of Ourselves, which is the First Step and necessary Means for obtaining of* Humility. 44

VII. *That*

The CONTENTS.

VII. *That the Principal Means for a Man's knowing himself, and obtaining* Humility, *is the Consideration of his Sins.* 49

VIII. *How to exercise ourselves in the Knowledge of what we are, that we may not be* dejected *or* dismayed. 57

IX. *Of the great Benefit and Profit arising from this Exercise of* Self-Knowledge. 64

X. *That the Knowledge of one's self, doth not dismay, but rather give Courage and Strength.* 70

XI. *Of other great Benefits and Advantages, arising from the Exercise of a Man's* Knowledge of himself. 75

XII. *How much it behoveth us to be continually exercised in the* Knowledge of ourselves. 79

XIII. *Of the* Second Degree *of* Humility, *and wherein this Degree consists.* 87

XIV. *Of some Steps, whereby a Man may rise to the Perfection of this* Second Degree *of* Humility. 97

XV. *Of the Fourth Step, which is, to re-*joice in Contempt, *and to be* glad thereof. 105

XVI. *That the Perfection of* Humility, *and of all other Virtues, consists in performing the Acts thereof, with* Delight *and* Chearfulness ; *and how much this contributes to our Perseverance in Virtue.*

115

The CONTENTS.

XVII. *Some Means are proposed, for the obtaining of this* Second Degree *of Humility, and particularly the Example of* CHRIST *our Lord*   120

XVIII. *Of some Human Reasons and Considerations, whereby we may be incited to the Pursuit of Humility.*   127

XIX. *Of other Human Reasons for promoting of* Humility   132

XX. *The true Way to be Valued and Esteemed by Men, is to addict ourselves to the Study of Virtue, especially the Virtue of Humility.*   140

XXI. *That by Humility is obtained true Peace of Mind, and cannot be had without it.*   148

XXII. *Of other Means more effectual for the obtaining the Virtue of Humility, to wit, the constant Exercise and Practice thereof.*   158

XXIII. *That we must studiously avoid all Words, that may turn to our own Praise.*   168

XXIV. *In what Manner we ought to examine our Consciences, concerning the Virtue of Humility.*   173

XXV. *How it may be compatible with Humility, to be accounted of by Men.*   189

XXVI. *Of the* Third Degree *of Humility.*   195

XXVII. *Whe-*

The CONTENTS.

XXVII. *Wherein the* Third Degree *of* Humility *consists.* 204

XXVIII. *The foregoing Argument is further deduced.* 210

XXIX. *The* Third Degree *of* Humility *is further explained, and how it comes, that the truly* Humble Man *thinks himself the* Least of All. 215

XXX. *How* Good *and* Holy Men, *may with Truth esteem themselves* less than others; *yea, and affirm themselves to be the* Chief of Sinners. 225

XXXI. *That this* Third Degree *of* Humility *is the most effectual Means to overcome all Temptations, and to acquire a Perfection in every Virtue.* 237

XXXII *That* Humility *is not contrary to* Magnanimity, *but rather the Foundation and Cause thereof.* 242

XXXIII. *Of the great Benefits and Advantages, which are contain'd in this* Third Degree *of* Humility. 252

XXXIV. *Of the great Graces and Favours, which* God *vouchsafes to the* Humble, *and the Cause why he so exalts them* 261

XXXV. *How much it imports us to have Recourse to* Humility, *to supply what is wanting in us of Virtue and Perfection, lest* God *take us in Hand to humble us by Correction.* 268

XXXVI. *How*

The CONTENTS.

XXXVI. *How* Children *may be trained up to the* Virtue *of* Humility. 282

A Prayer *against* Pride. 300
Praise *of* Humility. 306
Character *of* Humility. 308
Self-Annihilation. 313
Self-Abnegation. 314
The Frontispiece *explained*. 315
A Table *of the* Authors *cited in this Treatise, and the Time they flourished in.* 317, 318

F I N I S.

ERRATA.

PAGE 20, l 23, dele *the*   p 66, l 19, *not He*, read *He not*
      p 67, l 3, for *who*, r *what*   p 68, l 25, *Nothing* in
Ital and l 26, *Sin*, ditto   96, l 16, a Comma after *that is.*
and l 17, dele the Comma after *Knowledge*   99, l 9, *of*, r
off.   120, l 7, r *prescribed*, and l 11, r *Isaiah*   139, l 9.
r *tho'*, and l 11, *yet*, in Roman Char   152, l 25, after
to him, a Semicolon.   163, l 30, r *resides*   191, l 26,
after *the*, r *been*   193, l 22, for *Person*, r. *one*, and l 27,
r *his Person*, and l 28, r *he teaches*   99, l 25, after *due*,
a Period, and l 29, after *serves*, r *indeed*   200, l 4, dele
but.   205, l. 20, after *Hands*, a Semicolon   232, l 7, *as*,
r *A.* 233, l 2, r *Servants.* 257, l. 3, for *strait*, r. *erect*

BOOKS *Printed for* C. RIVINGTON,
at the BIBLE *and* CROWN *in St.* PAUL'*s*
Church-Yard.

1. **T**HE Right Ufe of Lent. or a Help to
Penitents Containing,
   1. A Preparatory Meditation on the Defign of
Lent, the Nature of Sin, &c.
   2. The Reafon, Inftitution, and Benefits of
Fafting.
   3. Some Rules and Advices concerning it.
   4 What we are to repent of
   5 The Way and Method of Repentance, with
fome Forms of Penitential Devotions
   The Second Edition. With fome Additions,
and Amendments.

   2. The Self-Deceiver plainly difcover'd to
himfelf Or, The Serious Chriftian inftructed
in his Duty to God, to Himfelf, and to his Neighbour In fome private Conferences between a
Minifter and his Parifhioner
   By *Clement Ellis*, M A late Rector of *Kirkby*
in *Nottinghamfhire*, Prebend of *Southwell*, and
Fellow of *Queen's-College, Oxon.* Pr 5 s

3 The Sick Man Vifited and Furnifh'd with Inftructions, Meditations, and **Prayers**, for Putting him in mind of his Change, for Supporting him under his Diftemper, and for Preparing him for, and Carrying him through, his laft Conflict with Death

By *Nathanael Spinckes*, A. M a Prefbyter of the Church of *England* The Fourth Edition Corrected To which is prefix'd,

A fhort Account of the Life of the Reverend Author, and his Effigies curioufly Engrav'd by Mr *Vertue* Price 5 s 6 d

4 Devotion Reviv'd Or, Safe and Eafy Directions for a truly Religious Life. With a Character of the Principal Virtues neceffary for a Chriftian.

By a Divine of the Church of *England* Compos'd at firft for his own private Ufe, and now publifh'd for the Common Good The Second Edition Pr 3 s.

5 An Expofition on the Thirty-nine Articles of the Church of *England* Founded on the Holy Scriptures, and the Fathers of the Three firft Centuries In Two Volumes

By *J Veneer*, Rector of St *Andrew's* in *Chichefter* The Second Edition with very large Additions Pr 10 s.

6 A New Expofition on the Book of Common Prayer Wherein the whole Service is Illuftrated and Defended by Inconteftible Proofs drawn from the Holy Scriptures By which is made appear, that there can be no Reafonable Objection urg'd by *Diffenters of any Denomina-*

tion

tion againſt joining in Communion with the Church of *England* Interſpers'd with proper Obſervations, and Anſwers to ſeveral popular Objections not conſider'd by other Writers To which is prefix'd an Introduction, demonſtrating the *Lawfulneſs* and *Expediency* of *Precompoſed Forms* of *Prayer*, in Anſwer to a Pamphlet, entitled, *Plain Reaſons for Diſſenting from the Church of* England, ſo far as relates to this Subject

By *J Veneer*, Rector of St *Andrew's* in *Chicheſter*. Pr. 5s.

7 The Sacred Claſſicks defended and Illuſtrated Or, An Eſſay humbly offered towards proving the Purity, Propriety, and true Eloquence of the Writers of the *New Teſtament* In Two Parts In the Firſt of which thoſe Divine Writers are vindicated againſt the Charge of barbarous Language, falſe *Greek*, and Soleciſms In the Second is ſhewn, that all the Excellencies of Style, and ſublime Beauties of Language and genuine Eloquence do abound in the ſacred Writers of the *New Teſtament* With an Account of their Style and Character, and a Repreſentation of their Superiority, in ſeveral Inſtances to the beſt Claſſicks of *Greece* and *Rome*. To which are ſubjoin'd proper *Indexes*

By *A Blackwall*, M.A Pr 6 s.

8 An Introduction to the Claſſicks Containing a ſhort Diſcourſe on their Excellencies, and Directions how to ſtudy them to Advantage, with an Eſſay on the Nature and Uſe of thoſe Emphatical and Beautiful Figures, which give Strength and Ornament to Writing

By *A Blackwall*, M A The Third Edition, with Additions, and an *Index* Pr 2s 6d.

3 The Sick Man Vifited and Furnifh'd with Inftructions, Meditations, and Prayers, for Putting him in mind of his Change, for Supporting him under his Diftemper, and for Preparing him for, and Carrying him through, his laft Conflict with Death.

By *Nathanael Spinckes*, A M a Prefbyter of the Church of *England* The Fourth Edition Corrected To which is prefix'd,

A fhort Account of the Life of the Reverend Author, and his Effigies curioufly Engrav'd by Mr *Vertue* Price 5 s. 6 d

4 Devotion Reviv'd Or, Safe and Eafy Directions for a truly Religious Life. With a Character of the Principal Virtues neceffary for a Chriftian

By a Divine of the Church of *England* Compos'd at firft for his own private Ufe, and now publifh'd for the Common Good. The Second Edition Pr 3 s

5 An Expofition on the Thirty-nine Articles of the Church of *England* Founded on the Holy Scriptures, and the Fathers of the Three firft Centuries In Two Volumes

By *J Vencer*, Rector of St *Andrew's* in Cirencefter. The Second Edition with very large Additions. Pr 10 s

6 A New Expofition on the Book of Common Prayer Wherein the whole Service is Illuftrated and Defended by Incontestable Proofs drawn from the Holy Scriptures. By which is made appear, that there can be no Reafonable Objection urg'd by *Diffenters of any Denomina-*

tion

tion againſt joining in Communion with the Church of *England* Interſpers'd with proper Obſervations, and Anſwers to ſeveral popular Objections not conſider'd by other Writers To which is prefix'd an Introduction, demonſtrating the *Lawfulneſs* and *Expediency* of *Precompoſed Forms* of *Prayer*, in Anſwer to a Pamphlet, entitled, *Plain Reaſons for Diſſenting from the Church of* England, ſo far as relates to this Subject

By *J Veneer*, Rector of St *Andrew's* in *Chicheſter.* Pr. 5 s.

7 The Sacred Claſſicks defended and Illuſtrated . Or, An Eſſay humbly offered towards proving the Purity, Propriety, and true Eloquence of the Writers of the *New Teſtament* In Two Parts In the Firſt of which thoſe Divine Writers are vindicated againſt the Charge of barbarous Language, falſe *Greek*, and Solecifms In the Second is ſhewn, that all the Excellencies of Style, and ſublime Beauties of Language and genuine Eloquence do abound in the ſacred Writers of the *New Teſtament* With an Account of their Style and Character, and a Repreſentation of their Superiority, in ſeveral Inſtances to the beſt Claſſicks of *Greece* and *Rome*. To which are ſubjoin'd proper *Indexes*

By *A Blackwall*, M A. Pr 6 s.

8 An Introduction to the Claſſicks Containing a ſhort Diſcourſe on their Excellencies, and Directions how to ſtudy them to Advantage, with an Eſſay on the Nature and Uſe of thoſe Rhetorical and Beautiful Figures, which give Strength and Ornament to Writing

By *A Blackwall*, M A The Third Edition, with Additions, and an *Index*. Pr 2 s. 6 d.

Books Printed for C. Rivington.

9. A New Latin Grammar. Being a short, clear, and easy Introduction of Young Scholars to the Knowledge of the *Latin* Tongue Containing an exact Account of the Two First Parts of *Grammar* With an *Index*
By *A Blackwall*, M A. Pr. 1 s 6 d.

10 The Church of *England* Man's Companion in the Closet Or, a Compleat Manual of Private Devotions, collected from the Writings of Archbishop *Laud*, Bishop *Andrews*, Bishop *Kenn*, Dr *Hickes*, Mr *Kettlewell*, Mr *Spinckes*, and other eminent Divines of the Church of *England*
With a Preface by the Reverend Mr. *Spinckes* Price 3 s.

11 A *Rationale*, or Practical Exposition of the Book of *Common-Prayer*, by the Right Reverend Father in God, *Anthony Sparrow*, D D. late Lord Bishop of *Norwich*. With his Caution to his Diocese against False Doctrines, and his famous Sermon of Confession, and the Power of Absolution The Seventh Edition To which are prefix'd, the Lives of the Compilers of the Liturgy, and an Historical Account of its several Reviews.
By the Reverend Mr. *Samuel Downes*, late of St *John's* College, *Oxon*. The Second Edition. Pr. 5 s 6 d.

12 The Christian's Sure Guide to Contentment, in several Practical Discourses on that Important Subject suited to the Conditions of a Christian Life
By a Divine of the Church of *England* Pr 18 d.
13 The

13 The Art of Dying Well Or, The Christian's Sure Guide to Heaven In 2 Parts.

Part I Containing Rules preparatory to a Happy Death in the Time of Health

Part II Such Instructions as are necessary in Times of Sickness.

Translated from the *Latin* of Cardinal *Bellarmin*, by *John Ball*, Presbyter of the Church of *England*. With Prayers suited to the Subject of each Chapter. Pr. 4 s.

14 Practical Discourses upon the most Important Subjects, *viz* Of Covetousness, Of Confession, Of Watching and Prayer, Of Christian Liberty, Of *Christ*'s Nativity, Of Purifying the Temple, On the Resurrection, Of the Possibility of Keeping God's Law, Of Feasting, Of Moderation, Of Superstition, On the Martyrdom of King *Charles* I All preach'd on particular Occasions in the Cathedral of St. *Patrick* and *Christ-Church*, *Dublin*,

By the Right Reverend Father in God, *William Sheridan*, D D Lord Bishop of *Kilmore* and *Ardagh*, In Three Volumes 8*vo* Pr. 15 s.

15 Fate and Destiny, Inconsistent with Christianity Or, The Horrid Decree of Absolute and Unconditional Election and Reprobation, fully Detected, shewing the Grand Error of Asserting, that *Christ* did not Die for All Men, but for an Elect Number only In Eight Conferences between *Epenatus* and *Eutychus* Wherein the most material Pretences, urg'd in Favour of those Principles, are clearly Stated and Answered, and Man prov'd to be the sole Efficient Cause of his own Destruction

By *Edward Birt*. Pr. 3 s.

Books Printed for C. Rivington.

16 A Preservative against Schism and Rebellion in the most Trying Times. Or, A Resolution of the most Important Cases of Conscience, relating to Government both in Church and State, in a Course of Lectures read in the Divinity-School at *Oxford* at the Time of the great Rebellion.

By *Robert Sanderson*, D. D. *Regius Professor,* and afterwards Lord Bishop of *Lincoln* In Three Volumes.

The First Volume concerning the Obligation of Promisary *Oaths.* Translated by the Special Command of his most Sacred Majesty King *Charles* I and afterwards Revised and Approved under his Majesty's own Hand. To which is added, The Judgment of the University, concerning the *Solemn League and Covenant.*

The Second and Third Volumes explaining the most Difficult *Cases of Conscience,* relating to Government Ecclesiastical and Civil. Translated by Mr *Lewis.* With the Life of the Author. Pr, 12 s.

17 The Christian's Exercise. Or, Rules to live above the World while we are in it; with Meditations, Hymns, and Soliloquies, suited to the several Stages of Christian Life. In Four Parts. By *Thomas a Kempis.*

To which is annexed, an Appendix of Letters, Dialogues, &c. Address'd to all true Lovers of Devotion, by *Robert Nelson*, Esq, The Second Edition Revis'd.

To which is added, a Prayer which Mr *Nelson* made for his own private Use. And a Letter wrote by Arch-bishop *Tillotson*, to his sick Friend. Pr 5 s.

18. An

18 An Hiſtorical Account of the ſeveral *Engliſh* Tranſlations of the Bible, and the Oppoſition they met with from the Church of *Rome*.

By *Anthony Johnſon*, A. M. Rector of *Swarkſton* in *Derbyſhire*.

19 Publick Prayer an Indiſpenſible Duty. A Diſcourſe, wherein is ſhewn,

I The Obligations from Reaſon and Scripture to attend the Publick Worſhip

II Some of the many Evils that ariſe from the Neglect of it, are remark'd, &c.

III The weak Excuſes Men pretend for not complying with this Duty, are endeavour'd to be removed

By *Anthony Johnſon*, A M Rector of *Swarkſton* in *Derbyſhire*. Pr. 1 s or 10 s. *per* Dozen.

20 A Letter to a Gentlewoman, concerning Baptiſm With a Prefatory Diſcourſe in relation to thoſe who differ in Opinion or Practice from the Church of *England*, touching that Sacrament Alſo an Office, or Form of Prayer for the Adult Perſons Pr 1 s

21 The Character of the Times delineated In Two Parts

I Containing a Deſcription of the moſt flagrant Enormities.

II A Detail of the moſt remarkable Blemiſhes in the Profeſſors of Virtue and Religion.

Deſign'd for the Uſe of thoſe who mourn in ſecret for the Iniquities of the Nation, and are convinced by ſad Experience, that *Private Vices* are *Publick* and *Real Miſchiefs* Pr 1 s

22, Reve-

22. Revelation examined with Candour Or, a fair Enquiry into the Senfe and Ufe of the feveral Revelations exprefly declared, or fufficiently implied to be given to Mankind from the Creation, as they are found in the Bible. With a Preface, containing the prefent State of Learning, Religion, and Infidelity in *Great-Britain*

By a profefs'd Friend to an honeft Freedom of Thought in Religious Enquiries. The Second Edition, corrected. In Two Volumes. Containing Differtations on the following Subjects, *viz*

VOL. I.

I Of the Forbidden Fruit.

II. Of the Knowledge of the Brute World convey'd to *Adam*.

III. Of his Knowledge of Marriage

IV Of the Skill of Language infufed into *Adam*

V. Of the Revelations immediately following the Fall

VI. Of the *Mofaic* Account of the Fall.

VII. Of Sacrifices

VIII Of the Corruptions of Mankind, which caufed the Deluge

IX Of the natural Caufes made Ufe of by God to flood the Earth

X Of the Ends of Divine Wifdom anfwered by the Deluge

XI Of the Objections to the *Mofaic* Account of the Deluge

XII Of the Concurrence of all Antiquity with the *Mofaic* Account of the Flood

XIII Of other Teftimonies relating to the Deluge.

XIV. Of

XIV. Of the Difficulties relating to *Noah's* Ark.

V O L II.

I Of the Grant of Animal Food made to *Noah*, after the Flood

II Of the Building ot *Babel*

III, Of the Predictions relating to *Ifhmael.*

IV. Of Circumcifion

V. Of the Deftruction of *Sodam* and *Gomorrah*

VI Of the Command given to *Abraham* to facrifice his Son.

23 Annotations on the Book of *Job*, and the Pfalms. Collected from feveral Commentators, and Methodized and Improved,

By *Thomas Fenton*, M A. Rector of *Nately-Scures* in *Hampfhire*, and fometime Student of *Chrift-Church* in *Oxford.*

24 The Scholar's Manual Being a Collection of Meditations, Reflections, and Reafonings, Defign'd for eftablifhing and promoting Chriftian Principles and Practice, In Irreligious and Sceptical Times. With fuitable Devotions Extracted from fome of the beft Antient and Modern Authors, chiefly in their Original Languages.

By a Gentleman of *Oxford.*

25 The Works of the Moft Reverend Dr. *John Tillotfon*, late Lord Archbifhop of *Canterbury*. Containing his Sermons, and other Difcourfes. Compleat in Three Volumes Folio

25. The

27 The Works of the Learned *Isaac Barrow*, D D late Master of *Trinity* College in *Cambridge* (being all his *English* Works) in Two Volumes, Folio.

Published by his Grace Dr *John Tillotson*, late Archbishop of *Canterbury*

28 The Christian Life, from its Beginning to its Consummation in Glory With proper and useful Indexes.

By *John Scott*, D D Rector of St. *Giles's in the Fields* The Ninth Edition, Folio

29 *Britannia* Or, A Chorographical Description of *Great-Britain* and *Ireland*, together with the adjacent Islands

Written in *Latin* by *William Cambden*, Clarencieux King at Arms, and Translated into *English*, with Additions and Improvements, revised, digested, and published, with large Additions,

By *Edmund Gibson*, D D Rector of *Lambeth*, and now Bishop of *London*, and Dean of his Majesty's Chapel Royal The Second Edition In Two Volumes, Folio.

30 Certain Sermons or Homilies Appointed to be read in Churches in the Time of Queen *Elizabeth* of Famous Memory Folio.

31. Certain

31 The Works of *Flavius Josephus*, translated into *English* by Sir *Roger l'Estrange*, Knight, viz

I The Antiquities of the *Jews*, in Twenty Books.

II Their Wars with the *Romans*, in Seven Books

III The Life of *Josephus*, written by himself.

IV His Book against *Apion*, in Defence of the Antiquity of the *Jews*, in Two Parts.

V The Martyrdom of the *Maccabees*

VI *Philo*'s Embassy from the *Jews* of *Alexandria* to *Caius Caligula*. All carefully revised, and compared with the Original *Greek*.

To which are added, Two Discourses, and several Remarks and Observations upon *Josephus* Together with Maps, Sculptures, and accurate Indexes

The Fourth Edition, with the Addition of a New Map of *Palestine*, the Temple of *Jerusalem*, and the Genealogy of *Herod the Great*, taken from *Villalpandus*, *Reland*, &c Folio.

32 The Archbishop of *Cambray*'s Pastoral Letter concerning the Love of God Together with the Opinion of the Fathers on the same Subject Now done into *English* To which is added a Circular Letter

By *George Bull*, D D late LordBishop of St *David*'s. His Visitation Sermon, and his Charge to his Diocese.

Published by *Robert Nelson*, Esq, in 12mo

33. Mo-

Books Printed for C. Rivington.

33. Modern Pleas for Schifm and Infidelity review'd Or, The prefent Principles of Deifm and Enthufiafm fairly reprefented, and the falfe Pretences of the moderate Man to the Intereft of the Church of *England* expofed.

Alfo Modern Pleas for Herefy review'd Or, A particular Defence of the *Athanafian* Creed againft the *Arians* and *Deifts*. In Two Parts. The Third Edition

With a Preface and Index, and feveral other Additions. By *Joſeph Smith*. Octavo.

34. An Effay concerning Marriage Shewing,
I The Preference of Marriage to a fingle Life
II. The Arguments for and againft Plurality of Wives and Concubines
III. The Authority of Parents and Governors, in regulating or reftraining Marriages.
IV. The Power of Husbands, and the Privileges of Wives.
V The Nature of Divorce, and in what Cafes it is allowable
VI The Reafons of prohibiting Marriage within certain Degrees
VII The Manner of contracting Efpoufals, and what Engagements and Promifes of Marriage are binding.
VIII The Penalties incurred by forcible and and clandeftine Marriages, and the Confequences attending Marriages folemnized by the Diffenters
To which is added An Hiftorical Account of the Marriage Rites and Ceremonies of the *Greeks* and *Romans*, and our *Saxon* Anceftors, and of moft Nations of the World at this Day. The Second Edition. By Mr *Salmon*. Pr. 4 s. 6 d.

Printed in the USA
CPSIA information can be obtained
at www.ICGtesting.com
LVHW080804251024
794733LV00009B/1583